# EVENTS,
# REFERENCE,
# AND
# LOGICAL FORM

## R. M. MARTIN

THE CATHOLIC UNIVERSITY OF AMERICA PRESS
Washington, D. C.

Other books by the same author:

TRUTH AND DENOTATION

THE NOTION OF ANALYTIC TRUTH

TOWARDS A SYSTEMATIC PRAGMATICS

INTENSION AND DECISION

BELIEF, EXISTENCE, AND MEANING

LOGIC, LANGUAGE, AND METAPHYSICS

WHITEHEAD'S CATEGOREAL SCHEME AND OTHER PAPERS

© 1978
The Catholic University of America Press

**Library of Congress Cataloging in Publication Data**

Martin, Richard Milton.
   Events, reference, and logical form.

   Includes bibliographical references.
    1. Events (Philosophy)—Addresses, essays, lectures.
2. Reference (Philosophy)—Addresses, essays, lectures.
3. Form (Logic)—Addresses, essays, lectures. I. Title.
B105.E7M37    160    77-24685
ISBN 0-8132-0538-7

# PREFACE

The various papers comprising this volume deal with closely interrclated topics of current interest in the philosophy of logic and mathematics, the philosophy of science, the philosophy of language, and analytic metaphysics. Some of them are primarily critical but the majority are constructive and cover new ground. The main novelty of the book is the outline of a systematic theory of events, which are construed so broadly as to embrace all kinds of entities whatsoever, physical objects, acts, states, processes, mental events, linguistic events, natural numbers, and so on. Such a theory is thought to be of special interest in providing a unified foundation for seemingly diverse approaches to contemporary philosophical problems.

In the first paper of the volume, I, foundations for a logico-metaphysical theory of events are presented somewhat summarily. Events and events only are taken as values for variables, and everything in heaven or earth is then construed in terms of them. In II, the theory is developed somewhat more deeply by enunciating various *fundamental principles*, comprising a tentative axiom system for event logic that should be useful as a basis for further elaboration and development.

In III the theory is expanded into a syntax and semantics containing a systematic theory of *linguistic acts*. On such a basis a semantical theory of *truth*, as relativized to both the speaker and linguistic occasion, may be developed. A characterization of the relation of *reference* is incorporated within it including a theory of *demonstratives* and of *pronouns*. In the light of this theory some of *Davidson's* recent work is discussed.

A somewhat novel philosophy of arithmetic is put forward in IV on *counting*, which is viewed pragmatically as a human activity, one among many. The concern is not only with formal arithmetic, but also with the use of numerical or numerosity words in ordinary language.

The problem of giving suitable *logical forms* for all manner of sentences of a natural language is one of the most important in contemporary philosophical logic. In V and VI a plethora of logical forms is presented providing for a great variety of English sentences. Nothing like a complete survey is attempted, but still the list of forms may be the most complete that has yet been given. Many kinds of sentences often thought intransigent or at least controversial are accommodated, not piecemeal, but as part of a comprehensive theory. One of the aims of such a theory is to provide a basis for an account of grammatical deep structure. Some hopefully useful steps in this direction are taken in these papers. VI is devoted primarily to *adjectives* and *adverbs*.

*Hiż's* "aletheic" semantics and its connection with the author's *non-translational* semantics is discussed in VII. Hiż is one of the most serious contemporary workers in the semantics of natural language, so that his work merits most careful attention. In VII other aspects of his work are compared and contrasted with *Carnap's semantics* and with the study of deep structure.

*Fitch's* view that so-called *propositions* are the sole and basic realities is discussed critically in IX. Fitch is one of the foremost contemporary proponents of propositions *sui generis*, and it is important therefore to see precisely just what that view consists of and why it is thought to be inadequate. Some features of *Quine's* philosophy of logic are discussed critically in X. In many respects Quine's views on this topic are the most satisfactory we have, so that a discussion of their seeming defects and inadequacies is urgently needed. And in XI, *Popper's "third world of objective spirit"* is discussed with more agreement than might appear on the surface. Truth, it is claimed, is the foremost denizen of the third world.

In XII some hopefully helpful, albeit rather loose, suggestions are put forward towards helping to clarify the logical structure of the *language of mathematical intuitionism.* Criticisms of some significant semantical and metaphysical points due to *Sellars* are given in XIII, concerning meaning, abstract entities, and events. In XIV *Lorenzen's* provocative John Locke Lectures, *Normative Logic and Ethics,* are examined rather thoroughly, including his remarks on the philosophy of mathematics. Finally, in XV, the *nominalistic* point of view, presupposed to some extent throughout, is defended against the recent attack by Hilary Putnam.

Although the papers of this volume are concerned with diverse philosophical topics ranging from the philosophy of logic and mathematics through metaphysics to the philosophy of the *Geisteswissenschaften,* the discussion is unified in its concern with a common methodology, with syntax, semantics, and systematic pragmatics, with event logic, and with logical form or grammatical deep structure. The unified methodological treatment of such seemingly disparate subjects is hopefully a step towards a "reunion" and a "meeting of extremes" in contemporary philosophy that is very much to be wished.

It is a pleasure to record gratitude to the National Science Foundation, Grants GS-273 and GS-3069, to the Vaughn Foundation, to New York and Northwestern Universities, and to the Universität Hamburg, for support of the work reported in this volume. All of the papers here were written prior to 1973 and none has previously been published.

For

"Socrates,"

whom one would like to have been like.

> "Degree being vizarded,
> The unworthiest shows as fairly in the mask.
> The heavens themselves, the planets, and this center
> Observe degree, priority, and place,
> Insisture, course, proportion, season, form,
> Office, and custom, in all line of order:
> And therefore the glorious planet Sol
> In noble eminence enthron'd and spher'd
> Amidst the other; whose med'cinable eye
> Corrects the ill aspects of planets evil,
> And posts, like the commandment of a king,
> Sans check, to good and bad: but when the planets
> In evil mixture to disorder wander,
> What plagues, what portents, what mutiny,
> What raging of the sea, shaking of earth,
> Commotion in the winds, frights, changes, horrors,
> Divert and crack, rend and deracinate
> The unity and married calm of states
> Quite from their fixture! O! when degree is shak'd,
> Which is the ladder to all high designs,
> The enterprise is sick."

*Troilus and Cressida,* I, iii.

# CONTENTS

# EVENTS

*"Dimidium scientiae, prudens quaestio."*

A realm of events should perhaps be included in our natural ontology. In addition to physical or "concrete" objects — whatever these are — there seem to be such things as *processes, changes, happenings, acts, states, utterances,* and so on. And such things, at first blush anyhow, seem to be of a kind very different from that of physical objects or concrete things. Perhaps these latter are themselves mere congeries of events in some fashion, in which case events would be the *only* item in our ontology. This is an intriguing possibility, the full logic of which seems not to have been explored.

There has been a good deal of talk about events in the recent philosophical literature, and for good reasons. Events seem needed for the analysis of *acts,* both physical and mental, and hence for moral theory as well as for discussions of the mind-body problem. Much of the contemporary preoccupation with language is focussed upon *linguistic* acts of various kinds. To *use* an expression, to assert, to deny, to question, and so on, it is thought, is to perform an act. Linguistic acts or events then presumably constitute an important species. In the *foundations of physics,* of course, events play a crucial role, and much effort has been devoted there to getting at their structure and interrelations. *Probability theory* is often regarded as a theory about events or kinds of events. Certain systems of *metaphysics* take events as over and against substances as the

1

fundamental entities, and there has been an almost perennial dispute between substance-oriented and process-oriented metaphysical views. There has been considerable discussion recently of the structure of *facts* and *propositions*. Some authors contrast these with events, some regard facts and events as the same. In either case, a clear theory of events is needed by way of background. Recent discussions of *causal relations* assume that events are to be taken as relata. In the fundamental sense, perhaps only an event can be said to be a "cause" or to be "caused." Events also seem needed for the logical analysis of *adverbs*, to say nothing of *verbs*, which have been a stumbling-block for some years in the logical analysis of language. Also much effort has been expended getting at the logic of *temporal flow* and of *tenses*, which are perhaps best treated in terms of a broader theory of events. Further, the study of *logical form*, which harks back to antiquity, is surely simplified and enriched with the admission of an event ontology. For all of these many reasons and purposes and no doubt many more, events have come to the fore in recent philosophical discussion.

A. **Preliminaries.** In several previous publications various alternative approaches to the problem of formulating a logic of events have been sketched.[1] In some of these a key feature has been that events have been taken as values for variables. Perhaps other kinds of entities are also admitted as values for variables, for example, concrete or physical objects in accord with reism or physicalism,[2] but at least events are. The need for recognizing a separate ontology for events seems to have been pointed out first by Reichenbach, but has been recently emphasized by Davidson.[3] One may recognize the

[1] See the author's "On Events and the Calculus of Individuals," *Akten des XIV. Internazionalen Kongresses für Philosophie* (Herder, Wien: 1968), Vol. III, pp. 143-157; *Belief, Existence, and Meaning* (New York University Press, New York and University of London Press, London: 1969), Chapter IX; and *Logic, Language, and Metaphysics* (New York University Press, New York and University of London Press, London: 1971), Chapters VII and VIII.

[2] See especially *The Philosophy of Rudolf Carnap*, ed. by P. A. Schilpp (Open Court Publishing Co., LaSalle, Ill.: 1963), pp. 869 ff. and 882 ff.

[3] H. Reichenbach, *Elements of Symbolic Logic* (The Macmillan Co., New York: 1947), pp. 268 ff. and Donald Davidson, "The Logical Form of Action Sentences," in *The Logic of Action and Preference*, ed. by N. Rescher (University of Pittsburgh Press, Pittsburgh: 1967), pp. 82-95 and "Causal Relations," *The Journal of Philosophy* 64 (1967): 691-713.

2

need without agreeing completely with the proposals to meet it that have been suggested. In the present paper the construction of an event ontology is carried a step further than previously by regarding events *and events only* as values for variables. The problem then arises as how best to accommodate other erstwhile types of entities: physical objects, sense data perhaps, persons, acts, sign events, linguistic acts, states of being, states of mind perhaps, chimeras, Homeric gods, objects or expressions taken in intension, and so on. Some "progress in clarification," in Hempel's splendid phrase, will hopefully be made in this paper in accommodating expressions for some of these types of entities upon the basis of a clear-cut ontology of events and events only.

One ought to be as clear as possible as to just what events are. The answer here is straightforward: *everything* is an event or a construct in terms of such. Constructs are mere logical fictions of one kind or another, handled as *manieres de parler,* so that the second disjunct of the foregoing statement may be dropped. This, in any case, is the thesis to be explored. Events constitute all there is; there is nothing more.

The first step in ushering in a kind of entity wholesale is to introduce variables over them. So now *event variables* are to be used fundamentally. Let these be '$e$', '$e_1$', '$e_2$', and so on, perhaps '$e''$', '$e'''$', and so on also. In addition to ordinary first-order logic with identity and virtual classes and relations, the calculus of individuals is to be employed.[4] The main notion here is that of part-to-whole interpreted spatio-temporally, so that '$e_1 \ P \ e_2$' expresses that the event $e_1$ is a spatio-temporal part of the event $e_2$. Spatio-temporally identical events, then, are those that are mutually spatio-temporal parts of each other. More will be said later, of course, about the part-whole and identity relations.

---

[4] See H. S. Leonard and N. Goodman, "The Calculus of Individuals and Its Uses," *The Journal of Symbolic Logic* 4 (1940): 45-55 and *Belief, Existence, and Meaning,* Chapter VI. Single quotes will be used throughout ambiguously as proper quotes or as quasi-quotes or corners. See W. V. Quine, *Mathematical Logic* (W. W. Norton Co., New York: 1940), pp. 33 ff. and the author's *Truth and Denotation* (University of Chicago Press, Chicago: 1958), pp. 34 f. Occasionally, especially *within* a formula, Quine's corners will be used in place of quotes. For more technical details, see II below.

# EVENTS, REFERENCE, AND LOGICAL FORM

Concerning events a certain kind of spatio-temporal topology or ordering is assumed. For the present only a very simple one is needed, sufficient for the kinds of spatio-temporal distinctions needed in ordinary discourse. Let '$e_1$ B $e_2$' express that $e_1$ is temporally wholly *before* $e_2$ in the sense of this topology. In terms of 'B' a suitable ordering of events is to be presumed given by means of which a theory of temporal flow may be accommodated.

B. **Event-Descriptive Predicates.** In addition to 'P' and 'B', or to primitive predicates in terms of which these are definable, a plethora of primitive predicates describing *event kinds* is introduced. It is important to distinguish events from event kinds.[5] The one are concrete occurrences, the other, kinds of occurrences. An event is a member of a kind, and the kind may be handled as a virtual class. The phrase 'Brutus's kissing Portia', for example, is ambiguous. It may designate the kind or denote many instances of the kind. Let

$$\langle b,K,p \rangle e$$

express that $e$ is a Brutus-kissing-Portia event, one, that is, of many no doubt similar events. '$\langle b,K,p \rangle$', although strictly an expression for a virtual ordered triple, is here taken as a *predicate* for an event kind. The specific notation is unimportant so long as the three ingredients, 'b' for Brutus, 'K' for kissing, and 'p' for Portia, are present in the appropriate order.

If concrete or physical objects are to be renounced (that is, as values for a special kind of variable) in favor of events, then 'b' and 'p' here are to be regarded as proper names of events or of complexes of such. Some complexes are ordinarily given thing names, others not. Those that do have thing names given to them have a high degree of personal or *genidentity*, it might be said; those that do not, do not. The complex event constituting Brutus has a proper name, and so does Portia. But the complex event constituting Brutus and Portia together (the *sum* of the two in the sense of the calculus of

[5] For an especially lucid statement of this, see R. Carnap, *Logical Foundations of Probability* (University of Chicago Press, Chicago: 1950), p. 35.

4

individuals) has no proper name ordinarily. Nor does any specific event of the kind Brutus's-kissing-Portia, although it might. So here, proper names of some complexes of events are admitted, but not of others.

Where 'b' is a proper name for Brutus, let '⟨b⟩' be a predicate of such a kind that '⟨b⟩$e$' expresses that $e$ is a Brutus-event, that is, one among all of the events comprising Brutus and his cosmic history. It is by means of predicates such as '⟨b⟩', *cosmic-sum* predicates, that the notion of *object,* and hence of personal identity, can be gotten at. Not only is '⟨b⟩' now a predicate descriptive of an event kind, but also '⟨$e$⟩', where '$e$' is a variable, this latter functioning even as a kind of predicate variable.

What now is an object? It is an event $e$ with the kind of personal identity built into '⟨$e$⟩', so to speak. Thus 'ObjEv $e$', read '$e$ is an object event', can be defined simply as '$(Ee')⟨e'⟩e$'. And any two events of the same object, that is, events $e_1$ and $e_2$ such that $⟨e⟩e_1$ and $⟨e⟩e_2$ for some object event $e$, are genidentical. '$e_1$ GenId $e_2$' may express that $e_1$ and $e_2$ are genidentical in this sense.

It might be thought that these definitions are too broad, for they condone as object events all manner of spatio-temporally scattered objects, in accord with the calculus of individuals. More useful, some might think, is the notion of an event for which there is a proper name in the language. For this, let us say that $e$ is a *designated object* or a *designated object event* — 'DesObjEv $e$' — if and only if there is some individual constant $e'$ such that $e'$ is a proper name of $e$. Brutus and Portia are then designated objects, but the complex sum or event consisting of Brutus and Portia together is not. (The $e'$ here is a *sign event* or inscription about which more will be said in a moment.)

A complex event is merely the fusion of a virtual class of events, again, in the sense of the calculus of individuals. Complex events are thus to be contrasted with events that might be called 'simple'. That there are simple events, that is, events not further decomposable into parts, may be disputed, but it seems not unreasonable to assume them. (A simple event, by definition, is one that is non-null and is a part of all its non-null parts — about which more later.) Simple events may also be referred to as *point* events. Let 'PtEv $e$' express that $e$ is a simple or point event in this sense. If the foundations of physics were to be developed in any detail, this notion would no doubt loom large. (There is fuller discussion of the problem of complex events in II and III below.)

      **C. States, Actions, Processes.**    Just as one gets at the notion of a designated object by reflection upon the proper names in language, one can get at the notion of a *designated state* of an object by reflecting upon certain kinds of verbs. Suppose a clear-cut division of verbs into process verbs, state verbs, and action verbs is available. Such a division has often been made in traditional grammar and has some intuitive reasonableness about it.[6] Process verbs involve change of some sort, such as 'becomes', 'grows', 'loses', 'dies', and so on. State verbs, such as 'sleeps', 'remains', 'waits', 'lives', involve some continuous condition, and action verbs, 'eats', 'breathes', 'kills', 'speaks', involve some action usually upon or to or with some object. (Action verbs may be further subdivided into accomplishments and achievements, but this need not be considered for the present.[7]) This division needs a careful looking at, but suppose for the moment it — or some similar division — were found to be theoretically sound. One could then distinguish designated process events, state events, and action events as follows.

      Each predicate is assumed to take a certain number of arguments. Thus 'Socrates runs' may well be a full atomic sentence, whereas 'Socrates gives' is not. This latter is presumably short for 'Socrates gives something to someone' or some similar sentence. Thus 'gives' may be handled as a three-place predicate, and 'runs' and the like as one-place predicates. In any case, these predicates all take events as arguments, and particularly interesting cases arise when the arguments are designated objects. Then one may say that $e$ is a designated process event — 'DesProcEv $e$' — if and only if there is a process predicate $e'$ of one place and a proper name $e''$ such that the predicate $\ulcorner \langle e', e'' \rangle \urcorner$ denotes $e$. (Note the informal use of Quine's

[6] See, for example, Otto Jespersen, *The Philosophy of Grammar* (Allen and Unwin, London: 1924) and H. Sweet, *A New English Grammar* (Clarendon Press, Oxford: 1892).
[7] See Zeno Vendler, *Linguistics in Philosophy* (Cornell University Press, Ithaca: 1967).

6

corners or quasi-quotes here.) Similarly, let 'DesStEv *e*' and, DesActEv *e*' express respectively that *e* is a designated state event or a designated action event.

Actually the matter is more complicated, for allowance should be made for process, state, and act predicates of two or more places. But these may readily be accommodated. One might also wish to say here that *e* is a DesProcEv *of* or *involving* the designated object *e'''*, where *e'''* is the object designated by *e''*. And similarly for state and act events of the designated objects involved. And similarly for all the objects involved if the predicates are of two or more places. If Brutus kisses Portia, the act is one of or involving Brutus as well as Portia. Note that these three definitions are metalinguistic, the classification of predicates as process, state, or act predicates being a grammatical one. (No doubt this classification can be transformed into a real one in terms of events rather than predicates.)

**D. Persons and Sign Events.** Human persons have thus far been relegated to objects. A human person is somewhat special, however — in his own eyes at least — and merits special handling. Suitable cognitive relations are to be presumed available for this purpose. *Acceptance* and its cognates here are perhaps as good as any, including *utterance*. Let '*e* Utt *e''*' express that *e* utters a sign event *e'* in the sense that *e* makes marks or sounds or other external signs suitably correlated with *e'*. It is to be understood that humans and only humans can bear Utt to anything in this sense. In all true instances of this sentential function, the place of '*e*' will be taken by a proper name of a human person, for humans are *par excellence* users of language. Hence one may say that *e* is a *person* or *person event* — 'Per *e*' — if and only if there is a sign event *e'* such that *e* Utt *e'*. Because every person has a proper name, every person is a designated object event, but not conversely. (For those not satisfied with the use of 'Utt' here for defining 'Per', an alternative will be given below.)

Throughout this paper, the expressions of the language are taken as sign events or inscriptions, rather than sign designs or shapes as is more customary. This is in accord with an ontology of events and events only. Because of the special importance in metalogic of variables for expression events, a new style of variable for them is often used, but here only the one style of variable is to be used. Suitable *shape predicates* for sign events are needed, 'LP' say for 'is a left parenthesis', 'Vee' for 'is a vee-shaped sign event', and so on. [8] Thus to be a sign event is definable as follows. An event $e$ is a sign event — 'SgnEv $e$' — if and only if $e$ is an LP or a Vee or and so on, or is the *concatenate* of any two distinct $e$'s.

Concatenation, the fundamental relation of logical syntax, is handled in terms of a three-place predicate 'C', so that 'C $e_1,e_2,e_3$' expresses that $e_1$ is the concatenate of $e_2$ and $e_3$, that is, $e_1$ is the expression consisting of $e_2$ followed by or juxtaposed with $e_3$ in that order. Among the axioms governing concatenation is included one now to the effect that if C $e_1,e_2,e_3$ then $e_1,e_2$ and $e_3$ are all distinct sign events. Among the sign events, certain ones are picked out and given certain labels. Thus proper names or individual constants (mentioned above) will be sign events of such and such shapes, and predicate constants, of such and such other shapes. The theory of concatenation and inscriptions is by now an old story, but like all good ones, worth the retelling. It will have to be told again, but in a somewhat new way, in a moment.

The recognition of sign events makes clear that event logic is to contain a syntax and a semantics. The object language may be taken as merely a part of the full event language, the translational part, the sign events then being just the linguistic expressions of that part.

Thus far the following species of events have been distinguished: object events, designated object events, point events, designated process, state, and action events, person events, and sign events. Important subspecies can also be distinguished: epistemic and deontic events and states, and various further kinds of linguistic acts and states. Just how these subspecies are distinguished will depend of course upon specifically what predicates are admitted in the system. Of this, more below.

---

[8] See N. Goodman and W. V. Quine, "Steps toward a Constructive Nominalism," *The Journal of Symbolic Logic* 12 (1947): 105-122, and *Truth and Denotation*, Chapter XI.

**E. Unitarian Pragmatics.** The point of view here is an event totalitarianism. With only slight modification of the above, it can be transformed into a kind of "unitarian pragmatics," to use Henry Hiż's happy phrase. Some notions of syntax and semantics have figured here and there in the above. The proposal now is to transform both of these areas of theory into branches of pragmatics as follows. In place of '$C$ $e_1,e_2,e_3$' one now writes '$e$ $C$ $e_1,e_2,e_3$', read '$e$ concatenates $e_2$ with $e_3$ to form $e_1$, where $e$ is a person and $e_1,e_2$, and $e_3$ are sign events'. Concatenates do not reside in thin air, they are human products or artifacts generated for specific human purposes. In fact all language likewise is now regarded as a human product, the result of countless human acts of various kinds. The syntactical study of language in terms of this new '$C$' is in accord with such a conception.

Semantics may now also be pragmatized. The relation of *multiple denotation* has been presupposed tacitly in the above as the basic relation of semantics, by use of which a one-place predicate may be said to denote severally each and every event to which it applies. Let 'Den' symbolize this relation.[9] In addition let

$$\text{'}e \text{ Ref } e_1,e_2,e_3\text{'}$$

express primitively that person $e$ uses sign event $e_1$ as occurring in sentence $e_3$ to refer to $e_2$. Suitable Rules of Reference should then be laid down. (See Essay III below.) And of course reference and denotation are closely interrelated. (If $e_1$ is a one-place predicate constant and $e_1$ denotes $e_2$, then every speaker of the language presumably uses $e_1$ to refer to $e_2$ in all sentences $e_3$ containing $e_1$ that he utters or asserts correctly. And similarly for *designation*, where $e_1$ is an individual constant and $e_1$ designates $e_2$.) It is human persons now who perform acts of reference or exhibit states of reference, just as they perform acts of concatenation or exhibit concatenational states.[10]

[9] Cf. *Truth and Denotation, passim.*

[10] It is interesting to note that this or some related notion seems needed in H. P. Grice's "Utterers' Meaning, Sentence-Meaning, and Word-Meaning," *Foundations of Language* 4 (1968): 225-242.

# EVENTS, REFERENCE, AND LOGICAL FORM

Consider now an event $e$ such that $\langle e_1, \text{Ref}, e_2, e_3, e_4 \rangle e$, that is, an event $e$ that is an $e_1$-using-$e_2$-to-refer-to-$e_3$-in-$e_4$ event. Is the predicate here to be regarded as an act predicate or a state predicate? Perhaps as either, depending upon the occasion. Perhaps the first time at which $e_1$ Ref $e_2, e_3, e_4$, the event is an act, but thereafter all such events are states. To lose one's virginity is an act, but to have lost it is a state. Thus, perhaps one can say that $e$ here is an act event provided there is no $e'$ bearing B to $e$ such that $\langle e_1, \text{Ref}, e_2 e_3, e_4 \rangle e'$ also. And otherwise any such event is a state event. The distinction here is not hard and fast and may be drawn differently if thought desirable.

**F. Rules or Patterns of Rationality.** What now do the syntactical and semantical rules of the system look like in this pragmatized version? First, even the shape predicates 'LP', 'Vee', and so on, must be pragmatized. LP's are not now sign events fixed as such unto eternity; rather human beings on certain occasions take certain events to be LP's or Vee's, just as they take a complex sign event to be a concatenate of its constituent sign events. Thus '$e_1$ LP $e_2$' is now to express that the person $e_1$ takes the event $e_2$ as a left parenthesis, '$e_1$ Vee $e_2$', that $e_1$ takes $e_2$ to be a vee-shaped sign event, and so on.

Syntactical rules may now be handled as follows. 'C', 'LP', 'Vee', and so on, are pragmatical predicates on a par with others, no more sacrosanct, no less so. The rules governing them should thus be empirical rules and not laid down *ex cathedra logicae*. On the other hand they should explicate certain *patterns of rationality* in order to carry the linguistic burden expected of them. One of the rules of concatenation, in the non-pragmatical version, is to the effect that no LP is a concatenate of any two sign events. In the pragmatized version, it is required rather that if $e_1$ LP $e_2$ then it is not the case that there are sign events $e_3$ and $e_4$ such that $e_1$ C $e_2, e_3, e_4$. This could be laid down as a rule, for all $e_1$ and for all $e_2$.

What are the means by which one can tell, in a given instance, whether $e$ LP $e_1$, $e$ Ref $e_1, e_2, e_3$, and so on? Well, one can ask $e$, one can ask others concerning $e$'s veracity in answering such

10

questions, one can observe his behavior, especially his linguistic behavior, to note whether it accords with the rules, and so on. As in most judgments concerning a fellow human, due allowance should be made for error, both on our part and his.

Persons par excellence are users of language. It is they and they alone who concatenate sign events or use them to refer. If one objects to using 'Utt' as above for defining the notion of a person, one could take instead 'C' or 'Ref' or even 'LP'. These latter are less behavioral, more conceptual, as it were, and hence might be regarded by some as more suitable for use in differentiating persons from physical objects.

In this pragmatized treatment of syntax and semantics, sign events can be anything whatsoever taken as such by someone or other. If person $e_1$ takes $e_2$ as an LP, for example, nothing is said concerning the inner structure of event $e_2$. It can be any manner of event whatsoever, but where $e_1$ LP $e_2$, $e_1$ will handle $e_2$ just as though it were a left parenthesis. $e_2$ will function in $e_1$'s vocabulary as a left parenthesis. Thus, on this view, any kind of events whatsoever may be taken as linguistic units, provided only that they function in the proper way in $e_1$'s vocabulary.

G. **Inference.** To the list above of kinds of events, several more have been added: concatenation events, reference events, LP-events, Vee-events, and so on. These are presumably the most fundamental types of syntactical and semantical events, and hence of linguistic acts generally. Several further types still remain to be distinguished. One important one is that of *inference.* Human beings carry out inferences, one of their most significant activities. Yet inference as a human activity seems not to have been given much attention. To be sure, there are *rules* of inference, but these are almost always rules of *valid deductive* inference. But there are many other kinds of inferences, and for general purposes a much broader theory seems needed than has been provided by the logicians. People infer invalidly, they infer inductively and statistically, perhaps abductively, as well as in other ways, including fallacious ones. For a general theory of inference, it is of interest to distinguish various *patterns* that a person's linguistic behavior actually does exhibit, as well as ideal or normative patterns that a person's inferences should (in some sense) exhibit.

Let 'Inf' be a new predicate significant in contexts of the form '$e$ Inf $e', e_1, \ldots, e_n$', read 'person $e$ infers $e'$ from $e_1, \ldots, e_n$'. How does one decide whether or not an instance of this holds? By asking person $e$, by observing his behavior, and so on, as with other atomic sentences of similar kind.

It is of interest to look briefly at the principles of logic themselves in terms of 'Inf'. By 'logic' here is meant first-order logic as throughout. Two kinds of formulation may be considered, in the first of which there are no axioms but only rules of inference. Suppose these are *Modus Ponens, Modus Tolens,* and so on. Let $e$ be a person. Then $e$ performs a *Modus Ponens act $e'$* provided there are sign events $e_1$, $e_2$, and $e_3$ such that $\langle e, \text{Inf}, e_1, e_2, e_3 \rangle e'$, where $e_3$ is of the form consisting of an LP concatenated with $e_2$ concatenated with a horseshoe sign ('$\supset$') concatenated with $e_1$ concatenated with a right parenthesis (that is, $\ulcorner (e_2 \supset e_1) \urcorner$, to use Quine's corners or quasi-quotes again). Similarly *Modus Tolens acts,* and so on, are introduced. A virtual class of $e$'s acts of inference is then said to *accord with logic* if and only if every one of those acts is a Modus Ponens act, a Modus Tolens act, and so on. If the formulation of first-order logic includes axioms, these are allowed to figure as additional premises wherever desired.

This pragmatized way of viewing of logic is of interest for several reasons. In the first place, it enables logic to be seen as a form of human activity and not as something far-off and removed from common toil. And this is done, not just in terms of a phrase however telling and eloquent, but in terms of an exact notation. Further, the principles of logic themselves, including rules of inference, are taken as definatory of rational patterns. Why is it important for a person's inferences to exhibit such patterns rather than others thought less desirable? Mainly, it would seem, because they have in fact been successful in conceptual practice. Starting with premises accepted or taken to be true, one is not led to unacceptable formulae, which he would not wish to take as true, if his inferences accord with idealized

12

patterns. This may be seen with especial clarity by studying inferences in mathematics and the sciences, where they are only rarely in error. The moment one steps beyond, however, one finds erroneous inferences at every turn. By means of 'Inf' erroneous inferences (including the traditional fallacies) may be studied, and even systematized, and the reasons for them gotten at clearly. The theory of error in general is a fascinating subject and should not be confined just to errors in perception, as is usually done. Much more significant for human knowledge generally, it would seem, are errors of inference and of conception. Perceptual errors one learns quickly to correct; inferential and conceptual ones require a tough schooling.

A word should be said about inferences of other than deductive type. The use of 'Inf' allows these to be viewed in the same way that deductive inferences are. There are, after all, such things as inductive inferences, which can now be systematized in terms of 'Inf', in accord perhaps with some suitable theory of confirmation. And similarly for statistical inference in terms of principles of statistical probability. Thus 'Inf' should play a fundamental role in any systematized methodology of science. If there is such a subject as the "logic of discovery" or of abduction, 'Inf' should play a role there also. (See XI below.) Perhaps no more than rules of thumb can be given for discovery, but even these may be useful when used cautiously, and it is surely of some interest to try to formulate them. For this the use of 'Inf" or some cognate locution would be indispensable. 'Inf' is thus a most useful pragmatical predicate, but one for the most part hitherto overlooked.

Enough now of this excursus on inference, which is intended in no way to change logic but merely to provide a somewhat new way of viewing it.

**H. The Null Event.** Thus far nothing has been said concerning a null event. The notion of a null individual has often been discussed, and it is perhaps remarkable how much of interest can be found to be said concerning it. One might have supposed that there would not be much, and that there would be agreement concerning even this. But not at all.

## EVENTS, REFERENCE, AND LOGICAL FORM

Mario Bunge thinks there are many null individuals[11] but J. W. Swanson apparently is content with just one.[12] If the individuals are subdivided into many sorts there would seem to be little reason for having a null individual in one sort and not in another. Bunge gives some interesting examples from optics, quantum mechanics, biology, psychology, and sociology. He thinks the description of the null individual as "that thing which is part of everything" should be supplanted by "that thing [of a given sort] which, added to an arbitrary individual of . . . [that sort] yields the latter." But these two descriptions are surely equivalent. In the calculus of individuals there is the theorem that an individual $a$ is a part of every individual if and only if for every individual $b$, the individual which is the sum of $a$ and $b$ is identical with $b$.

Bunge thinks that "null individuals are far from being nondescript" — they were not so regarded in "Of Time and the Null Individual" — but "may be assigned definite [physical] properties." For Swanson, on the other hand, the null individual (if for him there is only one (?)) has *no properties at all,* physical or otherwise. So here there are apparently three positions to consider, depending upon whether one regards the null individual(s) as having no properties at all, physical or otherwise (as with Swanson), as having no physical properties but having certain properties as required in the calculus of individual (R.M.M.), or as being assigned definite physical magnitudes (Bunge).

It is a little difficult to see how Swanson's position can be maintained, however, for the null individual or individuals must surely have some properties. Of course much depends upon just what a "property" is. They would seem best construed as virtual classes (or as virtual classes *in intension*[13]) and the null individual (of any sort) is surely a member of the virtual class of all self-identical individuals (of that sort). No harm would seem to arise from assigning physical magnitudes to the null individual(s). (But these

[11] In "On Null Individuals," *The Journal of Philosophy* 63 (1966): 776-778, in response to the author's "Of Time and the Null Individual," *ibid.* 62 (1965): 723-736.
[12] In "The Singular Case of the Null Individual in the Empty Domain," *ibid.*, 772-776.
[13] See especially *Belief, Existence, and Meaning,* Chapter VII, and §. I below.

14

magnitudes in turn are, in appropriate senses, null in all of the examples Bunge cites.) The assignment of a null magnitude does result in the possession of a physical "property" in however Pickwickian a sense. Further the null individual must surely be self-identical, and thus (contrary to Swanson) has at least this property. (Swanson's schema (4), i.e.,

$$(x) (Fx \supset \sim x = a_0 )$$

is thus to be rejected and hence also the alternative sketched in his last three paragraphs (pp. 774-6). For from (4) one can validly infer

$$a_0 = a_0 \supset \sim a_0 = a_0.$$

If Swanson wishes to prohibit this inference he does not state how. Further, his schema (2) is logically equivalent to

$$(Ex)\sim x = a_0,$$

which ascribes a certain "property" to $a_0$. There is no question then of (2)'s coming out true or false depending upon how one construes 'F' in (2). (2) is true or false factually depending upon whether the domain at hand contains an individual other than $a_0$ or not. Swanson's alternative proposal must therefore be rejected as untenable.)

The question now arises: should a null *event* be admitted or not? If one objects to so ghostly an entity, it may be asked why admitting such should be thought any worse than admitting a null class or set or relation. It would be difficult to give a cogent answer to this, and no doubt the matter should be settled on purely technical grounds. For the present this need not be decided either way. In a more formal development of the theory, however, it is convenient technically to admit such an entity, as in II below.

I. Concepts. Just as there are Russellian descriptions of individuals in ordinary logic, there are of course Russellian descriptions of events in event logic, phrases read 'the one and only event *e* such that $-e-$'. Often there are phrases of this kind that fail to describe any event, in which case one can say that they describe the null event. Often one and the same event is described in many different ways, and the way in which it is described — Frege's *Art des Gegebenseins*[14] in effect — may be significant. Here it is the event *under the given description* that is needed.

This phrase 'under a given description' frequently occurs in talk of events. How precisely is it to be accommodated? This question leads to the general topic of *concepts*. Concepts seem best handled as objects under a given linguistic description, and hence event concepts as events under a given description. But first let us reflect for a moment upon concepts in their own right.

'Concept' is of course used in various ways. These seem roughly classifiable into three, the purely logico-semantical use, the epistemological use, and a mixture of the two. The logico-semantical use seems fundamental, and in terms of it one would hope to accommodate the epistemological one. The pure semantics of concepts should make only incidental (if any) reference to the user of language. Perhaps 'concept' should be reserved for the logico-semantical use, and 'conception' for the epistemological one. In any case, concepts and conceptions ought surely to be given a respectable ontic status.

Very roughly, a concept is what a person "has" or entertains in conceptual thought. Like Frege's ideas, concepts are "had," but in a different sense. Concepts are objective and may be "had" by many persons. Concepts enter into thinking in fundamental ways and along with "ideas" furnish one of the primary means of apprehending the world and everything in it.

According to the *Oxford English Dictionary* a concept is "[t]he product of the faculty of conception; an idea of a class of objects, a general notion or idea." This account has a thick nineteenth century grime upon it, which, if removed, may still reveal some luster underneath. Even so, all of these rough preliminary statements are

---

[14] See "On Sense and Reference." tr. of "Über Sinn und Bedeutung," *Translations from the Philosophical Writings of Gottlob Frege*, ed. by P. Geach and M. Black (Blackwell's, Oxford: 1952), pp. 56-78.

16

woefully inadequate. And one knows scarcely where to begin to make sense of them. Perhaps it would be good to start the other way around, namely, to fix upon a clear notion of what concepts are, by identifying them with suitable entities already available in the underlying semantics. When we know not what even to look for, it may be good to try to make the best of what we already have.

The germ of what will be presented here is to be found in Frege's notion of the *Darstellungsweise* or *Art des Gegebenseins,* already referred to. In the *Begriffsschrift*, it will be recalled, Frege had noted that "the same content [*Inhalt*] of a name can be completely determined in different ways; but that in a particular case two ways of determining it really yield the same result is the content of a *judgment.* Before this judgment can be made, two distinct names, corresponding to the ways of determining the content, must be assigned to what these ways determine."[15] Then again, in "Über Sinn und Bedeutung," Frege notes that "it is natural to think of their being connected with a sign (name, combination of words, letter), besides that to which the sign refers, which may be called the *reference* of the sign, also what I should like to call the *sense* of the sign, *wherein the mode of presentation is contained* [these last italics added] ." It is not Frege's distinction of reference and sense that is of interest here, but rather the notion of an object's being presented in different ways by means of different expressions. This may be used as a guide to finding an appropriate ontology for concepts in event logic.

As thoughout, individual constants are of course to be distinguished sharply from predicate constants. Also individual constants should be distinguished from Russellian descriptions of individuals, although in many cases the former may be taken as abbreviations for the latter. If one follows the *O.E.D.,* concepts are always "of a class of objects" and thus are "general." In accord with this there are presumably no concepts of individuals. Let us go along with the

---

[15] *Translations*, p. 11 and p. 57. (The translation here, however, is that of Stefan Bauer-Mengelberg in *From Frege to Gödel*, ed. by J. van Heijenoort (Harvard University Press, Cambridge: 1967).) Cf. also the discussions in Chapter X of *Belief, Existence, and Meaning* and Chapter II of *Logic, Language, and Metaphysics.*

*O.E.D.* for the moment, a good companion anyhow, and then note later that parity of method allows the introduction of concepts of individuals as well.

Rather than of classes, let us speak of virtual classes only, as throughout, for they are usually a pretty good surrogate for the "real thing," as in effect already noted above. Let $\{e\ni(-e-)\}$ be a virtual class, and let some sign event $e_1$ be a name for it. And let $e_2$ be some other name for it. The names $e_1$ and $e_2$ both embody a way of determining or presenting the given class. They might yield the same "content" or not. Let us form, in the semantical metalanguage, the ordered couple $\langle\{e\ni(-e-)\},e_1\rangle$ of the class $\{e\ni(-e-)\}$ and of the expression $e_1$. This ordered couple may be regarded as a *class concept*, more particularly, as a class concept *of* $\{e\ni(-e-)\}$. But so can $\langle\{e\ni(-e-)\},e_2\rangle$. A class concept has two components, a class and an expression naming it. The class may be referred to as the *object* of the class concept and the expression as its *condition* or content or mode of presentation. Every class concept must have both components. Clearly there can be no class concept without a class, and no class concept without some conceptual component, here provided by a "way of determining" the class. Of course the class might be null but there would still be a class concept of it. There is a concept of unicorn even though there are no unicorns, and a concept of round square even though there are no round squares.

In similar fashion concepts for individuals may be introduced. Let '$e_0$' be an individual constant and $e$ some expression designating it. Then $\langle e_0,e\rangle$ is the individual concept of the object $e_0$ under the condition or mode of presentation $e$. The expression $e$ here may be a primitive individual constant designating the event $e_0$ or it may be a Russellian description of it. If $e$ fails to be either, then $\langle e_0,e\rangle$ fails to be an individual concept.

Given a virtual class or an individual, how many concepts of it are there? To answer this one must reflect upon the condition for the identity of concepts. Given, say, $\langle\{e\ni(-e-)\},e_1\rangle$ and $\langle\{e\ni(...e...)\},e_2\rangle$ as class concepts, under what circumstances are they to be regarded as the same? Well, surely, $\{e\ni(-e-)\}$ and $\{e\ni(...e...)\}$ must be the same virtual class. But also $e_1$ and $e_2$ must

stand in some close semantical relation. Perhaps it is enough to
require that they be *L-equivalent* in essentially Carnap's sense. Or
perhaps L-equivalent and have a certain structural similarity, that is,
contain only the same non-logical constants, say, occurring perhaps
in the same left-to-right order. In fact, there are *many* interesting
semantical relations to consider here. Finer and finer requirements
can be put on L-equivalence to arrive at various kinds of *synonymy*.
For the present, one need not settle on any one of these as final.
Meanwhile, sheer identity of concepts can be taken in the very strict
sense as identity of objects and identity of conditions, if it is
recognized that further significant relations, of L-equivalence and
synonymy, may obtain among the conditions. And similarly for
individual concepts.[16]

It is interesting to compare the use of 'concept' here with that of
Stephan Körner, with which there is welcome kinship.[17] Körner
distinguishes predicates and concepts as follows. "By adding a
synonymity rule to the rules which govern the use of a sign as a
predicate we ... change its use. The sign is then being used no longer
as a predicate but as a concept. If we are not free to substitute for
the sign any of its synonyms that we please, then we are using the
sign as a predicate. If we are so free we are using it as a concept. In
order to identify a particular concept it is necessary to mention one
of the synonymous conceptual signs and to specify the rules
governing its use." A concept for Körner carries its synonymity rule
on its sleeve, so to speak, and this rule might even be interlinguistic.
In contrast, the notion above does not depend upon synonymity or
any other such semantical relation. Further it is intralinguistic, but
of course interlinguistic semantical relations can be studied one by
one as needed or as they arise. And concepts for Körner are linked
only with predicates, whereas here they may be linked with all
manner of designative expressions including individual constants and
Russellian descriptions.

There is another point of contrast. Körner's use of 'concept' is
very linguistically oriented. Concepts are for him mere linguistic

[16] Somewhat similar comments are made in *Belief, Existence, and Meaning*, Chapter VII.
[17] S. Körner, *Conceptual Thinking* (Cambridge University Press, Cambridge: 1955), p. 14.

19

expressions with their synonymity rules tagging along. All expressions are always subject to rules, however, to all of the rules of the system at hand. If only syntactical rules are given, the expressions remain uninterpreted. If semantical rules are added, the expressions become interpreted in just the fashion laid down by those rules. But once the rules are specified, expressions are used in accord with *all* of them. One is not free to say that such and such a use is in accord with one rule, but that another use is not. One does not use words of ordinary language in such variable ways, nor of language systems. The rules of language "interanimate" each other fundamentally. Thus the tagging along of a synonymity rule is not a satisfactory way of differentiating concepts from predicates. Concepts have objects that enter into them constitutively, so to speak. Concepts are *of* objects always and the notation for them should contain an expression for the object, not just an expression for the expression for the object, as with Körner.

The notion of an object, or class, under a given description or mode of designation, does seem periphrastic nonetheless. When one writes '$\langle e_0, e \rangle$', where 'e' is some Russellian description, say, designating the event $e_0$, one could write '$e_0$' alone just as well. One would then recall that 'e' designates $e_0$ in accord with the semantical and other rules of the language. The notation '$\langle e_0, e \rangle$' carries a semantical rule on its sleeve, whereas '$e_0$' alone does not. But this periphrasis surely does no harm and may frequently serve as a useful reminder of the relevant semantical rule or rules. Formally speaking, the simpler notation could be made to work, no doubt, but it would fail to capture the intuitive notion of an individual or class *under a given description,* and thus to capture the structure of concepts as involving both objects and conditions.

Of course event concepts are now mere logical constructs or fictions, in the sense that they are not themselves values for variables. Virtual ordered couples are merely a kind of virtual relation, and virtual entities never, never, never, it should be remembered, can be values for variables. Even so, such fictitious entities can be put to good service.

J. **Conceptions.** What service is expected of concepts? How do they function in human thought and discourse? By being ingredients of *conceptions,* as Frege in effect pointed out. It was tentatively suggested above that 'conception' be taken in an epistemological sense, more particularly, as an event or act word. It is persons who may be said to "conceive" or "have" or entertain concepts. Let 'Has' be now significant in the contexts

(1) $\qquad$ '$e$ Has $\langle \{e_1 \ni (-e_1-)\}, e_2 \rangle$'

and

(2) $\qquad$ '$e$ Has $\langle e_1, e_2 \rangle$',

one for virtual-class expressions and one for individual constants. *Conceptual acts* or *states* involving individual events are then events $e'$ such that

(3) $\qquad$ $\langle e, \text{Has}, \langle e_1, e_2 \rangle \rangle e'$

for some person event $e$, some event $e_1$, and some sign event $e_2$. And a conceptual act or state involving the virtual class $\{e \ni (-e-)\}$ is any $e'$ such that

(4) $\qquad$ $\langle e, \text{Has}, \langle \{e \ni (-e-)\}, e_1 \rangle \rangle e'$

The use of ordered triples here, one factor of which is itself an ordered couple, is a natural extension of the notation above.

'Has' and the notation for concepts suggested seem to provide suitable tools for exploring conceptual thought and its relation to language, and this within an event ontology. The next step is to construct interesting patterns for rational conception. These no doubt would be closely based on some of the patterns already mentioned above, as well as upon various others.

One additional comment. The phrase 'event under a description' is ambiguous. It may refer to an event $e$ under a linguistic description or to $e$ as being of such and such a kind. The former is merely $\langle e, e' \rangle$ where $e'$ is a proper name or Russellian description of $e$. The latter is $\langle e, e' \rangle$ where $e'$ is a predicate ascribing to $e$ some event property or kind.

To simplify, (1) and (2) may be written, in non-conceptual terms, as

$$'e \text{ Has } \{ e_1 \ni (-e_1-) \}, e_2 '$$

and

$$'e \text{ Has } e_1, e_2 '',$$

where $e_2$ is understood to be the mode of description. Similarly (3) and (4) may be written without the inner half-diamonds.

**K. Epistemic Events.** The theory of events has spilled over into the theory of reference, the theory of inference, the theory of the null event, the theory of concepts, and the theory of conception. If everything whatsoever is an event, then of course event theory can legitimately spill over where'er it will. Everything must be accommodated in one way or another. If this can be done successfully, one has in the notion of event a truly unifying philosophical notion of great power.

Nothing has been said about perception, and this is not the occasion to take sides on the hoary issues involved in the percept theory as over against those involving sense data.[18] If sense data are admitted they are then a special kind of event requiring special handling. Instead of exploring this, consider locutions such as

'Person $e_1$ Sees object $e_2$ under the description $e_3$',
'Person $e_1$ Sees person $e_2$ under the description $e_3$',
'Person $e_1$ Sees event $e_2$ under the description $e_3$',

[18] See, for example, Roderick Firth's useful "Sense-data and the Percept Theory," *Mind* 68 (1949): 434-465 and 69 (1950): 35-56.

and the like. 'Sees' here is an additional predicate and seeing-events are then events $e'$ such that $e'$ is a person-$e_1$-seeing-$e_2$-under-the-linguistic-description-$e_3$ event for some $e_1$ and $e_2$ and $e_3$. All three forms of locution are common in ordinary speech. Especially interesting here is the third, an instance of which is 'Caesar sees Brutus kiss Portia'. The logical form here may be taken as

$$\text{`(E}e\text{) (E}e'\text{) (}\langle b,K,p\rangle e \cdot c \text{ Sees } e,e' \cdot \text{`}\langle b,K,p\rangle\text{' } e'\text{)',}$$

where 'b', 'K', and 'p' are as above and 'c' is 'Caesar', and "'$\langle b,K,p\rangle$'$e'$" expresses that $e'$ is of the appropriate shape.

In citing various forms of locution, here and throughout, one is not *analyzing* the notions involved therein. The citation of a logical form and the analysis of it are quite separate enterprises but are frequently confused with one another. The point of view here is that the first step in analysis is the settling upon a suitable form. Without this, just what is being analyzed may not be clear.

'Know', other than in the sense of knowing *that,* likewise can be embodied in different forms of locution. Thus

'Person $e_1$ Knows person $e_2$ under the description $e_3$',
'Person $e_1$ Knows object $e_2$ under $e_3$',
'Person $e_1$ Knows act event $e_2$ under $e_3$'

are typical and basic forms. The last one allows of iteration in the sense that $e_2$ can be an $e_1$'s-knowing-something-event. Caesar may know that he knows that Brutus kisses Portia. Of course he may know that he sees Brutus kiss Portia, and so on, also.

Note that there do not seem to be similar cognate forms for 'Believes', except as ellipses. Person $e_1$ cannot properly be said to believe person $e_2$ except as ellipsis that $e_1$ believes what $e_2$ utters or writes or thinks. One can believe *in* a person or object or event but not believe them *simpliciter.* Believing is to be contrasted with knowing in this respect. On the other hand 'believing that' is very much like 'knowing that', the "objects" of both being propositional constructs, which in turn can be characterized in terms of events under given modes of presentation.[19]

Note that these various epistemic relations are intentional, the hallmark of intentionality throughout being the *Art des Gegebenseins*. This will become clearer from some examples to be given below and in V and VI.

L. **Spatio-Temporal Location.** Let us return now to more mundane matters concerned with spatio-temporal location.

Physical objects are regarded as consisting of point events as their ultimate components and thus to have them as parts. Physical objects occupy space-time, because their ultimate parts do. Happenings, acts, processes, and the like, do not occupy space-time, however, but rather *occur* or *take place* therein. This is a significant difference that we will do well to reflect upon.

First, an *object* event $e_1$ can be said to *occupy* a point event $e_2$ — '$e_1$ Ocpy $e_2$' — provided $e_1$ has $e_2$ as a part. And the object event $e$ can be said *wholly* to occupy $e_2$ provided $e_2$ is the fusion, in the sense of the calculus of individuals, of the virtual class of all point events $e_3$ such that $e_1$ Ocpy $e_3$.

The following notions are also useful. First, event $e_1$ is said *temporally to overlap* with event $e_2$ — '$e_1$ TO $e_2$' — if and only if neither bears B to the other. (The 'B', recall, is available from the underlying space-time topology.) Then $e_1$ may be said to be a *temporal part* of $e_2$ — '$e_1$ TP $e_2$' — if and only if for every $e$, if $e$ TO $e_1$ then $e$ TO $e_2$. Then $e_1$ is *simultaneous* with $e_2$ if and only if every $e$ is such that $e$ TP $e_1$ if and only if $e$ TP $e_2$. One can say now that process or act $e_1$ *occurs at* the point event $e_2$ — '$e_1$ Occr $e_2$' — if and only if $e_1$ is a DesProcEv *of* some ObjEv $e_3$ or a DesActEv *of* some $e_3$ and $e_4$, either $e_3$ or $e_4$ Ocpy $e_2$, and $e_2$ TP $e_1$. 'Occr' should be read, more accurately, 'takes place in part at'. The process or act $e_1$ then occurs *wholly* at the fusion of the class of all point events that $e_3$ and $e_4$ occupy at the time, so to speak. Processes and acts are thus located spatio-temporally in terms

---

[19] See *Belief, Existence, and Meaning,* Chapters V and IX.

of the location of the objects to which they happen. To require this seems not unreasonable. Finally, a process or act $e_1$ occurs *within* an $e_2$ provided the fusion of point events at which it wholly occurs is itself a part of $e_2$.

Consider again Brutus's kissing Portia. Brutus and Portia are each given spatio-temporal location by reference to the point events that are parts of their bodies. How now is some act of Brutus's kissing Portia to be located? Various parts of the bodies of Brutus and Portia at the time could be singled out as somehow especially relevant. The kissing takes place wherever those parts of their bodies are at the time. More particularly, it occurs *at* just those point events that the relevant parts of their bodies occupy at the time, *wholly* at the fusion of those point events, and *within* any $e$ containing that fusion.

Not all acts or processes, however, need be spatio-temporally localized with respect to *all* the objects involved. An intentiona. act, such as Caesar's remembering that he saw Brutus kiss Portia, seems best localized in terms of Caesar's body at the place-time of his remembering. The place-time wholly at which the kissing took place seems irrelevant.

Spatio-temporally identical events or processes occur at the same PtEv's, but may of course differ in other respects. All manner of differences in intension may be accommodated by bringing in the *Arten des Gegebenseins*, the modes of description.

**M. Parts and Wholes.** By reference to their spatio-temporal location, the part-whole relation between object events is to have the characteristic that object event $e_1$ is a part of object event $e_2$ if and only if every PtEv that $e_1$ Ocpy, $e_2$ does also.

When is one *act* a part of another? Or a process a part of another? Or a state a part of another, or of an act or a process? A few comments, intended to illumine reasonable approaches to these difficult questions, are as follows.

The part-whole relation between events is sharply to be distinguished from that of *inclusion* between *event kinds*. Event kinds are handled virtually in terms of predicate couples, triples, and so on, such as '$\langle b,K,p \rangle$'. Consider any two such predicates, say '$\langle e_1,R_1,e_2 \rangle$' and '$\langle e_1,R_2,e_2 \rangle$' and suppose that

$$'(e)\,(e_1)\,(e_2)\,(\,\langle e_1,R_1,e_2 \rangle\,e\ \supset\ \langle e_1,R_2,e_2 \rangle\,e)'$$

holds in the theory. Any action kind $\langle e_1,R_1,e_2 \rangle$ is then clearly *included in* the action kind $\langle e_1,R_2,e_2 \rangle$. Suppose, for example, that every kissing of $e_2$ by person $e_1$ is a pressing of $e_1$'s lips against $e_2$. (The converse need not hold.) Then the action kind of kissing is included in the action kind pressing-one's-lips-against. This observation, however, throws little light upon 'P' as between expressions for events.

For specificity, and for sheer philosophic sport, the *O.E.D.* may be consulted again, this time on 'kiss'. In the primary entry, the verb is transitive and is to mean 'to press or touch with the lips (at the same time compressing and then separating them), in token of affection or greeting, or as an act of reverence . . .'. This may be symbolized as follows. Let 'b Pr p' express that Brutus presses Portia with his lips, 'b Tch p' that Brutus touches Portia with his lips, 'Cmprs b' that Brutus compresses his lips, 'Sep b' that Brutus separates them, and 'b Intd R,p' that Brutus intends to perform an act of the kind R on p.[20] 'b Aff p', 'b Gr p', and 'b Rev p' respectively express that b shows affection for p, greets p, and shows reverence for p. 'b (Aff ∪ Gr ∪ Rev) p' is short for the disjunction of 'b Aff p', 'b Gr p', and 'c Gr p', essentially as in *Principia Mathematica*, *23.03. Finally let '$e_2$ Fu $\{ e_3,e_4 \}$' express that $e_2$ is the fusion of the virtual class whose only members are $e_3$ and $e_4$ that is, that $e_2$ is just the sum of $e_3$ and $e_4$. One may then define, essentially in accord with the *O.E.D.*, using the usual symbols for notions of logic,

---

[20] Strictly, 'Intd' should itself be taken here intentionally, so that 'c Intd R,p' is short for '(E$e$) (E$e'$) (c Intd $e',e$ • '$\{e'' \ni \langle c,R,p \rangle e'' \}$ '$e$)'.

'⟨b,K,p⟩e' as '(⟨b,(Pr ∪ Tch),p⟩ e · (E$e_1$) (E$e_2$) (⟨Cmprs,b⟩ $e_1$ · ⟨Sep, b⟩ $e_2$ · $e_1$ B $e_2$ · ~ (E$e'$) ($e_1$ B $e'$ · $e'$ B $e_2$) · (E$e_3$) ($e_3$ Fu { $e_1$,$e_2$ } · $e_3$ P e)) · ⟨b,Intd,(Aff ∪ Gr ∪ Rev),p⟩ e)'.

The clause beginning '(E$e_3$)' here requires that the sum of $e_1$ and $e_2$ be a part of $e$. It need not of course be the whole of it.

What now are the parts of $e$ where ⟨b,K,p⟩$e$? The definiens of the definition above contains three separate conjuncts, each of which gives a necessary condition for $e$ to be a ⟨b,K,p⟩. But note that each of these conjuncts concerns $e$ as a whole, even the second. Thus the kind of meaning analysis involved here sheds more light upon the action *kinds* involved in ⟨b,K,p⟩ than upon the parts of $e$. Clearly now ⟨b,K,p⟩ is *included* in ⟨b, (Pr ∪ Tch), p⟩, in accord with the definition of 'inclusion' above. (Strictly, of course, a fully general definition is assumed here, of '⟨$e_1$,K,$e_2$⟩e' for variable '$e_1$' and '$e_2$'.) But are we not inclined to say here also that some action of the kind ⟨b, (Pr ∪ Tch), p⟩ is a *part* of one of the kind ⟨c,K,p⟩? It seems so. A kind of *inverse variation* law seems to obtain between the part-to-whole relation as between actions and inclusion as between action types. In fact it seems to hold that

$$(e_1) (e_2) (e_1 \text{ R } e_2 \supset e_1 \text{ S } e_2) \supset (e) (e_1) (e_2) (⟨e_1, R, e_2⟩ e \supset \supset (Ee') (e' \text{ P } e · ⟨e_1,S,e_2⟩e') ).$$

(See II below).

All events, including processes, acts, and states can easily and naturally be decomposed into temporal slices. Let 'Mom e' express that $e$ is a *momentary* event in the sense that $e$ is non-null and bears TP to every non-null event that bears TP to it. More particularly, then, every event can be sliced into a series of consecutive momentary events. The non-null parts of events are then these momentary parts plus all possible sums of them. This statement gives a necessary condition for a non-null $e_1$ to bear P to $e_2$, namely, that $e_1$ is a Mom or a fusion of a virtual class of Mom's.

Consider again the cosmic-sum predicate '⟨b⟩'. Some of the events $e$ such that ⟨b⟩$e$ may be PtEv's (or fusions of such) that are parts of

b. But one should recognize here primarily the processes, states, and acts involving b. Any *e*, where ⟨b,K,p⟩*e*, is also a ⟨b⟩. The events that involve or "happen" to Brutus are as much Brutus-events in the sense of '⟨b⟩' as are the PtEv's that *e* occupies. (Cf. the *Principle of Process, EvR 7*, in II below.)

N. **Natural Numbers.** A strong and workable theory of events cannot be developed without the introduction of natural numbers. These are needed for counting, for measurement, and various derivative purposes. Sophisticated methods of measurement require not only the natural numbers but real numbers as well. It will be noted in a subsequent essay (IV), however, that the natural numbers may be built up in terms of a pragmatic primitive 'Crrlt' for correlation regarded as a human activity. In terms of this arithmetic a kind of constructive theory of real numbers may also be developed, using more or less standard mathematical procedures.

Kronecker claimed that God made the integers and that all the rest is the work of man. But he was wrong, it seems, and for two reasons. God favored the *real* numbers by giving nature the kind of complex structure that can be measured only in terms of them. If God had really favored the integers, he would have seen to it that there are no incommensurable magnitudes. Secondly, even the integers are the work of man, as the development of arithmetic in terms of 'Crrlt' will show.

Perhaps it is possible to regard geometry, like arithmetic, as also a product of human correlation. Human beings assign numbers to PtEv's in certain ways, some of them leading to certain kinds of patterns determinative of special geometries. Thus it might be possible, in terms of 'Crrlt', to define the various notions needed in the spatio-temporal topology.

Among all the events discussed, it should be noted, some may be singled out and called 'mental events'. Utterance events, LP-events, correlational events, and the like, are examples of such. And of course, the having of conceptions, especially of things that are not, seems as mental as anything can be. In the event totalitarianism ample means are at hand for handling all manner of mental phenomena. It thus should not be urged against the considerations here that they are based too much on the physical at the expense of the mental.

Event logic here has been discussed wholly on the basis of first-order logic with virtual classes and relations. This is a restriction imposed from without and not dictated by the analysis of events itself. With only slight changes a higher-order logic or set theory could be used instead. The result would be an out-and-out platonistic theory of events of greater power than the first-order one. However, it is not clear that this greater power is ever needed.

**O. Causal Connection.** It has been suggested that event logic should be of interest for the study of the exact logical forms of sentences of natural language. But how? In partial answer to this — see also V and VI below — let us consider some of Stevenson's "if-iculties".[21]

Stevenson's valuable paper calls attention to a number of discrepancies between 'if' in English and its usual translation into the horseshoe sign of material implication. "This is not a reason for distrusting the horseshoe," he notes, "which is useful so long as it is taken to mean just what it is defined to mean; and it is not a reason for distrusting our English if's, which in spite of their ambiguities are indispensable to our daily discourse." Accordingly, Stevenson proposes to develop a "richer logic" than the ordinary one, by adding as primitives certain sentential connectives. He speaks throughout in the old terminology of "propositions" rather than in that of the sentences or statements used to express them. Thus he speaks of atomic and molecular propositions, somehow no doubt as real entities in the world, where talk of atomic and molecular sentences would save him from implicit involvement in the notorious difficulties connected with atomic propositions and facts. Finally, the inner structure of atomic sentences, and therewith of molecular ones, is never considered. Many molecular sentences contain quantifiers in

[21] Charles L. Stevenson, "If-iculties," *Philosophy of Science* 37 (1970): 27-49. The following paragraphs are adapted, with the kind permission of the editor, from the author's "On Stevenson's If-iculties," *Philosophy of Science* 39 (1972): 515-521.

interesting ways, the clarification of which would seem essential in getting at their structure. Stevenson, however, has no concern with quantifiers, and does not exhibit the quantificational structure of the English sentences considered.

Stevenson's paper is important in pointing out the seriousness of these discrepancies between 'if —— then' and '⊃' and it is certainly as erroneous to read the latter as 'if —— then' as it is to read it 'implies' or 'entails'. In fact, one can go further and say that it is an "error" to read *any* of the logical symbols in the usual way that is done. *Precisely* what is the connection between 'not' and '∼', or between 'or' and 'v' and 'and' and '·'? Examples showing that the one does not always translate properly into the other can be given *ad nauseam*. An exhaustive classification of the various uses of 'not', 'and', 'or', and so on, in English is needed before their exact connection with the symbols of logic can be fully characterized.[22] The same is true of '⊃' and its various translations into English. In the absence of such a classification of English uses of 'if', let us examine some of the sentences Stevenson considers from a point of view rather different from his.

Stevenson's "richer logic" is an extension of ordinary truth-functional logic, with propositional variables and quantifiers over them, gained by adding one or more intensional sentential connectives together with some probability theory. In place of this kind of "logic," the proposal here is to gain the additional logical power needed in the resources of the event logic above.

Consider Stevenson's first example,

(α)     'If you strike this match it will light; therefore, if you both wet this match and strike it, it will light.'

To strike a match is to perform a certain act, and for it to light is for it to undergo a certain process. In both cases we can speak of an event. Let

---

[22] For similar comments, see *Logic, Language, and Metaphysics.*

'⟨you,strike,this match⟩e'

express that e is an act or event of your striking this match. Similarly,

'⟨this match,lights⟩e'

expresses that e is an event of this match's lighting.

From the point of view of its surface structure, the first clause of (α) does seem to have the form of an 'if — then' sentence. However, from the point of view of its deep structure in terms of event logic, the first clause of (α) seems to have the form rather of a *causal* sentence, such as

'(e) (⟨you,strike,this match⟩ e ⊃ (Ee') (⟨this match, lights⟩ e' ·
· e Cs e'))',

where 'e Cs e'' expresses that e causes e'. This form reads: any event of your striking this match is a cause of some event of its lighting. But this form would not be quite adequate.

It has frequently been urged that causation should be construed rather as a relation between events *under a given linguistic description.* Thus in place of 'e Cs e'' it is proposed to use

'⟨e,a⟩ Cs ⟨e',a'⟩',

which may read: the event e as described by the predicate (or Russellian description) a is a cause of the event e' under the description a'. The first clause of sentence (α) then becomes

(β) '(e) (⟨you,strike,this match⟩ e ⊃ (Ee') (Ea) (Ea') (⟨this match,lights⟩ e' · '⟨you,strike,this match⟩'a · '⟨this match, lights⟩'a' · ⟨e,a⟩ Cs ⟨e',a'⟩) )'.

This may read: any event of your striking this match under this description causes some event of its lighting under that description.

EVENTS, REFERENCE, AND LOGICAL FORM

("'⟨you,strike,this match⟩' a' expresses here that $a$ is a sign event of the appropriate form.) No form simpler than this would seem to be adequate if the sentence is regarded as a causal one.

The second clause of sentence ($\alpha$) now becomes

($\gamma$) '$(e)(e_1)(e_2)($ (⟨you,strike,this match⟩ $e_1$ · ⟨you,wet,this match⟩ $e_2$ · $e = (e_1 \cup e_2)$ ) ) ⊃ $(Ee')$ $(Ea)$ $(Eb)$(⟨this match,lights⟩ $e'$ · '(⟨you, strike,this match) ∩ ⟨you,wet,this match⟩ )'$a$ · '⟨this match,lights⟩' $b$ · ⟨e,a⟩ Cs ⟨e',b'⟩) )'.

This reads: any complex event that consists of your striking this match and your wetting it causes (under this description) an event of its lighting (under that description). The '∩' here is borrowed from *Principia Mathematica*, *22.02, the event-descriptive predicates standing in effect for virtual classes of events.

Note that ($\beta$) is a true sentence if it is regarded as an instance of a causal law to the effect that striking matches causes them to ignite. ($\gamma$) however is false because it is not the case that striking *and* wetting matches — the temporal order has been disregarded here — causes them to ignite. Thus, although ($\alpha$) is a valid argument if its constituent sentences are rendered as 'if — then' sentences, it is clearly not valid if its constituents are regarded as causal and rendered in terms of their deep structure in event logic. Not that the renditions ($\beta$) and ($\gamma$) are final or cannot be improved upon, but only sufficient to protect us from an if-iculty.

'Cs', which designates here a dyadic relation of causation between events under given descriptions, has been used without analysis. So far as the forms of the sentences involved are concerned, this does not matter. For present purposes it could be analyzed in any way, perhaps even in a Humean way according to which 'Cs' could be replaced in ($\beta$) and ($\gamma$) by 'IP' for immediately precedes (in the temporal sense). An event under a given description ⟨e,a⟩ then bears Cs to some ⟨e',a'⟩ provided every event under the description $a$ bears IP to some event under the description $a'$, where $a$ and $a'$ themselves are interrelated by a law of proper causal form. The matter becomes complicated as soon as it is looked at deeply, and metalinguistically, and in any case need not be considered here. One is surely entitled to exhibit logical forms for English sentences without providing an analysis of all the non-logical words occurring.

**P. Some Further If-iculties.** Stevenson proposes some delightful exercises "to be added to any of our present-day texts," namely, to prove the validity of certain arguments that hang on an if-iculty. Let us reflect on at least some of these.

Consider

(1)  'Logic is not confusing. So logic is confusing only if it isn't.'

The play here is upon the notion 'only if', a variant of 'if — then'. Just how should 'only if' be read? If it is to be symbolized by '⊃', then the best readings are no doubt the harmless ones in terms of '∼', 'v,' and '·'. Hence, one should read '⊃' here in terms of 'not' and 'or' or in terms of 'not' and 'and'. The conclusion of (1) becomes, on the first reading, 'So logic is not confusing or it isn't', and on the second reading, 'It is not the case that logic is confusing and is not not confusing'. Any difficulties, if such they are, with these readings reduce to difficulties with the laws of tautology (or idempotence) and double negation as applied to the English 'or' and 'not'.

(2)  'If he dies tonight he will visit us tomorrow; because he will visit us tomorrow.'

Here 'because' is the giveaway. Presumably (2) states that his visiting us tomorrow is the cause of something or other, but just what is not too clear. If someone were to assert (2) to us, we would be puzzled as to what he intended to convey. What is it that will happen because he will visit us tomorrow? we might ask. Or, we might point out to the assertor the truism (meaning postulate?) that no one who dies today will visit us tomorrow. In any case, we would be well advised to ask the assertor to paraphrase (2) into a clearer form, before we try to determine its deep structure in order to decide whether it is supposed to contain a valid inference or not.

# EVENTS, REFERENCE, AND LOGICAL FORM

The third exercise likewise seems to require causal forms.

(3)     'It isn't true that if he breaks a mirror he will have bad luck. So if he *doesn't* break a mirror he will have bad luck.'

Superficially here again we might try to symbolize these sentences in terms just of '⊃', but to do so would not reveal their deep structure. (3) may be paraphrased as

(3')     'It isn't true that whenever he breaks a mirror he has bad luck. So whenever he doesn't break a mirror he has bad luck,'

and this in turn as

(3")     'It isn't true that his breaking a mirror causes him bad luck. So his not breaking a mirror causes him bad luck.'

(3") may be symbolized in causal form, as with the examples above, and the invalidity of the argument brought to light.
    Consider next

(4)     'He is a former communist. So if he is smiling he has a bomb in his pocket, or else if he has a bomb in his pocket he is smiling.'

The supposed validity of this argument is presumed to depend on the tautology

$$\text{'}(\text{---} \supset \cdots) \text{ v } (\cdots \supset \text{---})\text{'},$$

where in place of '---' and '····' sentences are inserted. But notice that there is an implicit time reference in the conclusion of (4), and not just to the now of the assertion but to all times. It seems to say that whenever he is smiling he has a bomb in his pocket, or else whenever he has a bomb in his pocket he is smiling. If the time were only the now of the assertion, the speaker would say that he is smiling *and* has a bomb in his pocket; the hypothetical form would not be used. Thus the conclusion of (4) becomes

34

'$(e)$ ($\langle$he,smiles$\rangle$ $e$ $\supset$ $(Ee')$ $(e$ Simul $e'$ $\cdot$ $\langle$he,has,bomb,pocket$\rangle$ $e')$ )
v $(e)$ ($\langle$he,has,bomb,pocket$\rangle$ $e$ $\supset$ $(Ee')$ $(e$ Simul $e'$ $\cdot$ $\langle$he,smiles$\rangle$ $e')$ )',

where '$e$ Simul $e'$' expresses that $e$ is simultaneous with $e'$. This form is not an instance of a logical or analytic truth. The premiss of (4) thus could be true but the conclusion false. Hence the argument is invalid.

Stevenson's other examples either involve causal forms, or references to time, or else depend upon "valid" inference either from contradictory premisses or to logically true or analytic conclusions. The examples involving causality may be handled as above. And when suitable temporal or tense references are provided, the if-iculties are lessened.

It almost always seems "unnatural" to regard an inference in English as valid if the premisses are contradictory or the conclusion is analytic. Accordingly the following definition of '*is validly inferrable in English*' is perhaps worth exploring. A declarative sentence $a$ of English is validly inferrable from English declarative sentences $b_1$, ... ,$b_n$ as premisses if and only if

(i)   $a$ is the deep structure of $a$, $b_1'$ of $b_1$, $\cdots$ , and $b_n'$ of $b_n$.
(ii)   $a'$ is not analytically true,
(iii)   no contradiction is a logical consequence of $b_1'$, $\cdots$ , $b_n'$,
(iv)   $a'$ is a logical consequence of $b'_1$, $\cdots$ , $b_n'$.

Perhaps some further clause concerning the form of $a'$ as in some way depending on those of $b_1'$, $\cdots$, $b_n'$ should be added, but at least these four requirements seem natural. On the basis of some such definition as this, many further kinds of if-iculties can be avoided.

'If someone pushes the button the doorbell will ring.'

Here also the form

# EVENTS, REFERENCE, AND LOGICAL FORM

'$(e)(\ (Ep)(\text{Per } p \cdot \langle p,\text{Push},b \rangle\ e) \supset (Ee')\ (Ea)(Ec)(\langle d,R \rangle\ e' \cdot\ '\{e''$
$\ni (Ep)(\text{Per } p \cdot \langle p,\text{Push},b \rangle\ e'')\}'\ a \cdot\ '\langle d,R \rangle'c \cdot \langle e,a \rangle\ \text{Cs } \langle e',c \rangle)\ )$',

with the obvious symbolization, is suggested.

To accommodate sentences of these various kinds, Stevenson characterizes a double horseshoe as a quasi-intensional connective in terms of some probability considerations. He also brings in modal operators and two or three additional propositional connectives of an intensional kind. Of course nearly every logically-minded philosopher nowadays complains that the logical apparatus used by other philosophers is too elaborate and complicated. First-order logicians complain that those who use second-order logic, set theory, model theory, and the like, presuppose too much. Modal logicians complain that model theorists use too much. Even model theorists complain that the extensions required of first-order logic for various philosophical purposes are too much. Mathematical constructivists declare a plague on all these houses. In spite of this occupational disease, however, it does seem that Stevenson's extended logic is too elaborate and that it has gone off in the wrong direction and in the wrong way.

Note in particular that his method makes fundamental use of unanalyzed propositions *sui generis* as values for variables. The use of quantifiers upon such entities condones their existence. Also, Stevenson introduces a notation for probability in the definiens of the definition of the double horseshoe, the special sentential connective he introduces. But probability matters seem irrelevant for the task of exhibiting the logical forms of the English sentences Stevenson considers — although of course there would no doubt have to be fundamental reference to them in handling some types of sentences. Validity of inference depends only on logical form, and on nothing else. There are also of course numerous objections to using modal notions object-linguistically in this day of sophisticated semantical interpretations of them.

Stevenson has certainly made his point that the reading of '$\supset$' as 'if ——then' is unwise. Many have been urging the dangers of this and

36

related readings for many years. Who was it who suggested it in the first place? Think of the harm this suggestion has done. It has blurred the distinction between logic and ordinary language in order to hold back the exact study of their relationship, in particular, of the ways in which logic can be helpful for the linguist.

Note that variables other than '*e*', '*e''*', and so on, have crept into the notation surreptitiously. This is harmless enough, and facilitates the reading of formulae, and is a usage that will be found throughout. In particular, '*a*', '*b*', and perhaps '*c*' will be used for sign events, '*p* for persons, and '*x*', '*y*', and so on, for physical objects, all with or without accents or numerical subscripts. All such entities, however, as remarked, are to be construed as events or congeries of such.

**Q. Some Rules of Thumb.** Let us try to get around these if-iculties, and all manner of other disparities between logic and ordinary language, in the following way. Let us realize that logic is not the simple thing Wittgenstein thought it was back in the days of the *Tractatus.* If that is all logic is, of course one would abandon it as Wittgenstein and his followers in effect have done. They have not been willing to allow the subject to grow, to include logical syntax, both an extensional and an intensional semantics (this latter constructively built upon the former), a pragmatics, and also now an event logic including a theory of tenses. Logic as conceived in this wide sense is a much more serious business philosophically than it has been in the hands of the Wittgensteinians. In terms of this kind of an extended logic, the deep structure of many English declaratives may be given. To avoid if-iculties, then, let us always try to get at the deep structures of the sentences involved as quickly as possible, and let us test the validity of an inference only in terms of them.

More specifically, the following rules of thumb are suggested for translating from ordinary English into logical notation:

(i) Read '... ⊃ —' as 'either not ... or —' or as 'not both ... and —' or some paraphrase of these, in nonquantified contexts.

(ii) Decompose sentences always into atomic sentences as far as seems required to reveal relevant structure.

(iii)  Always seek quantificational structure. Do not try to use only the truth functions.

(iv)  Supply suitable time or event references wherever relevant.

(v)  Seek to express necessity in terms of universal quantifiers or semantically in terms of the notion of analytic truth.

(vi)  `Use quotation marks correctly where needed. We often wish to mention expressions as well as use them. Do make use of the lessons of logical syntax and semantics.

(vii)  Be careful that quantifiers over all manner of obscure entities are not introduced. Reference to an obscure kind of entity usually conceals lack of depth of analysis.

(viii)  Be suspicious of any excessive complexity. Keep to the simplest forms wherever possible, but do not oversimplify.

(ix)  Seek to handle differences of "meaning" in the most concrete, Fregean way as differences in the *Arten des Gegebenseins.*

(x)  If the sentence is ambiguous, "disambiguate" it and consider separately the various pertinent "readings."

(xi)  Do not bring in epistemological or other contextual matters irrelevant to form. Deep structure and the validity of inferences depend solely on form, not on extra-linguistic context.

(xii)  Bring in semantical notions, such as 'designates', 'true', 'is true of', and so on, where needed.

(xiii) The use of syntactical, semantical, and pragmatical notions almost always can be made to take the place of reference to real classes, real relations, models, and the like.

Very little has been said here concerning distinctions of tense. The Reichenbachian handling of them, discussed in *Logic, Language, and Metaphysics,* may now easily be adopted. That theory, however, needs a careful looking at from a more linguistically oriented point of view. Different natural language handle tenses in different ways. Some provide for more tenses than others. Does the Reichenbachian theory really provide a theory of tenses universally applicable to all languages? Can all possible tenses be handled within it? To attempt to answer these difficult questions would lead beyond present considerations. For most English sentences, the Reichenbachian analysis seems to suffice, certainly as a first approximation anyhow.

R. **Event Metaphysics.** Event logic quickly develops into an event metaphysics. In fact, it would be difficult to draw a line of demarcation between the two. It is clear also that the metaphysics is one of Whiteheadian type. Metaphysics (or "speculative philosophy") is, according to Whitehead in a famous passage, "the endeavor to frame a coherent, logical, necessary system of general ideas in terms of which every element of our experience can be interpreted. It will be observed that logical notions must themselves find their places in the scheme of philosophic notions."[23] The use of 'necessary' here need not be explicated in terms of modality, but rather in terms of universal quantifiers. The principles are "necessary" in the sense that they are principles of vast generality, stated by means of universal quantifiers. " 'Coherence', as here employed," Whitehead states, "means that the fundamental ideas, in terms of which the scheme is developed, presuppose each other so that in isolation they are meaningless." Note that the whole scheme is a *system* of notions, namely, a language system based on ideas of great generality or defining power. It is clear that the event logic of the foregoing pages, in essentials anyhow, provides the foundations for a speculative philosophy of Whiteheadian type. The coherence, the logicality, the necessity-in-universality, the explication of logical notions themselves (in terms of 'Inf', 'Ref', and so on), as well as other notions of vast generality and defining power are all present.

Whitehead emphasizes that the speculative system must be "adequate" and "applicable" in the sense that "everything of which we are conscious, as enjoyed, perceived, willed, or thought, shall have the character of a particular instance of the general scheme." In particular, then, acts and states of perception, enjoyment, thinking, and so on, must be accommodated, as well as whatever is perceived, enjoyed, or thought about. The foregoing framework is sufficiently

---

[23] *Process and Reality* (Cambridge University Press, Cambridge: 1929), pp. 3-4. See also *Logic, Language, and Metaphysics*, Chapter 1 and the author's *Whitehead's Categoreal Scheme and Other Papers* (Martinus Nijhoff, The Hague: 1974).

broad to allow development in areas concerned with all such entities.

Some acts, states, or processes are said to be *obligatory,* others *prohibited,* and so on, in accord with a moral, social, or religious code. Deontic predicates such as 'is obligatory' and the like are natural adjuncts to event logic. Usually the theory of these terms is developed on the basis of suspect entities such as "propositions" and other unanalyzed entities of intensional type. From the foregoing, however, it is clear that such notions are not needed and that the real purport of the deontic notions may be achieved without them and without loss.

Even with dykes put up all along the line, event theory has overflown its banks, in this all too cursory outline. This no doubt attests to the intrinsic power and fertility of the subject.

# II

# SOME
# LOGICO-METAPHYSICAL
# PRINCIPLES

*"Fungar inani munere. Fungor vice cotis, acutum*
*Reddere quae ferum valet, excors ipsa secandi."*

The subtitle of this paper could be that of Frege's *Gundgesetze; Begriffsschriftlich Abgeleitet.* Any translation would be highly indeterminate. The point is, as has often been noted, that a proper notation is like a live teacher, gently guiding us into the clear and keeping us from error and wooliness. A real effort should be made to express logico-metaphysical principles in as perspicuous a notation as possible. Many advantages would be gained thereby and with no sacrifice of comprehensiveness, or even of grandeur.[1] Of course a notation must be available, and one cannot do better than to use that of the standard classical logic.

In I above and elsewhere various approaches to a logico-metaphysical theory of events, acts, processes, happenings, states, and the like, have been discussed somewhat loosely. It is now time to attempt a more rigorous formulation of the preferred theory in which events (and the like) and such only are taken as values for the

[1] Cf. J. Maritain, *The Degrees of Knowledge* (The Centenary Press, London: 1937), pp. 1-23.

variables. The logical framework is to be that of the first-order theory of the truth-functional connectives with identity and virtual classes and relations — a simple, applied functional calculus of first order. Moreover, fundamental use is made of the calculus of individuals with individuals taken as events. In addition, a simple ordering of events is given in terms of a primitive relation of *earlier than*. Actually the system is at least a metametalanguage, so as to contain not only an object-language part, but a first-order inscriptionalized syntax and semantics for that part, and then also a first-order syntax and semantics for all of that.

Let us begin at the beginning and outline the entire system, essentially that of I, *de novo,* thus making more explicit some items introduced there.

Let '~' and 'v' be the primitive truth-functional connectives for negation and alternation (or disjunction) respectively. The '·' (for conjunction), '⊃' (for material implication), and '≡' (for material equivalence) are then readily definable in the usual way. The variables are *'e'* with or without accents or numerical subscripts, ranging over events of all kinds indiscriminately. These are the only variables admitted, and everything is to be construed in terms of them. (In addition, *'p'*, *'a'*, *'x'*, and so on, may perhaps be used.) The universal quantifier is expressed in the usual way with a variable flanked by parentheses. The existential quantifier '(Ee)' is then short for '~ (e) ~' where in place of 'e' any variable is inserted.[2]

Suitable non-logical predicates applicable to events, a finite number of them, each of appropriate degree, are taken as primitive. Many of these will be mentioned more specifically later, and others are to be presumed introduced by definition. Some, as already suggested, are to be one-place predicates, some two-place, and so on.

The formula $'e_1 = e_2'$ as usual expresses that $e_1$ is identical with $e_2$, where '=' is the primitive for the relation of identity.

Virtual classes and relations are expressed by means of the inverted epsilon '϶' together with braces, as in I. Thus, where '——$e$——' is

---

[2] Bold-face letters are used here and throughout as informal syntactical variables. Single quotes, to simplify, are used ambiguously here and subsequently both in their usual sense as well as in the sense of Quine's corners as already noted in I.

some formula containing '$e$' as its only free variable, the predicate or abstract '$\{e \ni (--e--)\}$' (also written '$\{e \ni --e--\}$') stands for the virtual class of all $e$'s such that $--e--$.

Governing these various notions the usual standard logical laws are presumed to hold, including laws fro the sentential connectives and quantifiers and for identity, and also the following principles or rules concerning virtual classes and relations.

*Principles of Concretion:*

VCR1a.　　$\vdash (e_1)(\{e \ni(--e--)\} e_1 \supset (--e_1--))$, where '$(--e_1--)$' differs from '$(--e--)$' only in containing free occurrences of '$e_1$' wherever there are free occurrences of '$e$' in '$(--e--)$',

VRR1b.　　$\vdash (e_1)(e_2)(\{ee' \ni (--e--e'--)\} e_1 e_2 \supset (--e_1 --e_2--))$, where (etc., as required).

and so on.[3]

*Principles of Abstraction:*

VCR2a.　　$\vdash (e_1)((--e_1--) \supset \{e \ni(--e--)\} e_1)$, if (etc.),

VRR2b.　　$\vdash (e_1)(e_2)((--e_1--e_2--) \supset \{ee' \ni(--e--e'--)\} e_1 e_2)$, if (etc.),

and so on.

Among the primitive and defined predicates, some may be called 'intentional'. Such predicates as 'knows', 'believes', 'wishes', 'remembers', and so on, are of this kind. The predicates other than the intentional ones are called 'physical' or perhaps just 'non-intentional'.

Let '$R$' and '$S$', perhaps with numerical subscripts or accents, stand for any $n$-place primitive predicates or abstracts ($n \geqslant 2$). And let '$F$' and '$G$' similarly stand for one-place primitive predicates or abstracts. Moreover, '$R$' and '$F$' will occasionally be used for virtual relations or classes themselves.

---

[3] The '$\vdash$' is to be read 'is a theorem'. It is to absorb all single quotes or corners around the context to which it is applied.

Clearly

'$F = G$' may abbreviate '$(e) (Fe \equiv Ge)$',

and

'$R = S$' may abbreviate '$(e_1) \cdots (e_n) (Re_1 \cdots e_n \equiv Se_1 \cdots e_n)$'
$\cdots e_n)$'

in familiar fashion. (Here '$e$' is understood not to occur freely in $F$ or $G$ nor $e_1, \cdots, e_n$ in $R$ or $S$.)

As *Principles of Identity* the following are needed.

IdR1.    $\vdash (e) e = e$.
IdR2.    $\vdash (e_1) (e_2) (e_1 = e_2 \supset (Fe_1 \equiv Fe_2))$.

In addition, because of the presence of the event-descriptive and cosmic-sum predicates, the following also are needed.

IdR3.      $\vdash (e) (e_1) (e_2) (e_1 = e_2 \supset (\langle e_1 \rangle e \equiv \langle e_2 \rangle e))$,
IdR4.      $\vdash (e) (e') (e'') (e_1) \cdots (e_n) (e') \cdots (e'_n) ((e_1 = e'_1 \cdots$
$\cdot e_n = e'_n \cdot e' = e'' \cdot R = S) \supset (\langle e', R, e_1, \cdots, e_n \rangle e \equiv \langle e'', S, e'_1, \cdots,$
$e'_n \rangle e))$.

The calculus of individuals is developed here in terms of a primitive '$P$' for the relation of part to whole. Thus '$e_1$ P $e_2$' expresses that $e_1$ is a part of $e_2$. Also terms of the form '$(e1\text{---}e\text{---})$' are admitted as primitives, where '$\text{---}e\text{---}$' is a formula containing '$e$' as a free variable. The '1' here is not the numeral for the number one but rather for an operation of *point-event summation*. The expression '$(e1\text{---}e\text{---})$', is thus to stand for the complex event containing as parts all point events $e$ such that $\text{---}e\text{---}$. This notion will become clearer in the next paragraph.

Let us say informally for the moment that an event is *null* if and only if it is a part of all events. Then a point event may be described as any event $e$ such that it is non-null and is a part of all of its non-null parts. More specifically, then,

'PtEv $e$' may abbreviate '$(\sim (e'') e \; \mathbf{P} \; e'' \cdot (e') ((\sim (e'') e' \; \mathbf{P} \; e'' \cdot e' \; \mathbf{P} \; e) \supset e \; \mathbf{P} \; e'))$'.

The definiendum reads '$e$ is a point event'. The point events are the smallest admissible units out of which the cosmos, physical and mental, is presumed to be built.

The null event is admitted here without qualms as a helpful technical device. It is not indispensable, however, and could readily be dropped if desired. The convenience of admitting it more than compensates for any uneasiness one may feel in so doing.

An event $e_1$ may be said to *overlap* an event $e_2$ if and only if they have a point event in common. Thus

'$e_1 \; O \; e_2$' may abbreviate '$(Ee) (\text{PtEv} \; e \cdot e \; \mathbf{P} \; e_1 \cdot e \; \mathbf{P} \; e_2)$'.

And events $e_1$ and $e_2$ are said to be (totally) *discrete* if and only if they do not overlap. Thus

'$e_1 \; D \; e_2$' abbreviates '$\sim e_1 \; O \; e_2$'.

Consider now $\{e \ni e = e\}$, the universal virtual class V, and then the event $(e 1 e = e)$. This latter is clearly the complex event containing all point events as parts. It is thus the entire cosmos, containing all point events whatsoever, past, present, and future, here, there, and everywhere. For short, it is called 'W', so that

'W' abbreviates '$(e 1 e = e)$'.

The admission of W, the *world* or *cosmos,* as an entity seems as natural as admitting the universal class V. Similarly

'N' may abbreviate '$(e 1 \sim e = e)$'.

N is the null event, and again, its admission seems as natural as admitting the null virtual class, that is, the class $\Lambda$ or $\{e \ni \sim e = e\}$.

Also let

'$-e$' abbreviate '$(e'1 \sim e' \mathrm{P} e)$'.

The *negative* event $-e$ thus consists of just those point events that are not parts of $e$. Similarly

'$(e_1 \cup e_2)$' may abbreviate '$(e1 \, (e \, \mathrm{P} \, e_1 \, \mathrm{v} \, e \, \mathrm{P} \, e_2))$'

and

'$(e_1 \cap e_2)$' may abbreviate '$(e1(e \, \mathrm{P} \, e_1 \cdot e \, \mathrm{P} \, e_2))$'.

The complex event $(e_1 \cup e_2)$ is the *sum* of the events $e_1$ and $e_2$, and $(e_1 \cap e_2)$ is their *product.*

The reader will note that with these five notions available, a kind of Boolean algebra may be developed. In fact, the calculus of individuals here is just this Boolean algebra, where the individuals are taken as events.

Some readers may object that in admitting all possible sums, products, and negatives here the universe is somehow being over-populated. Given any events $e_1$ and $e_2$, however remote from each other in space or time, their sum is assumed also to be an event, and their product also (even if null). As a matter of fact, however, proper names and descriptions are often admitted for just such sums. 'World War II', for example, names the sum of a vast motley of scattered events, whereas 'the statue of Liberty' names a motley of adjacent parts, arms, head, body, torch, and so on.

The following notion is useful in what follows, the notion of the *fusion* of a virtual class of events. Let '$F$', '$G$', and so on, hereafter stand for any virtual class. Then

'Fu'$F$' may abbreviate '$(e1(\mathrm{E}e') \, (F \, e' \cdot e \, \mathrm{P} \, e'))$'.

## SOME LOGICO-METAPHYSICAL PRINCIPLES

The fusion of $F$ is thus the event consisting of all point events that are parts of members of $F$. Similarly

‘Nu‘$F$’ may abbreviate  ‘$(e1(e')(F e' \supset e \text{ P } e'))$’,

so that the *nucleus of $F$* is the event consisting of all point events that are parts of all members of $F$.

To the foregoing principles the following are now to be added, as stipulating principles of the calculus of individuals.

*Principle of Reflexivity for P:*

CIR 1.    ⊢ $(e) e \text{ P } e$.

*Principle of Transitivity for P:*

CIR2.   ⊢ $(e_1)(e_2)(e_3)((e_1 \text{ P } e_2 \cdot e_2 \text{ P } e_3) \supset e_1 \text{ P } e_3)$.

*Principle of Antisymmetry for P:*

CIR3.    ⊢ $(e_1)(e_2)(e_1 \text{ P } e_2 \cdot e_2 \text{ P } e_1) \supset e_1 = e_2)$.

*Principle of Summational Parts:*

CIR4.    ⊢$(e')((e1Fe) \text{ P } e' \equiv (e)((\text{PtEv } e \cdot Fe) \supset e \text{ P } e'))$.

*Principle of Summational Wholes:*

CIR5.    ⊢ $(e')(e' \text{ P } (e1Fe) \equiv (e)((\text{PtEv } e \cdot e \text{ P } e') \supset Fe))$.

*Principle of Existence for Point-Event Parts:*

CIR6.    ⊢ $(e)(\sim e = \text{N} \supset (Ee')(\text{PtEv } e' \cdot e' \text{ P } e))$.

*General Principle of Non-Nullity:*

## EVENTS, REFERENCE, AND LOGICAL FORM

*CIR7.*    $\vdash (e_1) \cdots (e_n) (Re_1 \cdots e_n \supset (\sim e_1 = \mathrm{N} \cdot \cdots \cdot \sim e_n = \mathrm{N}))$, for all non-intentional primitive $R$ and for $n \geqslant 1$

*CIR1-3* are familiar kinds of rules. *CIR4* stipulates that the sum of all point events $e$ such that $Fe$ is a part of $e'$ if and only if every point event $e$ such that $Fe$ is a part of $e'$. And *CIR5*, similarly, that $e'$ is a part of the sum of all point events $e$ such that $Fe$ if and only if every point event $e$ that is a part of $e'$ is such that $Fe$. Clearly it is to be assumed that every non-null event has a point-event part, as in *CIR6*. And further it is assumed, in *CIR7*, that the null event cannot be a relatum of any of the primitive physical relations. Clearly the null event is not to be blue, red, or the like, it is not to weigh so many grams, it is not to attract some entity with such and such a force, and so on.

Let hereafter

'E!$e$'   abbreviate    '$\sim e = \mathrm{N}$'.

The definiendum here may read '$e$ exists' or '$e$ occurs' or '$e$ is actual', these readings being merely short for '$e$ is not the null entity'.

Let '$e_1$ B $e_2$' express primitively, as in I above, that $e_1$ is earlier than or before $e_2$ in a suitable temporal ordering. Concerning this relation the following principles are assumed.[4]

*Principle of Asymmetry for B:*

*BR1.*    $\vdash (e_1)(e_2)(e_1 \text{ B } e_2 \supset \sim e_2 \text{ B } e_1)$.

Clearly B is an asymmetrical relation.

*Principles of Before-Than for Point-Event Sums:*

*BR2.*    $\vdash (e')((e1Fe) \text{ B } e' \equiv (e)((\text{PtEv } e \cdot Fe) \supset e \text{ B } e'))$.

*BR3.*    $\vdash (e')(e' \text{ B } (e1Fe) \equiv (e)((\text{PtEv } e \cdot Fe) \supset e' \text{ B } e))$.

---

[4] Cf. R. Carnap, *Introduction to Symbolic Logic and Its Applications* (Dover, New York: 1958), p. 214.

SOME LOGICO-METAPHYSICAL PRINCIPLES

Clearly a point-event sum $(e1Fe)$ is before $e'$ if and only if every point event $e$ such that $Fe$ is before $e'$, and $e'$ is before $(e1Fe)$ if and only if $e'$ is before every point event $e$ such that $Fe$.

The next two principles serve to interrelate P and B.
*Interrelational Principles of P and B:*

 *BR4.*  ⊢ $(e_1)(e_2)((e)((E!e \cdot e \, P \, e_1) \supset \sim e_2 \, B \, e) \supset (e)$ $(e_2 \, B \, e \supset e_1 \, B \, e))$.

If $e_2$ is before no non-null part of $e_1$, then $e_1$ is before every event that $e_2$ is.

 *BR5.*  ⊢ $(e_1)(e_2)((e)((E!e \cdot e \, P \, e_1) \supset \sim e \, B \, e_2) \supset (e)$ $(e \, B \, e_2 \supset e \, B \, e_1))$.

If no non-null part of $e_1$ is before $e_2$, then every event before $e_2$ is also before $e_1$.

In addition it is assumed that the null event N and the cosmic world-event W do not bear B to anything.
*Principle of N-exclusion for B:*

 *BR6.*  ⊢ $(e_1)(e_2)(e_1 \, B \, e_2 \supset (E!e_1 \cdot E!e_2))$.

*Principle of W-exclusion for B:*

 *BR7.*  ⊢ $(e_1)(e_2)(e_1 \, B \, e_2 \supset (\sim e_1 = W \cdot \sim e_2 = W))$.

Clearly no event is either before or after the null event, and no event is either before or after W. These rules exclude them altogether from the temporal ordering.

Let us turn now to the event-descriptive predicates.

The rules of formation, or definitions of 'formula' and 'term' for the above, have not been given. For the sake of explicitness, they may be formulated as follows. The clauses are to be taken together as providing a definition (by simultaneous recursion) of 'term' and 'formula' within the metalanguage:

1. If **e** is variable or primitive individual constant, **e** is a term.

2. If **e** is a variable and $A$ is a formula, then '$(e1A)$' is a term.

3. An $n$-place primitive predicate followed by $n$ terms ($n \geqq 1$) is a formula.

4. If $e_1$ and $e_2$ are terms, '$e_1 = e_2$', '$e_1 \ P \ e_2$', and '$e_1 \ B \ e_2$' are formulae.

5. If $A$ is a formula, so is '$\sim A$'.

6. If $A$ and $B$ are formulae, so is '$(A \lor B)$'.

7. If $A$ is a formula and **e** is a variable, '$(e)A$' is a formula.

8. If **e** is a variable, $A$ is a formula, and $e'$ is a term, '$\{e \ni A\} e''$ is a formula.

9. If $e_1, \cdots, e_n$ ($n \geq 2$) are distinct variables, $A$ is a formula, and $e'_1, \cdots, e'_n$ are terms, then '$\{e_1 \cdots e_n \ni A\} e'_1 \cdots e'_n$' is a formula.

10. If $e, e_1, \cdots, e_n$ ($n \geq 1$) are terms and $Q$ is an $n$-place primitive predicate, '$\langle e_1, Q, e_2, \cdots, e_n \rangle e$' is a formula.

11. If $e, e'_1, \cdots, e'_n$ ($n \geqq 1$) are terms, $e_1, \cdots, e_n$ are distinct variables, and $A$ is a formula, '$\langle e'_1, \{e_1 \cdots e_n \ni A\}, e'_2 \cdots, e'_n \rangle e$, is a formula.

12. If **e** and $e'$ are terms, '$\langle e \rangle e''$ is a formula.

The full formational grammar, the so-called formation rules, of the object language is spelled out by means of these rules.

The following are *inter alia* fundamental principles characterizing the event-descriptive and cosmic-sum predicates.

First there is the *Principle of Event Existence*.

$$EvR1. \qquad \vdash \ (e)(e_1) \cdots (e_n)(Ree_1 \cdots e_n \ \equiv \ (Ee') \ \langle e, R, e_1, \cdots, e_n \rangle e').$$

Clearly where $Ree_1 \cdots e_n$, there is at least one event $e'$ of the kind described. There may of course be many, but the Principle requires at least one.[5]

Next is the *Principle of Cosmic Summation*.

---

[5] Cf. H. Reichenbach, *loc. cit.*, Chapter VII.

# SOME LOGICO-METAPHYSICAL PRINCIPLES

*EvR2.* $\quad \vdash (e)(e')(e_1) \cdots (e_n)(\langle e,R,e_1. \cdots e_n\rangle e' \supset (\langle e\rangle e'$
$\cdot \langle e_1\rangle e' \cdot \cdots \cdot \langle e_n\rangle e'))$.

Any event of the kind described is one of the events comprising the cosmic sums of the various "subjects."

There is also the *Principle of Distinctness of the Event from its Subjects.*

*EvR3.* $\quad \vdash (e)(e')(e_1) \cdots (e_n)(\langle e,R,e_1, \cdots ,e_n\rangle e' \supset (\sim$
$e' = e \cdot \sim e' = {}'e_1 \cdot \cdots \cdot \sim e' = e_n))$.

The null entity is to be excluded from the cosmic sum of anything. This is required by the *Existence Principle for Cosmic-Sum Events.*

*EvR4.* $\quad \vdash (e)(e')(\langle e\rangle e' \supset E!e')$.

Next is the *Principle of Event-Kind Inclusion,* a special case of which was already discussed in I.

*EvR5.* $\quad \vdash (e)(e_1) \cdots (e_n)(Ree_1 \cdots e_n \supset See_1 \cdots e_n) \supset (e)$
$(e_1) \cdots (e_n)(e')(\langle e,R,e_1, \cdots ,e_n\rangle e' \supset (Ee'')(e'' \text{ P } e' \cdot \langle e,S,e_1, \cdots ,$
$e_n\rangle e'))$.

The *Principle of Event-Parts* is to the effect that every non-null part of an *e*-event is itself an *e*-event.

*EvR6.* $\quad \vdash (e)(e_1)(e_2)((\langle e\rangle e_1 \cdot E!e_2 \cdot e_2 \text{ P } e_1) \supset \langle e\rangle e_2)$.

If *e* is some Caesar-event then every non-null spatio-temporal part of *e* is also a Caesar-event.

And finally, in accord with the attitude that everything non-null in heaven or earth is to be regarded as an event, there is the *Principle of Process.*

51

## EVENTS, REFERENCE, AND LOGICAL FORM

*EvR 7.*         ⊢ $(e)(e') ( (E!e \cdot e$ P $e') \supset \langle e' \rangle e). e).$

These principles by no means exhaust all that are needed to characterize the event-descriptive and cosmic-sum predicates, but they will suffice for present purposes.

It was mentioned above that the theory of events includes an inscriptionalized syntax and semantics. The metalanguage incorporating this is to contain then a translation of all the foregoing, as well as suitable additional predicates for its syntax and semantics. Sign events are merely one more species of events, so that it seems eminently natural to add an inscriptionalized syntax to a translation of the foregoing.

What now are sign events? Usually they are contrasted with sign designs or shapes, and sign events are regarded as instances of them occuying space-time. But anything at all, except N or W, can be taken as a sign event provided only that it be taken to behave in the desired way. More specifically, then, sign events are to be relativized throughout to the *user* of language. It is the user who takes certain objects or events and regards them as sign events of such and such a kind. Thus, as in I, let

'*e* LP *e*''

express primitively that person *e* takes the event *e'* as a *left parenthesis,*

'*e* RP *e*'',

as a *right parenthesis,* and so on. No matter what actual event *e'* is here, the user *e* regards it as being a left or right parenthesis. Notation is a human artifact and not confined just to certain configurations of ink-marks throughout the cosmos.[6]

Similarly, let

[6]As in N. Goodman and W. V. Quine, "Steps toward a Constructive Nominalism."

'*e* VEE *e'* ',
'*e* TILDE *e'* ',
'*e* EE *e'* ',
'*e* AC *e'* ',
'*e* ID *e'* ',
'*e* PEE *e'* ',
'*e* INVEP *e'* ',
'*e* LB *e'* ',
'*e* RB *e*'',
'*e* ONE *e'* ',
'*e* BEE *e'* ',
'*e* LHD *e'* ',

and

'*e* RHD *e'* '

express primitively that person *e* takes *e'* to be a 'v', a '∼', an '*e*', an
'' or accent, an '=', a 'P', an 'ǝ', a '{' or a left brace, a '}' or
right brace, a '1', a 'B', a '⟨' or left half-diamond, or a '⟩' or right
half-diamond, respectively. All variables of the translation part of the
metalanguage may now officially be written as '*e*', '*e*'', '*e*''', and so
on, although informally we can continue to use '$e_1$', '$e_2$', and so on.
Again, officially, let all primitive predicates be 'Q', 'Q'', and so on,
and all primitive individual constants be 'a', 'a'', and so on, although
again others may be used informally. Then, in addition to the
foregoing,

'*e* QUEW *e'* '

is needed for 'Q', and

'*e* Ay *e'* '

for 'a'.

Each of the relations here is a *shape-descriptive relation,*

53

supplanting the shape predicates of non-pragmatized inscriptional syntax. In addition, of course, a relation for concatenation is needed, as in I. Let

$$'e \ C \ e_1, e_2, e_3'$$

express now primitively that person $e$ takes $e_1$ to be the result of concatenating $e_2$ with $e_3$, that is, $e$ regards the complex expression $e_1$ as being the result of putting $e_2$ and $e_3$ end to end, as it were, in proper orientation to each other.

Let us turn now to the syntactical rules, only a few of which will be given.

Clearly it is desirable that the user should not mix up the various basic symbols of his notation. He should not mix up a 'v' with a '∼', or an 'ə' with a '∼', and so on. This requirement is reminiscent of Ernst Schröder's *Axion der Inhärenz der Zeichen*.[7] "It guarantees us that throughout all our arguments and deductions the symbols remain constant in our memory — or preferably on paper." Thus the following may be postulated.

*Principle of Discreteness for Basic Signs:*

*InSynR1.* ⊢ $(e) \ (e_1) \ (e_2) \ ( \ ( \ (e \ LP \ e_1 \ \bullet \ e \ RP \ e_2 \ ) \ ) \supset e_1 \ D \ e_2 \ )$ $\bullet \ ( \ (e \ LP \ e_1 \ \bullet \ e \ VEE \ e_2 \ ) \supset e_1 \ D \ e_2 \ ) \ . \ ... \ . \ ( \ (e \ Quew \ e_1 \ \bullet \ e \ Ay \ e_2 \ )$ $\supset e_1 \ D \ e_2 \ ) \ )$.

Here all possible combinations are to be presumed filled in.

Let

$'e$ Char $e''$ abbreviate $'(e$ LP $e' \ v \ e$ RP $e' \ v \ \cdots \ v \ e$ Ay $e')'$.

The definiendum reads then '$e$ takes $e'$ to be a typographical character or symbol'. There is then the principle that $e$ takes no

---

[7] Referred to in G. Frege, *The Foundations of Arithmetic* (Blackwells, Oxford: 1950), p. VIII$^e$.

character to be the result of concatenation.
*Principle of Simplicity of the Characters:*

*InSynR2.* ⊢ $(e)(e')(e$ Char $e' \supset \sim (Ee_1)(Ee_2) e$ C $e', e_1, e_2)$.

Also clearly, if $e$ takes $e_1$ as the concatenate of $e_2$ and $e_3$ then $e$ does not take $e_1$ as the concatenate of $e_3$ and $e_2$.
*Principle of Quasi-Asymmetry for C:*

*InSynR3.* ⊢ $(e)(e_1)(e_2)(e_3)(e$ C $e_1, e_2, e_3 \supset \sim e$ C $e_1, e_3, e_2)$.

Also if $e$ C $e_1, e_2, e_3$ then $e_2$ and $e_3$ are discrete and $e_1$ is their sum. (Let 'Per $e$' express that $e$ is a person.)
*Principle of Discrete Sums:*

*InSynR4.* ⊢ $(e)(e_1)(e_2)(e_3)(e$ C $e_1, e_2, e_3 \supset$ (Per $e \cdot e_2$ D $e_3 \cdot e_1 = (e_2 \cup e_3)))$.

Clearly no character is null or universal.
*Principle of Non-Nullity and Non-Universality for Characters:*

*InSynR5.* ⊢ $(e)(e')(e$ Char $e' \supset$ (Per $e \cdot E!e' \cdot \sim e' = W))$.

It follows from these two principles that

$(e)(e_1)(e_2)(e_3)(e$ C $e_1, e_2, e_3 \supset (E!e_1 \cdot E!e_2 \cdot E!e_3 \cdot \sim e_2 = W \cdot \sim e_3 = W))$,

so that this need not be postulated separately. It follows from the preceding also that

$(e)(e_1)(e_2)(e_3)(e$ C $e_1, e_2, e_3 \supset (\sim e$ C $e_2, e_1, e_3 \cdot \sim e$ C $e_2, e_3, e_1 \cdot \sim e$ C $e_3, e_1, e_2 \cdot \sim e$ C $e_3, e_2, e_1))$.

# EVENTS, REFERENCE, AND LOGICAL FORM

The principle under which two concatenates are taken to be identical is as follows.

*Principle of Concatenational Identity:*

*InSynR6.*  $\vdash ((e)(e_1) \cdots (e_6)((e \ C \ e_1,e_2,e_3 \ \cdot \ e_3 \ C \ e_4,e_5, e_6) \supset (e_1 = e_4 \equiv ((e_2 = e_5 \ \cdot \ e_3 = e_6) \ v \ (Ee_7)(e \ C \ e_3,e_7, e_6 \ \cdot \ e \ C \ e_5,e_2,e_7) \ v \ (Ee_7)(e \ C \ e_2,e_5,e_7 \ \cdot \ e \ C \ e_6,e_7e_3))))).$

Next let

'*e* SgnEv *e''* abbreviate '(*e* Char *e'* v (E*e*$_1$)(E*e*$_2$) *e* C *e'*, *e*$_1$,*e*$_2$)',

so that *e* takes *e'* to be a sign event provided *e* takes *e'* to be a character or a concatenate.

Additional principles, which need not be given here, and indeed additional syntactical primitives, are required for a full delineation of pragmatized inscriptional syntax.[8]

According to the above, the user *e* is free to take anything he wishes as a character. But for most languages, there is of course a standard or canonical notation, in use throughout the speaking or writing community. This may be provided for here by picking out some one person as the paradigmatic or expert user and taking his notation as canonical. Let 'WVQ' be the proper name of such a person. To be a canonical left parenthesis is then to be like some sign event taken as a left parenthesis by WVQ. Let '*e*$_1$ Like *e*$_2$' express that the sign event *e*$_1$ is sufficiently like *e*$_2$ to be taken as a sign event of the same kind. Then

'LP *e*' may abbreviate '(E*e'*) (WVQ LP *e'* · *e* Like *e'*)'.

And similarly for other characters, for concatenates in general, and for the various defined notions.

Such a delineation will be given in the author's *Semiotics and Linguistic Structure* (The State University of New York Press, Albany: to appear).

# SOME LOGICO-METAPHYSICAL PRINCIPLES

Little of a technical kind has thus far been said about truth and reference. It seems best to reserve these subjects for the next essay, III below. Also little has been said concerning intentional as over and aginst the physical predicates. However, a good deal of doctrine concerning these will emerge from the various material of V and VI below.

Just as from the object language, a semantical metalanguage was formed by adding a syntax, a semantics, and a theory of reference, so also now a metametalanguage is to be formed from the foregoing metalanguage in essentially the same way. As already noted, the full theory must be regarded as at least metametalinguistic.

The foregoing represents the first attempt apparently to suggest some axioms for a comprehensive theory of events in which syntax and semantics may be accommodated. The list of axioms put forward is thus merely provisory and subject to correction and improvement in the light of subsequent research. Whatever its shortcomings, the foregoing appears to provide the only known system of its kind based on first-order logic and without the infinite complexities and obscurities necessitated if sets (or real classes) are introduced as values for variables. All such entities have been eschewed here with a resulting gain in ontic simplicity.

Some metaphysical readers may feel that logic has been pressed too far in the foregoing and that somehow metaphysics has been lost. "Logica sunt, non leguntur," they say in effect. The proper reply is not "Metaphysica sunt, non leguntur," as Frege noted correctly, but rather that a fruitful syncretism of the two is now eminently desirable. Hopefully the foregoing provides a few useful first steps in this direction.

# III

# ON TRUTH, REFERENCE, AND OCCASIONS OF UTTERANCE

*"Simplex ratio veritatis."*

It has been suggested by many writers in recent years that 'true' should be regarded as adjectival of acts or occasions of utterance or assertion or the like. The semantic predicate for truth, it will be recalled, whether characterized in terms of a defined relation of satisfaction or a primitive relation of designation or denotation, or in some other way, is adjectival only of declarative sentences of the language at hand.[1] Unfortunately, those writers who favor acts of utterance and the like have not been too clear as to just what *theory* is involved in their contention. The purpose of this present paper is to fill this lacuna, in terms of event logic including a theory of linguistic acts.

Donald Davidson is prominent among those writers who have called attention to the occasions-of-utterance theory of truth, as it may be called. "We could take truth to be a property [class?], not of sentences, but of utterances, or speech acts, or ordered triples of sentences, times and persons; but it is simplest just to view truth as a

---

[1] See especially A. Tarski, "The Concept of Truth in Formalized Languages," in *Logic, Semantics, Metamathematics* (Clarendon Press, Oxford: 1956); R. Carnap, *Introduction to Semantics* (University of Chicago Press, Chicago: 1942); and *Truth and Denotation.*

relation between a sentence, a person, and a time."[2] It is far from clear that this latter proposal is actually the simplest, however. Nor is it clear whether speech acts are here identified with ordered triples of sentences, times, and persons or not. In any case, the speech-act or occasions-of-utterance theory seems never to have been worked out. It would involve, in Davidson's words, "a fairly far-reaching revision in the theory of truth."

Davidson suggests that his theory, of regarding truth as a relation among a sentence, a person, and a time, would (pp. 319-320) "entail sentences like the following:

[1]     'I am tired' is true as (potentially) spoken by $p$ at $t$ if and only if $p$ is tired at $t$.
[2]     'That book was stolen' is true as (potentially) spoken by $p$ at $t$ if and only if the book demonstrated by $p$ at $t$ is stolen prior to $t$."

In particular, then, Dividson's proposal is intended to enable us to handle sentences containing personal pronouns, demonstratives, and tensed verbs in the way suggested. This proposal is not without interest, but several doubts concerning it are in order.

There is Davidson's dangerous use of 'potentially' in the metalanguage, with neither a logical form given for it nor an analysis. There is the introduction of a new style of variables or names for times that would seem unsatisfactory to some. Times are not entities *sui generis* but are perhaps best handled as constructs in terms of events or occasions.   Also it is not clear whether expressions for Davidson are to be handled as sign designs or shapes or as sign events or inscriptions. The distinction is rather important, and an enormous difference in theory will result in the choice made. Also, even persons may be analyzed away as sequences of fusions of genidentical events. Thus, if sign events are chosen, sentences, persons, and times may all be handled in terms of an underlying theory of events. The gist of Davidson's proposal may be accommodated, however, in this alternative treatment.

    [2] D. Davidson, "Truth and Meaning," *Synthese* 17 (1967): 304-323, p. 319. Cf. also G. H. von Wright, *Norm and Action* (Routledge and Kegan Paul, London: 1963), pp. 22 ff.

# ON TRUTH, REFERENCE, AND OCCASIONS OF UTTERANCE

The objects of speaking, of uttering, of writing, and so on, are best regarded, it would seem, as concrete entities constituting the converse domain of certain relations. Let

$$\text{'}p \text{ Spk } e\text{'},$$
$$\text{'}p \text{ Utt } e\text{'},$$

and

$$\text{'}p \text{ Wrt } e\text{'}$$

be used to express respectively that the person $p$ speaks, utters, or writes the sign event $e$.[3] If persons are assimilated to vast fusions of genidentical events, as in I and II above, an event variable can be used in place even of '$p$'. (The fundamental forms become then '$e_1$ Spk $e_2$', '$e_1$ Utt $e_2$', and '$e_1$ Wrt $e_2$'). The analysis of the key relations mentioned in these forms need not be given at the moment, in accord with Davidson's policy of distinguishing sharply "between questions of logical form or grammar, and the analysis of individual concepts." Only when some semblance of order is gained concerning the forms is it fruitful to go on to analysis.

The notion of reference was discussed only in passing in I above. Here let us be more explicit. One should ask: precisely what is it that is supposed to refer to what? Words, it will be answered, and these refer to the objects of the discourse at hand. However, different people use the same word to refer to different objects and different words on different occasions of use to refer to the same object. In reference five factors thus seem important: the user, the word, the thing, the linguistic context, and the occasion of use. In accord with this, we could construe reference as a pentadic relation and bring in these five factors explicitly. Thus

(3) $\qquad\qquad\qquad$ '$e_1 \text{ Ref}_e \text{ } e_2, e_3, e_4$'

[3] Cf. Chapter I of *Logic, Language, and Metaphysics*.

could be taken to express primitively that person $e_1$ uses word or sign event $e_2$ as occuring in the sentence $e_4$ to refer to the object $e_3$ in the linguistic act or occasion $e$. However, reference to the act or occasion $e$ is already provided for by writing, in place of (3),

(4)  $'\langle e_1, \text{Ref}, e_2, e_3, e_4 \rangle e'$

In fact, (3) may be regarded as short for (4) if 'Ref' is taken as a primitive for a quadratic relation. The form

(4')  $'e_1 \text{ Ref } e_2, e_3, e_4\,'$

may thus be regarded now a primitive sentential form.

Let the vocabulary of the object language be augmented now to include the personal pronouns '$I$', '$you$', '$he$', '$she$', and '$it$', and the demonstrative '$that$' as prefixed to one-place predicates. The phrases '$that\ F$', '$that\ G$', and so on, are now to be significant as terms for events or individuals, where in place of '$F$' and '$G$' one-place predicates are inserted. The personal pronouns likewise are to be significant as individual terms.

The plural forms of both the personal pronouns and of the demonstrative may also be regarded as referring, provided a suitable syntax for them has been given. Thus if '$Q$' is some one-place predicate applicable to persons, '$Qe$' is now to be significant where in place of '$e$' a plural personal pronoun is inserted. '$Q\ we$', '$Q\ you_p$', and '$Q\ they$' express respectively that we have Q, that you (in the plural) have Q, and that they have Q. Similarly '$Q\ (those\ F)$' is significant and expresses that those $F$'s have Q. Syntactically there seems to be no problem in admitting these plural forms. They become interesting when their reference is to be characterized, and for this the person and the acts of reference must be brought in explicitly. And of course all the persons and entities referred to by pronouns and demonstratives are understood to be among the values for variables of the language at hand.

To handle pronouns and demonstratives, let

$$\text{'}e \text{ I } e\text{'',}$$
$$\text{'}e \text{ YOU}_s \ e\text{'',}$$
$$\text{'}e \text{ HE } e\text{'',}$$
$$\text{'}e \text{ WE } e\text{'',}$$
$$\text{'}e \text{ YOU}_p \ e\text{'',}$$
$$\text{'}e \text{ THEY } e\text{'',}$$
$$\text{'}e \text{ THAT } e\text{'',}$$

and

$$\text{'}e \text{ THOSE } e\text{''}$$

be introduced to accommodate shape-descriptive relations additional to those of II. Let 'PerPrn $e$' express that $e$ is a canonical personal pronoun, that is, an inscription of the proper shape '$I$', '$you_s$' (in the singular), '$he$', '$she$', '$it$', '$we$', '$you_p$' (in the plural), and '$they$'. And let 'Dmtv $e$' express that $e$ is a canonical demonstrative, of the shape '$that$' or '$those$' as concatenated with a one-place predicate constant. Thus 'WE $e$' may express that $e$ is a canonical '$we$'-shaped inscription, and so on.

It is now time to consider *Rules of Reference* for the object language as thus argued. The following constitute apparently the first attempt in this direction on the basis of a theory of inscriptions and for a language containing personal pronouns and demonstratives. Some of the Rules may therefore not be wholly satisfactory but still may be useful in helping to get at the real "roots of reference" and as heuristics for more adequate formulations.

The first rule, *RefR1,* is a *Rule of Limitation,* to the effect that persons use certain expressions to refer to non-linguistic entities.

*RefR1.* $\vdash$ $(e)(e_1)(e_2)(e_3)(e \text{ Ref } e_1,e_2,e_3 \supset (\text{Per } e \ \cdot$ (InCon $e_1$ v PredConOne $e_1$ v PerPrn $e_1$ v Dmtv $e_1$ v PtEvSumTrm $e_1$) $\cdot$ Sent $e_3$ $\cdot$ $e_1$ Occ $e_3$ $\cdot$ $\sim$ SgnEv $e_2$)).

Here 'InCon $e_1$' expresses that $e_1$ is a canonical individual constant 'PredConOne $e_1$' that $e_1$ is a canonical one-place predicate

63

constant, 'PtEvSumTrm $e_1$' that $e_1$ is a canonical term for a point-event sum containing no free variables (that is, an expression of the form '$(e1--e--)$' *where* '$--e--$' is a sentential form containing '$e$' as its only free variable), and '$e_1$ Occ $e_3$' that $e_1$ and $e_3$ are in canonical notation and $e_1$ has at least one occurrence in $e_3$.

The next rule is the *Rule of Unique Reference for Individual Constants and Point-Event Summation Terms.*

*RefR2.*     ⊢ $(e)$ $(e_1)$ $(e_2)$ $(e_3)$ $(e_4)$ $(e_5)$ $(\,(e$ Ref $e_1,e_2,e_3$ ·
(InCon $e_1$ v PtEvSumTrm $e_1$) · $e$ Ref $e_1,e_4,e_5) \supset e_2 = e_4$).

If person $e$ uses the individual constant or point-event summation term $e_1$ to refer to $e_2$ and also to $e_4$, then $e_2$ and $e_4$ are the same, even if the sentential contexts are not.

*RefR3, RefR4,* and *RefR5* are respectively the *Shape-Descriptive Rules* for InCon's, PtEvSumTrm's and for PredCon-One's, as one might expect.

*RefR3.*     ⊢ $(e)$ $(e_1)$ $(e_2)$ $(e_3)$ $(\,(\Gamma\ e_1 \cdot e$ Ref $e_1,e_2,e_3) \supset e_2 =$
e), where in place of '$e$' an individual constant is inserted whose shape description is $\Gamma$.[4]

*RefR4.*     ⊢ $(e)$ $(e_1)$ $(e_2)$ $(e_2)$ $(\,(\Gamma\ e_1 \cdot e$ Ref $e_1,e_2,e_3) \supset e_2 =$
e), where in place of '$e$' an expression (with no free variables) for a point-event sum is inserted whose shape description is $\Gamma$.

*RefR5.*     ⊢ $(e)$ $(e_1)$ $(e_2)$ $(e_3)$ $(\,(\Gamma\ e_1 \cdot e$ Ref $e_1,e_2,e_3) \supset (e$
Ref $e_1,e_4,e_3 \equiv --e_4--)\,)$, where (i) '$--e_4--$' is a sentential form containing $e_4$ as its only free variable (if any) and $\Gamma$ is the shape-description of the abstract '$\{e_4 \ni --e_4--\}$' or (ii) '$--e_4--$' consists of a one-place primitive predicate constant concatenated with the variable $e_4$ and $\Gamma$ is the shape description of that constant.

[4]Cf. *Truth and Denotation*, p. 247.

# ON TRUTH, REFERENCE, AND OCCASIONS OF UTTERANCE

The rules concerning PerPrn's and Dmtv's are as follows. *RefR6* is the *Rule of Unique Self-Reference for 'I'*.

*RefR6.* $\vdash (e)(e_1)(e_2)(e_3)((I\ e_1 \cdot e\ \text{Ref}\ e_1,e_2,e_3) \supset e = e_2)$.

And *RefR7* is the *Rule of Multiple Self-Reference for 'We'*.

*RefR7.* $\vdash (e)(e_1)(e_2)(e_3)((\text{WE}\ e_1 \cdot e\ \text{Ref}\ e_1,e_2,e_3 \supset (e\ \text{Ref}\ e_1,e,e_3 \cdot (Ee_4)(\text{Per}\ e_4 \cdot \sim e = e_4 \cdot e\ \text{Ref}\ e_1,e_4,e_3)))$.

Similarly there are *Rules of Unique Reference for 'You$_s$'* and of *Multiple Reference for 'You$_p$'*.

*RefR8.* $\vdash (e)(e_1)(e_2)(e_3)((\text{YOU}_s\ e_1 \cdot e\ \text{Ref}\ e_1,e_2,e_3) \supset (\text{Per}\ e_2 \cdot (e_4)(e\ \text{Ref}\ e_1,e_4,e_3 \supset e_2 = e_4)))$.

*RefR9.* $\vdash (e)(e_1)(e_2)(e_3)((\text{YOU}_p\ e_1 \cdot e\ \text{Ref}\ e_1,e_2,e_3) \supset (\text{Per}\ e_2 \cdot (Ee_4)(\text{Per}\ e_4 \cdot \sim e_2 = e_4 \cdot e\ \text{Ref}\ e_1,e_4,e_3)))$.

In similar vein there are *Rules of Unique Reference for 'He', 'She', and 'It'*, and of *Multiple Reference for 'They'*. Let 'Male *e*' and 'Fem *e*' express respectively that *e* is a male and that *e* is a female.

*RefR10.* $\vdash (e)(e_1)(e_2)(e_3)((\text{HE}\ e_1 \cdot e\ \text{Ref}\ e_1,e_2,e_3) \supset (\text{Male}\ e_2 \cdot (e_4)(e\ \text{Ref}\ e_1,e_4,e_3 \supset e_2 = e_4)))$.

*RefR11.* $\vdash (e)(e_1)(e_2)(e_3)((\text{SHE}\ e_1 \cdot e\ \text{Ref}\ e_1,e_2,e_3) \supset (\text{Fem}\ e_2 \cdot (e_4)(e\ \text{Ref}\ e_1,e_4,e_3 \supset e_2 = e_4)))$.

*RefR12.* $\vdash (e)(e_1)(e_2)(e_3)((\text{IT}\ e_1 \cdot e\ \text{Ref}\ e_1,e_2,e_3) \supset (\sim \text{Male}\ e_2 \cdot \sim \text{Fem}\ e_2 \cdot (e_4)(e\ \text{Ref}\ e_1,e_4,e_3 \supset e_2 = e_4)))$.

*RefR13.* $\vdash (e)(e_1)(e_2)(e_3)((\text{THEY}\ e_1 \cdot e\ \text{Ref}\ e_1,e_2,e_3) \supset (Ee_4)(\sim e_2 = e_4 \cdot e\ \text{Ref}\ e_1,e_4,e_3))$.

# EVENTS, REFERENCE, AND LOGICAL FORM

The next rules are *Principles of Unique Reference for 'that'* and of *Multiple Reference for 'those'*.

*RefR14.* ⊢ $(e)(e_1)(e_2)(e_3)(e_4)(e_5)$ ((THAT $e_4$ · PredCon-One $e_5$ · C $e_1,e_4,e_5$ · $e$ Ref $e_1,e_2,e_3$) ⊃ $(e_6)$ ($e$ Ref $e_1,e_6,e_3$ ⊃ $e_2 = e_6$)).

*RefR15.* ⊢ $(e)(e_1)(e_2)(e_3)(e_4)(e_5)$ ((THOSE $e_4$ · PredConOne $e_5$ · C $e_1,e_4,e_5$ · $e$ Ref $e_1,e_2,e_3$) ⊃ $(Ee_6)$ ($\sim e_2 = e_6$ · $e$ Ref $e_1,e_6,e_3$)).

Also there is a *Shape-Descriptive Principle for 'that' and 'those'*.

*RefR16.* ⊢ $(e)(e_1)(e_2)(e_3)(e_4)(e_5)$ (((THAT $e_4$ v THOSE $e_4$) · Γ $e_5$ · C $e_1,e_4,e_5$ · $e$ Ref $e_1,e_2,e_3$) ⊃ $Fe_2$), where in place of '*F*' a PredConOne is inserted whose shape-description is Γ.

This rule clearly requires that whenever a person uses a '(that *F*)' or '(those *F*)' clause to refer correctly to an entity, that entity is in the virtual class *F*. (To simplify, the outer parentheses around '(that *F*)' and '(those *F*)' have not been indicated in the rules here.)

Whereas it seems that all uses of InCon's, PredConOne's, and of the Dmtv's and PtEvSumTrm's are referential, not all uses of some of the personal pronouns in ordinary language are. Pronouns are sometimes used to express cross-reference in the translations in ordinary language of universal conditionals, for example. In the present theory, only direct referential uses are considered, although the extension to cross-referential uses could easily be given. Hence there is also here a *Rule of Closure*.

*RefR17.* ⊢ $(e_1)(e_2)(e_3)$ (( InCon $e_1$ v PredConOne $e_1$ v PtEvSumTrm $e_1$ v PerPrn $e_1$ v Dmtv $e_1$) · Sent $e_3$ · $e_1$ Occ $e_3$ · $e_2$ Uses $e_3$)) ⊃ $(Ee_4)e_2$ Ref $e_1,e_4,e_3$).

Here '$e_2$ Uses $e_3$' expresses that $e_2$ uses $e_3$ in the sense of apprehending it, uttering it, accepting it, asserting it, doubting it, questioning it, commanding it, or what-not. The rule states that all inscriptions that are InCon's or PredConOne's or PerPrn's or Dmtv's or PtEvSumTrm's that occur in a sentence used by $e_2$ are used by $e_2$ referentially.

These rules lay down standards for the correct use of 'Ref'. They are in effect meaning postulates in essentially Carnap's sense, and are to be added to the rules of inscriptional syntax. They are by no means intended to exhaust the Rules of Reference needed, but are sufficient for present purposes.

Note that in the present account variables are not regarded as referring expressions. The variables are rather said to *range* over the entities of the object language but do not refer to them.

In order to define a predicate for truth some semantical ingredients are needed. Let 'Den' for denotation be a new primitive and governed by the following *Rules of Denotation.*[5]

*DenR1.*   $\vdash (e_1)(e_2)(e_1 \text{ Den } e_2 \supset \text{PredConOne } e_1)$,

*DenR2.*   $\vdash (e_1)(\Gamma e_1 \supset (e_1 \text{ Den } e_4 \equiv (--e_4--)))$, where (as in *RefR5*).

A relation of designation of InCon's and PtEvSumTrm's is now definable. We may let

'$e_1$ Des $e_2$' abbreviate '$((\text{InCon } e_1 \text{ v PtEvSumTrm } e_1) \cdot (Ee_3) \cdots (Ee_{15})(\text{LB } e_3 \cdot \text{EE } e_4 \cdot \text{INVEP } e_5 \cdot \text{EE } e_6 \cdot \text{ID } e_7 \cdot e_8 \text{ Like } e_1 \cdot \text{RB } e_9 \cdot \text{C } e_{10},e_3,e_4 \cdot \text{C } e_{11},e_{10},e_5 \cdot \text{C } e_{12},e_{11}, e_6 \cdot \text{C } e_{13},e_{12},e_7 \cdot \text{C } e_{14},e_{13},e_8 \cdot \text{C } e_{15},e_{14},e_9 \cdot e_{15} \text{ Den } e_2))$'.

Forthcoming then are the *Rules of Designation.* [6]

*DesR1.*   $\vdash (e_1)(e_2)(e_1 \text{ Des } e_2 \supset (\text{InCon } e_1 \text{ v PtEvSumTrm } e_1))$.

*DesR2.*   $\vdash (e_1)(\Gamma e_1 \supset e_1 \text{ Des } e)$, where (etc. as in *RefR3* or *RefR4*),

---

[5] Cf. *ibid.*, pp. 109-110.
[6] Cf. *ibid.*, pp. 167-168.

# EVENTS, REFERENCE, AND LOGICAL FORM

*DesR3.* $\vdash (e_1)(e_2)(e_3)((e_1 \text{ Des } e_2 \cdot e_1 \text{ Des } e_3) \supset e_2 = e_3)$.

Mass or bulk predicates can be introduced together with an additional individuating notion of being a bit of.[7] The extensions in the foregoing theory of reference required for these seem to pose no fundamental problems. 'That water', 'those bits of earth', and so on, may then also, it would seem, be regarded as referential phrases.

Following Quine in essentials, let an *eternal* sentence be one containing neither personal pronouns nor demonstratives, an *occasion* sentence containing at least one such.[8] Thus

'EtSent $e$' may abbreviate '(Sent $e \cdot \sim (Ee_1)(e_1 \text{ Occ } e \cdot$ (PerPrn $e_1$ v Dmtv $e_1$)))'.

'OcsnSent $e$' may abbreviate '(Sent $e \cdot \sim$ EtSent $e$)'.

Let us turn now to the semantical notion of truth, distinguishing the truth of eternal sentences from that of occasion sentences, and then in turn distinguishing various kinds of true speech acts.

Eternal-sentence truth may be defined immediately in terms of 'Den' as follows.

'TrErSent $e$' may abbreviate '(EtSent $e \cdot (Ee_1)(Ee_2)(Ee_3)$ $(Ee_4)(Ee_5)(Ee_6)(Ee_7)(Ee_8)(\text{LB } e_1 \cdot \text{Vbl } e_2 \cdot \text{INVEP } e_3 \cdot \text{RB }$ $e_4 \cdot \text{C } e_5,e_1,e_2 \cdot \text{C } e_6,e_5,e_3 \cdot \text{C } e_7,e_6,e \cdot \text{C } e_8,e_7,e_4 \cdot (e_9)$ $(\sim \text{SgnEv } e_9 \supset e_8 \text{ Den } e_9))$'.

Here 'Vbl $e_2$' expresses that $e_2$ is of the canonical shape of a variable. An eternal sentence '———' is thus true if and only if some abstract of the form '$\{ e' \ni ——— \}$' denotes all entities that are not sign events, in other words, all non-linguistic entities.

[7]Cf. W. V. Quine, *Word and Object* (The Technology Press of the Massachusetts Institute of Technology and John Wiley and Sons, New York and London: 1960), pp. 91 ff. Cf. also *Logic, Language, and Metaphysics*, p. 57.

[8] *Word and Object*, pp. 35 ff. and *passim*.

# ON TRUTH, REFERENCE, AND OCCASIONS OF UTTERANCE

A theory of truth for occasion sentences and for speech acts cannot be expected to be less powerful than the full semantical theory of truth. On the contrary, it must consist of that theory together with the extensions required for handling acts and events. Thus it would not be apposite or at all helpful to complain that the definition of 'TrEtSent' here is somehow too complicated. The notions needed in the definiens are also needed in the various definitions to follow. And in any case, the foregoing definition is much simpler than the orginal one of Tarski.

The notion of being a *true act of utterance of an eternal sentence* may be introduced as follows.

'TrUttEtSent $e$' abbreviates '$(Ee_1)(Ee_2)(\text{TrEtSent } e_2 \cdot \text{Per } e_1 \cdot \langle e_1, \text{Utt}, e_2 \rangle e)$'.

And similarly for true acts of speech, acts of writing, acts of acceptance, acts of assertion, acts of remembering, and so on, of eternal sentences. Forms relativized to the user may also be introduced, by deleting the quantifier '$(Ee_1)$' in the definiens here and adding '$e_1$' as a parameter in the definiendum. Thus

'TrUttEtSent $e,e_1$' may abbreviate '$(Ee_2)(\text{TrEtSent } e_2 \cdot \text{Per } e_1 \cdot \langle e_1, \text{Utt}, e_2 \rangle e)$'

and may be read '$e$ is one of $e_1$'s true utterance acts of an eternal sentence'. And similarly for other types of linguistic acts.

(The condition of adequacy for 'TrEtSent' may be established by noting that

$$\vdash (e)(\Gamma e \supset (\text{TrEtSent } e \equiv (\cdots\cdots)))\,,$$

where (i) in place of '$\Gamma$' a shape-descriptive predicate is inserted, (ii) in place of '$(\cdots\cdots)$' an eternal sentence of the translation part of the metalanguage is inserted having $\Gamma$ as its shape description, and (iii) '$\vdash$' is short for 'is a theorem of the metalanguage'.)

Before giving the definition of truth for occasion sentences, let us return to Davidson's examples (1) and (2). Let times be handled here in terms of events. Let '$TI$' express that I am tired, and let

$$\text{`}TI\text{' } e\text{'}$$

express that $e$ is an inscription of the shape '$TI$'. Also let '$e_1$ T $e_3$' express that $e_1$ is tired at or during the time of $e_3$. In effect then, Davidson seems to have in mind a definition something like the following.

$$\text{`Tr } e_1, e_2, e_3\text{'} \quad \text{for} \quad \text{`}(\langle e_2, \text{Utt}, e_1 \rangle e_3 \; \cdot \; \text{`}TI\text{' } e_1 \; \cdot \; e_2 \text{ T } e_3)\text{'}.$$

Davidson's (1) then, in the form

$$\text{`}(e_1)(e_2)(e_3)((\langle e_2, \text{Utt}, e_1 \rangle e_3 \; \cdot \; \text{`}TI\text{' } e_1) \supset (\text{Tr } e_1, e_2, e_3 \equiv e_2 \text{ T } e_3))\text{'}$$

is forthcoming as a theorem.
  Similarly, (2), where

$$\text{`}(that \text{ B}) \; was_e \text{ S'}$$

expresses that that book was stolen (the 'was' relative to some present event $e$, as in *Logic, Language, and Metaphysics*, p.112) and

$$\text{`}((THAT \text{ B}) \text{ WAS}_E \text{ S})e_1\text{'}$$

expresses that $e_1$ is an inscription of such and such a shape, is forthcoming as

$$\text{`}(e_1)(e_2)(e_3)((\langle e_2, \text{Utt}, e_1 \rangle e_3 \; \cdot \; ((THAT \text{ B}) \text{ WAS}_E \text{ S}) e_1) \supset (\text{Tr } e_1, e_2, e_3 \equiv ((that \text{ B}) \; was_e \text{ S} \cdot e \text{ B } e_3)))\text{'},$$

where in place of '$e$' the name of some present event is inserted and in place of '$E$' the shape-descriptive name of that name.
  An appropriate generalization of the definition just given (of

'Tr') is of course in order.

Let

$$'e_1 \; SF' \; e_2,e_3,e_4 \;'$$

be presumed defined (in inscriptional syntax) to express that sign event $e_1$ differs from $e_2$ only in containing occurrences of a variable $e_3$ not occuring in $e_2$, wherever the personal pronoun or demonstrative phrase $e_4$ occurs in $e_2$. Then

'TrOcsnSent$_e$ $e_1,e_2,e_3$' may abbreviate '(OcsnSent $e_1$ · ~ SgnEv $e_2$ · Per $e_3$ · (E$e_4$) (E$e_5$) (E$e_6$) (E$e_7$) (E$e_8$) (E$e_9$) (E$e_{10}$) (E$e_{11}$) (E$e_{12}$) (E$e_{13}$) ( (PerPrn $e_4$ v Dmtv $e_4$) · $e_4$ Occ $e_1$ · ~ (E$e_{14}$) ( (PerPrn $e_{14}$ v Dmtv $e_{14}$) · $e_{14}$ Occ $e_1$ · ~ $e_{14}$ Like $e_4$) · $e_5$ SF' $e_1,e_6,e_4$ · LB $e_7$ · INVEP $e_8$ · RB $e_9$ C $e_{10},e_7$, $e_6$ · C $e_{11},e_{10},e_8$ · C $e_{12},e_{11},e_5$ · C $e_{13},e_{12},e_9$ · $e_{13}$ Den $e_2$ · $e_3$ Ref $e_4,e_2,e_1$ · $\langle e_3$, Uses, $e_1 \rangle$ $e$) )'.

Let '——e——' be an occasion sentence $e_1$ used by person $e_3$ in speech act $e$ and containing a personal pronoun or demonstrative $e_4$ in place of 'e'. Such a sentence is a true occasion sentence of entity $e_2$ (and relative to $e_3$ and $e$) provided $e_3$ Ref $e_4,e_2,e_1$ and, moreover, some abstract of the shape '$\{y \; \ni \; ——y——\}$' denotes $e_2$.

This definition may be further generalized to allow any finite number of arguments in place of '$e_2$'.

In his "On Saying That"[9] Davidson has put forward further considerations closely related to the foregoing. He proposes to handle sentences such as

(5)              'Galileo said that the earth moves'

as

---

[9] *Synthese* 19 (1968): 130-146. Cf. also J. Hintikka, *Knowledge and Belief* (Cornell University Press, Ithaca, New York: 1962), pp. 13 ff., where the demonstrative character of 'that' in contexts such as (5) below is briefly considered. This character is made much of in the discussion to follow.

(6a)                         'The earth moves.
(6b)                         Galileo said that.'

or

(7a)                         'Galileo said that.
(7b)                         The earth moves.'

Sentences in indirect discourse "wear their logical form on their sleeve," he notes (p. 142). "They consist of an expression referring to a speaker, the two-place predicate 'said', and a demonstrative referring to an utterance. Period. What follows [the period in (7a)] gives the content of the subject's saying, but has no logical or semantic connection with the original attribution of a saying." Davidson does, note, regard the 'that' in (6a) as referring to an utterance. Thus, merely by filling in a tacit blank, the 'that' of (6b) or (7a) becomes 'that utterance'.

What now are utterances? Are they acts of uttering (by someone of some expression) or are they rather the expressions uttered? The expressions uttered are sentences, but Davidson tells us that "the 'they' is a demonstrative singular term referring to an utterance (not a sentence)." Very well then, utterances are presumably to be taken as acts of uttering. There is nothing else for them to be, it would seem.

Let 'Mv e' (with roman 'e', note) express that the earth moves. How now do we express 'Galileo said that'? Where Ut is the virtual class of acts of sentential utterances, that is, the class $\{e \ni (E e_1)(E e_2)(\text{Per } e_1 \cdot \text{Sent } e_2 \cdot \langle e_1, \text{UTT}, e_2 \rangle e)\}$,

$$\text{'g S (\textit{that} Ut)'}$$

seems to give the logical form for (7a), with 'g' for 'Galileo' and 'S' for 'said'. '(*that* Ut)' is a demonstrative phrase used by the speaker to refer to some one act of utterance. It is difficult to see how '(*that* Ut)' could be regarded as a demonstrative phrase and lack such reference. However, Davidson's point is that what follows the period in (7a) "has no logical or semantic connection with the original attribution of a saying." Rather '(*that* Ut)' might be taken by the speaker to refer to the utterance that immediately follows. This is not quite Davidson's view, but let us play with it for a moment. Let now $e_1$ be the speaker's act of utterance of 'g S (*that* Ut)'. The *speaker* goes on to utter 'Mv e'. To what then does the speaker's use of '(*that* Ut)' refer? To the speaker's subsequent act of uttering 'Mv e', that is, to the one occasion $e$ such that there is an inscription $e'$ of the shape 'Mv e', $e$ is an act of the speaker's uttering $e'$ and $e_1$ is immediately before $e$.

More precisely, where '$e_1$ ImB $e_1$' expresses that $e_1$ is immediately before $e_2$ in temporal order, and

$$\text{'(MV E)}e\text{'}$$

and

$$\text{'(G  S  (\textit{THAT}  Ut))}e\text{'}$$

express respectively that $e$ is of the appropriate shape, (7a) and (7b) may be construed as follows.

(7a')             'g  S  (*that*  Ut)',
(7b')                 'Mv  e',

where the speaker DD accepts that

$(\textit{that}\ \text{Ut}) = (\imath e)\,(E e')\,((\text{MV E})e' \cdot \langle \text{DD,Utt},e'\rangle\, e \cdot (\imath e_1)\,(E e'')$
$((\text{G S (THAT Ut)})e'' \cdot \langle \text{DD,Utt},e''\rangle\, e_1 \cdot --e''--)\ \text{ImB}\ e)$,

where '$--e''--$' specifies that the place-time of the inscription $e''$ is such and such.

The foregoing does not agree however, with Davidson's account in one crucial respect. "Assuming the 'that' [in (7a)] refers [p. 144], we can infer that Galileo said something from 'Galileo said that'; but this is welcome." From (7a'), however, it does not follow that Galileo said anything at all, but only that the speaker does. Still worse, it would seem that (7a′) is false, for whatever Galileo may have said, he did not make the utterance referred to by the speaker.

To forestall the difficulty just mentioned, Davidson construes (7a) rather as

(8)   '(E$x$) (Galileo's utterance $x$ and my utterance immediately to follow make us samesayers).'

The relation of making-us-samesayers is presumably quadratic. Let

$$‘e_1,e_2 \text{ SmUttrs } e_3,e_4’$$

express that person $e_1$ in uttering $e_2$ makes himself a samesayer with person $e_3$ in uttering $e_4$. Using this relation, the foregoing may be patched up so that (7a′) is not only true but entails that Galileo said something. Consider now two languages, $L$ and $L'$, the one $L$ used by the speaker DD and the other by Galileo. Let 'Sent$_L$'  $e$' express now that $e$ is a sentence of $L'$. The condition on (7a) becomes then that DD accepts that

$$( \text{ that Ut}) = (\imath e) (Ee_1) (Ee_2)((\text{MV E})e_1 \cdot \langle DD, Utt, e_1 \rangle \ e \cdot DD,$$
$$e_1 \text{ SmUttrs } g, e_2 \cdot \text{Sent}_{L'} \ e_2 \cdot (\imath e') (Ee_3) ( (G \ S \ \textit{THAT} \ Ut ) )$$
$$e_3 \cdot \langle DD, Utt, e_3 \rangle \ e' \cdot \text{ --} e_3 \text{-- }) \ ImB \ e),$$

where '$-\!\!-e_3-\!\!-$' specifies the time and place of $e_3$.

The exhorbitant price one has to pay in introducing (8) should be emphasized. The relation SmUttrs is after all the synonymy relation all over again, disguised now as a relation of pragmatics. Worse yet, it is *interlinguistic*, where even a proper *intra*linguistic account raises difficult problems. Note that the pragmatical meta-metalanguage here must be a very complicated one in which the two languages $L$ and $L'$ may be compared. Further, the use of 'samesayers' is scarcely consistent with approval of (and acceptance of) Quine's thesis of the indeterminacy of translation. The arguments in favor of that thesis surely can be turned against Davidson's account. To paraphrase his own words: "All that the indeterminacy shows (p.138) is that if there is one way of getting it right there are other ways that differ substantially in that non-synonymous sentences are used . . ." as arguments of the relation of samesaying. "And this is enough to justify our feeling that there is something bogus about the sharpness questions of . . ." samesaying "must in principle have . . ." And in any case, Davidson merely introduces (8) without giving any *theory* concerning it. It is merely a promissory note. The foregoing considerations suggest that the note can probably never be paid, if the thesis of the indeterminacy of translation is taken seriously.

Both of the foregoing accounts being inadequate, how can matters be patched up? One way suggests itself by introducing

(10) $\qquad\qquad$ '$e$ Prphrs $e''$

to express that $e$ is a paraphrase of $e'$, in essentially the sense of Hiż.[10] (10) may be construed so broadly that $e$ and $e'$ may be in different languages. The condition on (7a) that DD accepts would be then to the effect that (*that* Ut) is some utterance of an inscription $e''$, where $e''$ is an Italian paraphrase of 'Mv $e$', that Galileo is supposed to have made. Or, alternatively,

(11) $\qquad\qquad$ '$g$ Utt$'_{It}$ $e$'

could be taken to express that Galileo utters an Italian paraphrase of $e$ (in $L$). Although (9) is intralinguistic, (11) is not. The use of (11) would enable us to avoid having to use a comparative metalanguage. The condition on (7a) that DD accepts would then be to the effect that (*that* Ut) is some utterance $e'$ such that there is an $e''$ such that $\langle g, \text{Utt}'_{It}, e'' \rangle$ $e'$ where (MV E)$e''$.

Note that paraphrase is very different from samesaying. Samesaying is presumably much stronger, and closer to synonymy. Paraphrase is more experimental and depends for its characterization

---

[10] See especially H. Hiż, "The Role of Paraphrase in Grammar," *Monograph Series on Language and Linguistics, Number 17* (1964): 97-104.

upon actual usage and the linguistic habits of the speakers. Where all hope might be abandoned that some one and only one proper notion of synonymy could be found, there is every reason indeed to expect from the fruitful notion of paraphrase precisely what one wants. Perhaps paraphrase should be made even more pragmatic. In place of (10) we could have

(10′)                          '$e$ Prphrs $e_1, e_2$ '

to express that person $e$ paraphrases $e_1$ as $e_2$.

Note also that the account of 'that' in terms of (10) or (10′) may be extended to provide logical forms for contexts concerned with believing, knowing, thinking, remembering, and so on. For Davidson each such extension would require new unstructured relations, believessame, knowssame, thinkssame, and so on, perhaps as primitives. No such additional relations are needed in the present account.

# IV

# THE PRAGMATICS
# OF COUNTING

*"Difficile est proprie communia dicere."*

It should be of interest to attempt to base formal arithmetic on the process of counting. Counting does seem very fundamental and important as a human activity, in science and elsewhere. This activity should be studied and a theory about it explicitly formulated. Out of that theory the arithmetic of the integers ought somehow to emerge. Such a theory, a *logic* or *pragmatics* of counting, will be developed in what follows.

Strokes and strings of them, often used as counters, are of no interest on their own account. They become so only when human beings *correlate* them suitably with objects they wish to count. In general, however, one does not count *objects* as such, but only objects *of a specific kind* — protons, wavicles, tables, chairs, the seasons, and so on. The mere notion of an object or individual is much too general to be used as a basis for the theory of counting. Let us consider for the moment then just objects of a given virtual class or kind $F$. In counting, a person $p$ might correlate a single stroke with a single object of the kind $F$. He would correlate a sequence of two strokes with two objects of the kind $F$. And so on. How now is this procedure to be incorporated in a suitable pragmatics, in which counting is explicitly taken as a human process?

# EVENTS, REFERENCE, AND LOGICAL FORM

Let 'AC $a$' express, as in the syntax above, that $a$ is a canonical accent-shaped sign event or stroke somewhere in space-time.[1] And let

$$\text{'}p \ \text{Crrlt} \ a,x,F\text{'}$$

express that person $p$ correlates the expression $a$ with the object $x$ where $x$ is of the kind $F$. (Suppose also that no proper part of $x$ is of the kind $F$.) That $p$ correlates an accent (or stroke) with $x$ is then expressed by

$$\text{'}(Ea) \ (AC \ a \ \cdot \ p \ \text{Crrlt} \ a,x,F)\text{'}$$

It might seem that sequences of two, three, or more accents could be accommodated by admitting forms

$$\text{'}p \ \text{Crrlt} \ a,x,y,F\text{'},$$

and so on. To do so, however, would not be technically sound. It would not give us a form

$$\text{'}p \ \text{Crrlt} \ a,x,F\text{'}$$

for variable '$x$', '$x$' ranging over individuals.

The devices of the calculus of individuals, however, may be brought in in a natural way. Let $(y \cup z)$ be the compound or sum-individual consisting of $y$ and $z$ together, as above. The individuals $y$ and $z$ may be either spatio-temporally contiguous or scattered, it matters not. (The calculus of individuals, it will be recalled, condones as individuals all possible sums of individuals, no matter how scattered in space-time.) Suppose now that $x = (y \cup z)$ where $y$ and $z$ do not overlap but are both of the kind $F$ where $x$ is not. Suppose further that no proper parts of $y$ or $z$ are of the kind $F$. In this case, person $p$ may properly correlate a sequence of two strokes with the compound individual $x$ with respect to the kind $F$.

[1] See *Truth and Denotation*, Chapter XI.

Note that in such correlation, the entities $y$ and $z$ are being counted or correlated only in so far as they are of the kind $F$.

Concerning 'Crrlt', we have thus far the following principles, using the familiar symbolization.

$\vdash (p)(a)(x)((p$ Crrlt $a,x,F$ · AC $a) \supset (Fx$ · $\sim (Ey)(y$ PP $x$ · $Fy))$.

$\vdash (p)(a)(x)((p$ Crrlt $a,x,F$ · $(Eb)(Ec)(AC$ $c$ · C $a,b,c))$ $\supset (Ey)(Ez)(x = (y \cup z)$ · $\sim y$ O $z$ · $Fy$ · $Fz$ · $\sim Fx$ · $\sim (Ew)(w$ PP $x$ · $Fw$ · $\sim w = y$ · $\sim w = z)))$.

And so on. ('$y$ O $z$' expresses here that $y$ and $z$ overlap, and '$y$ PP $x$' that $y$ is a proper part of $x$.)

If one wishes, numerical expressions may be introduced in context as follows. Let

'$p$ Crrlt $1,x,F$' abbreviate '$(Ea)(AC$ $a$ · $p$ Crrlt $a,x,F)$',
'$p$ Crrlt $2,x,F$' abbreviate '$(Ea)(Eb)(Ec)(AC$ $b$ · AC $c$ · C $a,b,c$ · $p$ Crrlt $a,x,F)$',

and so on.

Let 'AcStr $a$' express that $a$ is a *string of accents*. 'AcStr $a$' may be defined by requiring that $a$ be a sign event such that every unit sign event that is a part of it is itself and AC. The sign event $a$ then could contain nothing but AC's and sequences of such.

Numerical addition may be introduced, again in context, as follows.

'$p$ Crrlt $(a + b),x,F$' for '$(Ec)(C$ $c,a,b$ · AcStr $a$ · AcStr $b$ · $p$ Crrlt $c,x,F)$'.

Multiplication is a little more difficult. Let '$c$ $S_{AC}^{AcStr}$ $a,b$' be defined to express that $c$ is a sign event differing from $b$ only in containing some AcStr equally long with $a$ in place of each AC of $b$. If $a$ and $b$ are themselves AcStr's then $c$ will be an AcStr also, and of

length, to speak loosely,

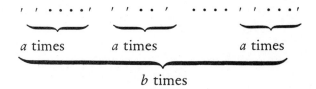

Then

'$p$ Crrlt $(a \times b), x, F$' may abbreviate '$(Ec)$ (AcStr $a$ · AcStr $b$ · $c$ $S_{AC}^{AcStr}\, a,b,$ · $p$ Crrlt $c,x,F)$'.

Note that the commutative law for multiplication follows from the syntactical principle that, where '$c$ EqLng $d$' expresses that $c$ is an inscription equally long with $d$,

$\vdash (a)(b)(c)(d)\,(\,($AcStr $a$ · AcStr $b$ · $c$ $S_{AC}^{AcStr}\, a,b$ · $d$ $S_{AC}^{AcStr}\, b,a) \supset c$ EqLng $d)$.

What on this view is a positive integer? Merely an AcStr correlated by someone to something (having $F$). Then

'$N_F\, a$' may abbreviate '(AcStr $a$ · $(Ep)(Ex)\, p$ Crrlt $a,x,F)$'.

And what is numerical identify? Merely a relation between equally long AcStr's taken to be integers. More stringent conditions could be required, but these seem hardly necessary. Thus

'$(a \approx_F b$' abbreviates '$(N_F\, a$ · $N_F\, b$ · $a$ EqLng $b)$'.

Note, incidentally, that Crrlt is not to be confused with a one-one dyadic relation of any kind. More particularly, the following hold:

80

$\sim (p)(q)((p \text{ Crrlt } a,x,F \cdot q \text{ Crrlt } a,x,F) \supset p = q),$
$\sim (a)(b)((p \text{ Crrlt } a,x,F \cdot p \text{ Crrlt } b,x,F) \supset a = b),$
$\sim (x)(y)((p \text{ Crrlt } a,x,F \cdot p \text{ Crrlt } a,y,F) \supset x = y).$

Also not all formulae of the form

'$(p)(a)(x)((p \text{ Crrlt } a,x,F \cdot p \text{ Crrlt } a,x,G) \supset F = G)$'

need hold.

All the foregoing definitions have been relativized to some given (virtual) class $F$ of objects. Nothing prevents these definitions from being relativized now to the universal class V of all objects in the domain of the variables '$x$', '$y$', and so on. In human practice, most correlations take place only with respect to some restricted class, as already mentioned. If one's interest, however, is to develop formal arithmetic for its own sake, this restriction would be undesirable. The restricted class might contain fewer objects than integers. Of course even the universal class might also be too small in this way. This is a difficulty to be circumvented in a moment.

We have now a notation in which the principles of the arithmetic of positive integers may be formulated. But nothing yet has been said of axioms other than that a syntax of sign events is being presupposed. Of particular interest here are the existence assumptions. Is there only a finite number of inscriptions in the whole cosmos, or are they infinite in number? Syntax is mute on the answer to this question and may be formulated in such a way that an infinity of sign events is neither assumed nor denied. Clearly, however, there are many of them. In particular there are enough AcStr's to enable us to do a good deal of arithmetic. Any arithmetical principles that depend upon the assumption of an infinity of AcStr's, however, must be provided for in some other way.

Peano's Postulates for the integers may now be stated and some of them proved. Clearly

(P1)    $\vdash N_V 1$

and

(P2)    $\vdash \sim (Ea)1 \approx_V (a + 1)$.

The principle that

(P3)    $\vdash (a) (N_V a \supset N_V (a + 1))$,

however, in effect asserts the existence of an infinity of AcStr's and might therefore be false. Rather than to assert this outright, it seems best here to use Russell's device, with respect to the Axiom of Infinity in *PM*, to take it as hypothesis where needed. Let 'InfAx' then abbreviate (P3) and be taken as an hypothesis to such theorems of arithmetic as depend upon it.

The fourth postulate, that

(P4)    $\vdash (a) (b) ((N_V a \cdot N_V b \cdot (a + 1) \approx_V (b + 1)) \supset a \approx_V b)$,

is provable using the syntactical principle that

$\vdash (a) (b) (a') (b') ((\text{AcStr } a \cdot \text{AcStr } b \cdot (Ec) (Ed) (\text{AC } c \cdot \text{AC } d \cdot \text{C } a',a,c \cdot \text{C } b',b,d \cdot a' \text{ EqLng } b')) \supset a \text{ EqLng } b)$.

What now about the Principle of Mathematical Induction? Let '$G(a)$' be some formula containing '$a$' as its only free variable and occurring only in contexts of the form '$p$ Crrlt $a,x,$V'. '$G(a)$' may thus be atomic or molecular of any complexity. The Induction Principle then states that

(P5)    $\vdash (G(1) \cdot (a) ((N_V a \cdot N_V (a + 1) \cdot G(a)) \supset G(a + 1))) \supset (a) (N_V a \supset G(a))$,

for any such *G*. This presumably may be proved for each suitable value of '$G$', from the induction schema of inscriptional syntax.

The various arithmetic principles concerning addition and multiplication are provable from syntactical principles concerning concatenation and the notion $S_{Ac}^{A cStr}$.

The foregoing is a loose sketch of a kind of "rational reconstruction" of the theory concerning arithmetic rather akin to that of Paul Lorenzen within a suitable pragmatical metalanguage.[2] It is not claimed that this reconstruction is of any "formal" interest in throwing new light on purely mathematical features of arithmetic. It is of interest rather only in showing that arithmetic may be given a suitable pragmatical foundation in terms of a theory of counting.

It might be objected that the foregoing does not sufficiently make room for the human making or "construction" of strokes and sequences of them in terms of which numbers are handled. It might be objected that all past, present, and future AcStr's are already presumed to be available in the foregoing account, whereas AcStr's ought themselves, in "constructive" arithmetic, to be regarded as human artifacts, perhaps even with a temporal date. There ought to be no AcStr unless or until someone makes or constructs it. Let us examine this contention a little in the light of some general comments concerning linguistic artifacts.

Artifacts are entities "made" by human beings. The constructivist might require that the AcStr's here should be "made" and thus that the values for the variables '$a$', '$b$', and so on, be restricted to just the expressions "made" by someone or other (or perhaps even to those "made" by just some one person). Moreover, the view seems to be that the strokes or sequences of such do not "exist" prior to their being made. Let us try to be clear about these requirements and then observe that they are neither sound nor viable.

The expressional variables and quantifiers upon them, on this view, become time-bound and person-bound in awkward ways. Strictly in place of '$(a)$' we should now write '$(a)_{p,t}$' with the relativization to the person $p$ and the time $t$ made explicit. Such a quantifier could be contextually defined as follows.

[2] See in particular his *Normative Logic and Ethics*, to be discussed in XIV below.

'$(a)_{p,t}Fa$'   for   '$(a)\,((p$ M $a,t$ v $(Et')\,(t'$ B $t \cdot p$ M $a,t))\supset Fa)$',

where '$p$ M $a,t$' expresses that $p$ makes $a$ at time $t$ (in the sense in which the constructivist wishes) and '$t'$ B $t$' expresses that the time $t'$ is wholly before the time $t$.

In this way numerical quantifiers would become restricted to just the AcStr's made by the arithmetician up to a certain time. The fact is, however, that he could never make enough to do arithmetic in the sense of (P1) $-$ (P-5) (together with the various principles concerning multiplication and addition). Nor would there be enough if another arithmetician were allowed to take over making AcStr's where he left off. Nor would there be enough even if all arithmeticians throughout history were just to work making AcStr's. Nor even if all humanity had done nothing but make AcStr's throughout these 10,000 years!

It should be noted also that the grammar of '$p$ M $a,t$' is such that the "entity" $a$ must be available as a value for a variable even before $p$ makes it. The values for variables, in other words, must be looked at timelessly in order to provide a grammar for expressions for objects that come into and pass out of being. Even if no name is yet available for an object, it must already be available as a value for a variable. Consider 'Paul will make a stroke mark on the blackboard in his lecture tomorrow'. To have this sentence mean what we intend it to, requires that that stroke mark be available as a value for a variable at the time the sentence is uttered. The form is roughly

'$(Ea)\,(AC\ a \cdot p$ M $a,t' \cdot t$ B $t')$',

where $t'$ is tomorrow's time, and $t$ is today's, this sentence being uttered today. (The clauses concerning the blackboard and the lecture are disregarded here.)

One can conclude then that general linguistic considerations concerning the logic of 'makes' or 'constructs' require that the objects made or constructed be available timelessly as values for

84

variables. If the constructivist thinks otherwise, it is by no means clear what his contention amounts to.

What now should be said concerning the nature of arithmetical truths on the basis of the foregoing pragmatical rational reconstruction? They become *empirical* truths, in essentially the same sense as the truths of syntax and of pragmatics. The proofs of non-trivial arithmetical principles involve either empirical existence (and other) assumptions concerning sign events, or empirical assumptions concerning who correlates what with what. Note that even the principles

$$\text{'}1 \approx_{\text{V}} 1\text{'}$$

here is empirical, for the clause '$N_{\text{V}}1$' is required in its proof.

More particularly, (P1) is clearly empirical, as in effect just noted. (P2) requires the empirical, syntactical principle that

$$\sim (Ea)\,(Eb)\,(Ec)\,(AC\ a\ \cdot\ AcStr\ b\ \cdot\ C\ c,b,a\ \cdot\ c\ EqLng\ a).$$

(P3) is clearly empirical, in effect stating the existence of an infinity of AcStr's. Similarly for (P4) and the Induction Schema, as in effect already noted.

It is evident that with the integers available, a full theory of rational numbers and a constructivistic theory of real numbers may be developed of sufficient power for most of the tasks for which numbers are needed in empirical science.

# V

# A PLETHORA OF
# LOGICAL FORMS

*"Haec oportebat facere, et illa non omittere."*

Events, states, acts, processes, and the like, may be regarded as actual happenings or goings-on in the spatio-temporal world, the "really real" entities of which all else is composed. An event concept, on the other hand, is an event taken under some linguistic description, an event under a Fregean *Art des Gegebenseins*.[1] Event concepts are thus to be handled metalinguistically, more precisely, semantically, and for their discussion therefore the distinction between use and mention should be maintained. To connect the use and mention of expressions, some rules of reference (or of denotation or designation) are needed, or some variants thereof.

In the preceding essays a rather wide-ranging theory of events has been put forward, including a semantics as based upon inscriptions or sign events. If events are to be taken seriously, it would not be appropriate to regard linguistic expressions as sign designs, for this would be to admit something quite foreign into the theory. It seems best therefore to construe expressions as sign events rather than sign designs and to face up to the semantical complexities

---

[1] See G. Frege, "On Sense and Reference" (p. 57) and *Begriffsschrift* (p. 11) in *Translations*.

in so doing. It will be of interest now to reflect further upon event identity and the problem of how events are to be individuated, topics that have come to the fore in several recent discussions. Along the way a plethora of tentative logical forms will be gained that should be useful for the study of natural language.

Under what circumstances are events $e_1$ and $e_2$ to be identified? There seems to be no need to abrogate the Leibnitzian definition in the case of events, any more than for any other type of object. The *criterion* for the identity of events $e_1$ and $e_2$ remains then the familiar one that every predicate applicable to one is also applicable to the other. This criterion cannot be stated within the language, for obvious reasons, but only in the metalanguage. The criterion is clearly not a definition. In fact, for present purposes '=' may be taken as primitive, with metaprinciples *IdR1-IdR4* taken to stipulate axioms, as in II above.

Among the predicates applicable to events will be some indicating spatio-temporal position. Events occur or take place at given times and at given places. Times may perhaps be taken as suitable fusions of *simultaneous* events, and places as fusions of events occurring *at the same place.* Let '$e_1$ CoPl $e_2$' express that $e_1$ and $e_2$ are *coplacial.* Some such notion as this would play in the theory of places essentially the same role that simultaneity plays in the theory of times. '$e_1$ At $e_2$' can then be used to express that $e_1$ occurs at the place of $e_2$, and '$e_1$ During $e_2$', that $e_1$ occurs during the time of $e_2$.

A logical consequence of *IdR2* is then that identical events occur at the same places and at the same times. Another consequence is that if $e_1 = e_2$ and $e_1$ is a spatio-temporal part of $e_3$ then $e_2$ is also. And so on.

Under what circumstances are event *kinds* to be identified? Being handled virtually, clearly

'$\langle e_1, F \rangle = \langle e_2, G \rangle$'  may abbreviate  '$(e) (\langle e_1, F \rangle e \equiv \langle e_2, G \rangle e)$',

'$\langle e_1, R, e_2 \rangle = \langle e_3, S, e_4 \rangle$'  may abbreviate  '$(e) (\langle e_1, R, e_2 \rangle e \equiv \langle e_3, S, e_4 \rangle e)$',

and so on.

88

Alvin Goldman has recently suggested that acts (act *tokens*, as he puts it) be identified in accord with the following:

"For any act $e_1$ and any $e_2$, where $e_1$ is the exemplifying of [act type] $\phi$ by [person] $X$ at [time] $t$ and $e_2$ is the exemplifying of $\psi$ by $Y$ at $t'$, $e_1 = e_2$ if and only if $X = Y$, $\phi = \psi$, and $t = t'$."[2]

This suggestion seems too strong but accords in part with the above with the time factor omitted. Strictly the time factor is not needed, for it may presumably be handled in terms of the underlying spatio-temporal topology for events. Note that Goldman has *exemplifyings* as values for variables as well as act kinds. Does not this, however, contradict his contention (p. 773) that "instead of treating actions (or events) as a primitive or irreducible category, our account reduces act tokens to persons, act properties, and times"? There is no genuine reduction if act tokens are taken as values for variables.

Goldman's account fails, however, for intentional contexts containing *Arten des Gegebenseins*. Not identity, but synonymy or paraphrase are required here. Further, his account contains simultaneously both a necessary and sufficient condition for identity where only a sufficient one is suitable. Here necessary conditions are given by *IdR1-IdR4*. A sufficient condition may be given as follows.

Let '$e_1$ Prphrs $e_2$' express that $e_2$ is a paraphrase of $e_1$, as in III above. Let 'Intl $R$' express that $R$ is an intentional relation, the primitive intentional relations being no doubt finitely enumerable. Further, let '$e$ IntlRltm $R$' express that the sign event $e$ is an *intentional relatum* of $R$, that is, an *Art des Gegebenseins*. Every intentional relation has at least one intentional relatum, perhaps more. Then

*IdR5a.*   $\vdash (e)\,(e')\,(e_1)\,(e_2)\,(e_3)\,(e_4)\,((\langle e_1,R,e_2\rangle\, e \cdot \langle e_3,S,e_4\rangle$ $e' \cdot e_1 = e_2 \cdot R = S \cdot ((\sim(\text{Intl } R \cdot e_2 \text{ IntlRltm } R) \cdot e_2 = e_4)\, \text{v}$ $(\text{Intl } R \cdot e_2 \text{ IntlRltm } R \cdot e_2 \text{ Prphrs } e_4)))\supset e = e')$,

[2] Alvin L. Goldman, "The Individuation of Action," *The Journal of Philosophy* 68 (1971): 761-774.

and so on for predicates of higher degree.

The discussion of event identity leads immediately to matters of intentionality (with a 't') and intensionality (with an 's'), for they go hand in hand.

Consider the adverb 'intentionally' itself. Although Oedipus married Jocasta intentionally and Jocasta is his mother, Oedipus did not marry his mother intentionally. (This example is due to Davidson.) Intentional adverbs can be handled in terms of the Fregean *Art des Gegebenseins*. Let '$\langle o,M,j \rangle e$' express that $e$ is an event of Oedipus' marrying Jocasta. It is not sufficient to add here merely that $e$ is also intentional, or intentional on Oedipus' part. The structure of the intention should be brought in by indicating that it is $e$ *as taken under the description* '$\langle o,M,j \rangle$' that is intentional.

Let '$e$ Intd $e_1, e_2$' express that person $e$ intends to do $e_1$ (or intends to bring $e_1$ about) under the event-descriptive predicate $e_2$. Then, although

$$(Ee) (\langle o,M,j \rangle e \cdot o \text{ Intd } e, {}'\langle o,M,j \rangle {}'),$$

and the person o is identical with the mother of o, Mo'o, it does not follow that

$$(Ee) (\langle o,M,Mo'o \rangle e \cdot o \text{ Intd } e, {}'\langle o,M,Mo'o \rangle {}').$$

The occurrence of 'j' in '$\langle o,M,j \rangle$' can be replaced *salva veritate* by 'Mo'o', but not of course the occurrence of "j" in "'$\langle o,M,j \rangle$'".

A notational remark is in order, making explicit a usage above. Single quotes are being used throughout as shape-quotes as is customary. The only linguistic objects that are values for variables, however, are inscriptions or sign events, not shapes or sign designs. Thus '$e$ Intd $e_1, e_2$' here is meaningful only where $e_2$ is a sign event. But '$e$ Intd $e_1$, '$\langle o,M,j \rangle$'' has been used above where the third argument is a shape. This latter, however, may be regarded as defined by

$$'(Ee_2) (e \text{ Intd } e_1, e_2 \cdot {}'\langle o,M,j \rangle {}' e_2 )',$$

where ' '$\langle o,M,j\rangle$'$e_2$' expresses that $e_2$ is a sign event of the shape '$\langle o,M,j\rangle$'. And similarly throughout.

In order to simplify, distinctions of tense will be disregarded here. The presumption is that they may all be handled in the somewhat Reichenbachian manner as in *Logic, Language, and Metaphysics.*

The late J. L. Austin claimed to have detected a difference between

'He clumsily trod on the snail'

and

'He trod clumsily on the snail'.[3]

The first is supposed to state that the trodding is one of a sequence of actions, whereas with the second "to tread on it is, very likely, his aim or policy." The second would be intentional, then, whereas the first not. Hence the first would become

'(E$e$) ($\langle he$, Trod, the Snail$\rangle$ $e$ · Cl $e$)',

and the second, somewhat simplified,

'(E$e$) ($\Gamma e$ · Cl $e$ · $he$ Intd $e$, '$\{e''$ $\ni (\Gamma e''$ · Cl $e'')\}$ ')',

where '$\Gamma$' is short for '$\langle he$,Trod,the Snail$\rangle$'. (To simplify, '$he$' here has been treated as a proper name.)

Although 'clumsily' is not always used intentionally, 'intentionally' itself no doubt is. In general, it seems, intentional phrases may often, perhaps always, be handled by bringing in the mode of description as a separate factor, as here. Adverbs such as 'reluctantly', 'carefully', 'voluntarily', 'deliberately', 'willingly', 'knowingly', and the like, may be handled similarly.

---

[3] J. L Austin, *Philosophical Papers* (Clarendon Press, Oxford: 1961), p. 147. A deeper discussion of adverbs is given in VI below.

'Johann reluctantly went to the concert',

where '$e$ Reluct $e_1, e_2$' express that $e$ is reluctant to do $e_1$ under the description $e_2$, becomes

'(E$e$) (⟨j,Went,the Concert⟩$e$ · j Reluct $e$, '⟨j,Went, the Concert⟩')'.

'Johann knowingly listened to the Sonata'

becomes, similarly,

'(E$e$) (⟨j,Listened,the Sonata⟩$e$ · j Knows $e$, '⟨j, Listened,the Sonata⟩')'.

'Johann listened to the Sonata knowingly'

is different, however, for this seems to be rather

'(E$e$) (⟨j,Listened,the Sonata⟩$e$ · j Knows the Sonata, '———')',

where '———' describes something or other about how the Sonata should be played. Note that

'Johann listened knowingly to the Sonata'

seems ambigious as between these two readings.

Let us bring in negation.

'Johann did not go reluctantly to the concern'

is a paraphrase of

'Johann went willingly to the concert'.

On the other hand,

'Johann reluctantly did not go to the concert'

becomes

'(E$e$) ($\sim$ ⟨j,Went,the Concert⟩ $e$ · j Reluct $e$, ' $\{e''$ ∍ $\sim$ ⟨j,Went,the Concert⟩$e''\}$ ')'.

The $e$ here may be thought of as a state, rather than as an event strictly. The formula expresses not only that he did not go to the concert but that he is (or was) in a state of reluctance at not going.

Consider now

'Reluctantly Johann listened to the Sonata knowingly'

as constrasted with

'Knowingly Johann listened to the Sonata relcutantly'.

The first seems to become

'(E$e$)(⟨j,Listened,the Sonata⟩$e$ · j Knows the Sonata, '———' · j Reluct $e$, ' $\{e'$∍(E$e''$)(⟨j,Listened,the Sonata⟩$e'$ · ⟨j,Knows,the Sonata, '———'⟩$e''$ · $e''$ During $e'$)$\}$ ')',

and the second

'(E$e$) (⟨j,Listened,the Sonata⟩ $e$ · j Reluct $e$, '⟨j,Listened, the Sonata⟩' · j Knows $e$, '$\{e'$ ∍ (E$e''$) (⟨j,Listened,the Sonata⟩$e'$ · ⟨j, Reluct,$e$, '⟨j,Listened,the Sonata⟩'⟩$e''$ ∘ $e''$ During $e'$)$\}$')'.

The adverbs initially placed here "modify" the entire sentence, to speak loosely, whereas the others modify only the appropriate adjacent phrases. The difference is accommodated here in construing the *Art des Gegebenseins* appropriately.

Consider now the relation H of *hunting for*.

# EVENTS, REFERENCE, AND LOGICAL FORM

'Johann is hunting for a suitable apartment'

does not become

$$\text{'(E}e\text{) (j H } e \cdot \text{Apt } e \cdot e \text{ Suit j)',}$$

for he may be hunting for a suitable apartment without there being one. This difficulty is circumvented if the appropriate linguistic description is brought in. Let

$$\text{'(E}e\text{) j H } e, \text{ '}\{e' \ni (\text{Apt } e' \cdot e' \text{ Suit j})\}\text{' '}$$

express that Johann is seeking something under the description of its being an apartment suitable for him, even if it should turn out that that something be null. Suppose every apartment suitable for him costs \$1,000 a month but that he is poor. From the first formula here it follows that he is seeking an apartment that costs \$1,000 a month, which he is not doing. From the second formula no such consequence follows. To hunt for an entity under one description is not always to hunt for it under another.

Consider also

'There is something Johann is seeking, namely, the fountain of youth'.

Here likewise the linguistic description is to be brought in, either as a Russellian description or as an event-descriptive predicate. If the former, we have

$$\text{'(E}e\text{)j S } e, \text{'(} \imath e_1 \text{) (FY}e_1 \text{)' '.}$$

One and the same event may of course be taken under many different *Arten des Gegebenseins,* due to the richness of our language, reflected here in the multiplicity of event-descriptive predicates available. In speaking of the event one predicate may be appropriate in one context, another in another. It may be known or

94

believed, or something of the sort, that one predicate applies, without its being known that the other does. A stabbing may be a killing without the stabber's knowing it at the time. A seeming loss or reverse of some kind may turn out to be a blessing in disguise.

It is convenient, following Quine, to distinguish between mass nouns and count nouns as suggested already in III. 'Many', 'a few', and so on, may be used to modify count nouns, 'much', 'a little', and so on, mass nouns.

'In Philadelphia, nearly everyone reads the Evening Bulletin'

becomes

'Few $\{ e\ni(\text{Per } e \cdot e \text{ In Phila. } \cdot \sim e \text{ Reads the } \textit{Eve. Bull.})\}$',

where *'Few F'* describes the numerosity of the virtual class $F$ as being a few.

'Many are called, but few are chosen'

becomes

'Many $\{ e\ni(\text{Per } e \cdot \text{Called } e) \} \cdot$ Few $\{ e\ni (\text{Per } e \cdot \text{Chosen } e)\}$'.

Perhaps the idioms 'Many $F$', 'Few $F$', and so on, may be handled in terms of the 'Crrlt' for arithmetic. Let

'$e$ Crrlt 'Many',$e'$,$F$'

express merely that person $e$ correlates 'Many' with (the parts of) the individual $e'$ with respect to the virtual class $F$. And similarly for 'few', 'several', 'most', 'nearly all', and so on. Some of these no doubt will turn out to be interdefinable.

Strictly numerical expressions, or idioms involving them, may be handled in terms of the pragmatics of counting. Let '$e$ Num $F$'

express that $e$ is the numerosity or cardinality of the virtual class $F$. Actually this is definable as follows.

‘$e$ Num $F$’ abbreviates ‘$(N_V\ e \cdot (Ee_1)\ (Ee_2)\ (Per\ e_1 \cdot e_1$ Crrlt $e,e_2,F)$’,

where ‘$N_V\ e$’ expresses that $e$ is a number (in the sense of being a correlated string of accents). To say that there are three oranges on the table is then to say that

$$3\ \text{Num}\ \{\ e\ni(Oe \cdot e\ \text{On the table})\},$$

for ‘3’ properly introduced.

Sentences involving numerical comparison may be handled in terms of the *greater than* or *less than* relations of arithmetic.

‘There are more apples than oranges on the table’

obviously becomes

‘$(Ee_1)\ (Ee_2)\ (e_1\ \text{Num}\ \{\ e\ni(Ae \cdot e\ \text{On t})\} \cdot e_2\ \text{Num}\ \{\ e\ni (Oe \cdot e\ \text{On t})\} \cdot e_1 > e_2)$’

in more or less obvious fashion.

‘There are many more apples than oranges on the table’

becomes, however,

‘$(Ee_1)\ (Ee_2)\ (e_1\ \text{Num}\ \{e\ni(Ae \cdot e\ \text{On t})\} \cdot e_2\ \text{Num}\ \{\ e\ni (Oe \cdot e\ \text{On t})\} \cdot e_1 > e_2 \cdot \text{Many}\ \{e\ni(N_V\ e \circ e_1 \geqq e \geqq e_2)\})$’.

The clause for ‘many’ is merely tacked on, as it should be. That there are many integers between (and including) the integer giving the numerosity of the apples on the table and that giving the numerosity of the oranges on the table gives here the desired effect.

Words such as 'frequently', 'often', 'rarely', and so on, are similar to 'many', 'most', and so on, but "modify" virtual classes of actions or processes or the like.

'He frequently calls on her'

becomes

'Many $\{e \ni \langle he,$ Calls on, $her \rangle e\}$'.

'Presidents of the United States frequently die in office'

becomes

'Many$\{e \ni (Ee_1)(Ee_2)(e_1$ is President of U.S. during $e_2$ ⋅ $\langle e_1, Dies \rangle e$ ⋅ $e$ During $e_2)\}$'.

Quantitative modifiers of mass or bulk nouns are handled a little differently. Let 'Bit' be available to express the relation of being a bit of. '$e_1$ Bit $e_2$', where $e_2$ is the total bulk individual (water, or etc.), expresses that $e_1$ is a bit of $e_2$. Then perhaps

'Much $e$' may abbreviate 'Many $\{e' \ni e'$ Bit $e\}$'

and

'Little $e$' may abbreviate 'Few $\{e' \ni e'$ Bit $e\}$'.

'He drank much wine'

then becomes

'$(Ee_1)(e_1$ = wine ⋅ Many $\{e \ni (e$ Bit $e_1$ ⋅ $he$ Dr $e)\})$'

or

97

'Many $\{e \ni (e \text{ Bit wine} \cdot he \text{ Dr } e)\}$'.

Consider the differences between

'Maria swims skillfully'

and

'Maria swims frequently'.

The latter says that the numerosity of Maria's acts of swimming is many. Thus

'Many $\{e \ni \langle m, \text{Swims} \rangle e\}$'.

The other does not say only that Maria is skillful at swimming, but rather that she does swim and that her acts of swimming are such as to exhibit skill. Thus

'$(Ee) \langle m, \text{Swims} \rangle e \cdot (e) (\langle m, \text{Swims} \rangle e \supset m \text{ Skill } e, '\{e' \ni \langle m, \text{Swims} \rangle e'\}')$',

On the other hand, perhaps

'Maria is skillful at swimming'

becomes merely

'$(Ee) m \text{ Skill } e, '\{e' \ni \langle m, \text{Swims} \rangle e'\}$''',

to the effect that Maria is skillful at doing something under the description of its being an act of her swimming. Better yet,

'$(Ee) m \text{ Skill } e, '\{e_1 \ni e_1 = \text{Fu } '\{e_2 \ni \langle m, \text{Swims} \rangle e_2\}\}$''',

to the effect that Maria is skillful at doing $e$ under the description of

98

its being the fusion (in the sense of the calculus of individuals) of all her acts of swimming.

Several of the sentences considered thus far contain adverbial phrases. Let us consider now a few more. Some of these will be recognized as interesting examples from the relevant literature, as indeed have been many of the foregoing.

Consider next the famous example,

'The three bitterly crying children walked home fast,'

due to Uriel Weinreich.[4] The 'the' here may be disregarded. To simplify, let us drop it for the moment. The sentence with the 'the' dropped becomes then

'$(Ee_1)$ $\cdots$ $(Ee_9)$ (Ch $e_1$ $\cdot$ Ch $e_2$ $\cdot$ Ch $e_3$ $\cdot$ $\sim$ $e_1 = e_2$ $\cdot$ $\sim$ $e_2 = e_3$ $\cdot$ $\sim$ $e_1 = e_2$ $\cdot$ $\langle e_1, \text{Cr} \rangle e_4$ $\cdot$ $\langle e_2, \text{Cr} \rangle e_5$ $\cdot$ $\langle e_3, \text{Cr} \rangle e_6$ $\cdot$ Bitter $e_4$ $\cdot$ Bitter $e_5$ $\cdot$ Bitter $e_6$ $\cdot$ $\langle e_1, W, e_1\text{'s home} \rangle e_7$ $\cdot$ $\langle e_2, W, e_2\text{'s home} \rangle e_8$ $\cdot$ $\langle e_3, W, e_3\text{'s home} \rangle e_9$ $\cdot$ Fast $e_7$ $\cdot$ Fast $e_8$ $\cdot$ Fast $e_9$ $\cdot$ $e_4$ During $e_7$ $\cdot$ $e_5$ During $e_8$ $\cdot$ $e_6$ During $e_9$ )'.

Bringing in now the 'the', 'the three bitterly crying children' is not taken to describe, but rather to indicate anaphorically that some condition, satisfied by just those children, has been left out. A paraphrase of the sentence is then of the form

'The three bitterly crying children of whom such and such is true walked home fast.'

For this we have the following logical form, where '—$e$—' indicates that such and such holds of $e$.

'$(Ee_1)$ $\cdots$ $(Ee_9)$ ([as above] $\cdot$ —$e_1$— $\cdot$ —$e_2$— $\cdot$ —$e_3$— $\cdot$ $(e)$ (—$e$— $\supset$ ($e = e_1$ v $e = e_2$ v $e = e_3$))))'

[4] See Uriel Weinreich, "On the Semantic Structure of Language," in *Universals of Language*, ed. by J. Greenberg (The M.I.T. Press, Cambridge, Mass. and London: 1966), p. 200.

# EVENTS, REFERENCE, AND LOGICAL FORM

This form is to be contrasted with the logically very much more complicated form suggested by Weinreich himself modelled after Reichenbach.

Sometimes of course numerical words are used adverbially. Consider

'Brutus kissed Portia twice',

which becomes

$$\text{'}(Ee_1)\,(Ee_2)\,(\langle b,K,p\rangle e_1 \cdot \langle b,K,p\rangle e_2 \cdot \sim e_1 = e_2)\text{'}$$

Again, consider

'Brutus kissed Portia twice, the second time more passionately than the first',

which becomes

$$\text{'}(Ee_1)\,(Ee_2)\,(\langle b,K,p\rangle e_1 \cdot \langle b,K,p\rangle e_2 \cdot e_1 \ B \ e_2 \cdot e_2 \ MP \ e_1)\text{'},$$

where '$e_1 \ B \ e_2$' expresses that $e_1$ takes place before $e_2$ does and '$e_2 \ MP \ e_1$' that $e_2$ is more passionate than $e_1$.

Adverbs such as 'while', 'during', and so on, may be handled as relations between events, as already noted.

'Nero played the harp while Rome burned'

becomes clearly

$$\text{'}(Ee_1)\,(Ee_2)\,(\langle n,Pl,h\rangle e_1 \cdot \langle r,B\rangle e_2 \cdot e_1 \ During \ e_2)\text{'}.$$

As values for the variables '$e$', etc., are included of course states of mind, states of the body, states of being this or that, and so on. Most of the examples considered thus far have been concerned with acts or actions involving change of state.

Aches, pains, and the like, are in effect bodily states.

'James has now a bodily pain similar to the one he had yesterday'

becomes

$(Ee_1)$ $(Ee_2)$ $(\langle j,P \rangle e_1$ · $e_1$ During *yesterday* · $\langle j,P \rangle$ $e_2$ · $e_2$ During *now* · $e_1$ Sim $e_2)$',

where '$\langle j,P \rangle e$' expresses that $e$ is a state of John's being in bodily pain.

Mental states, dispositions, and the like, may be handled similarly.

'Michael's modesty prevented his having any conspicuous success in the competitive world'

translates into

$(Ee_1)$ $(\langle m,M \rangle e_1$ · $(e)$ $(\langle m,M \rangle e \supset e\ P\ e_1)$ · $(e_2)$ $(\ (\langle m,S,cw \rangle e_2$ · Consp $e_2) \supset e_1$ Prvnt $e_2))$'.

Here the second clause is inserted to assure that all states or acts of Michael's being modest are *parts* of $e_1$ so that $e_1$ is the maximal or longest state of his being modest. It is this maximal state that prevents any state or act of his being conspicuously successful in the competitive world.

Consider the following sentences containing 'persuaded' or 'expected':

'I persuaded John to leave'

and

'I expected John to leave'.

Both of these seem to involve intentional relations, and hence the

*Art des Gegebenseins* is to be brought in. Expectation seems to be triadic and persuasion quadratic. Thus

$$\text{`}e_1 \text{ Expct } e_2,e_3\text{'}$$

may express that person $e_1$ expects the event or state $e_2$ under the event-descriptive predicate $e_3$.

$$\text{`}e_1 \text{ Prsd } e_2,e_3,e_4\text{'}$$

may express that person $e_1$ persuades person $e_2$ to bring $e_3$ about as described by the event-descriptive predicate $e_4$. The first sentence then becomes

$$\text{`}(Ee)\ I\ \text{Prsd } j,e\text{`}\langle j,L\rangle\text{'' '},$$

and the second,

$$\text{`}(Ee)\ I\ \text{Expct } e,\ \text{`}\langle j,L\rangle\text{'' '}.$$

Consider next

'I persuaded a specialist to examine John'

and

'I persuaded John to be examined by a specialist'.

These two may have different truth values, although the difference between them seems to be merely using the passive voice in the second in place of the active voice in the first. However, the difference is clearly much deeper than this. The first becomes

$$\text{`}(Ee_1)\ (Ee_2)\ (Ee)\ (\text{Spec } e_1\ \cdot\ I\ \text{Prsd } e_1,e,\ \ulcorner\langle e_2,\text{Exmn},j\rangle\urcorner\ \cdot\ e_2\ \text{Des } e_1)\text{'}.$$

(Note the need here again of using Quine's corners.) The second, however, turns into something quite different:

'(E$e$) $I$ Prsd j,$e$, ' { $e''$ɜ(E$e_1$) (Spec $e_1$ ∙ ⟨$e_1$,Exmn,j⟩$e''$) } ' '.

Consider also the variants of these sentences with 'expected' in place of 'persuaded'.

'I expected a specialist to examine John'

becomes

'(E$e_1$) (E$e_2$) (E$e$) (Spec $e_1$ ∙ $I$ Expct $e$, ⌜⟨$e_2$,Exmn,j⟩⌝ ∙ $e_2$ Des $e_1$)'

and

'I expected John to be examined by a specialist'

becomes merely

'(E$e_1$) (E$e_2$) (E$e$) (Spec $e_1$ ∙ $I$ Expct $e$, ⌜⟨j,∪Exmn,$e_2$⟩⌝ ∙ $e_2$ Des $e_1$)',

where ∪Exmn is merely the converse of the dyadic relation Exmn (as in *P.M.*, *31.02).

Enjoying seems similar to expecting and persuading in requiring reference to a suitable description. Let

'$e_1$ Enj $e_2$,$e_3$'

express that $e_1$ enjoys the act, process, state, or event, or whatever $e_2$ under the description $e_3$.

'Maria enjoyed dancing with the Duke of Regalia'

then becomes

'(E$e_1$) (m  Enj  $e_1$, '⟨m,D,duke⟩'  ·  ⟨m,D,duke⟩$e_1$ )'.

If the Duke of Regalia happens to be the worst dancer anywhere, it does not follow that

Maria enjoyed dancing with the worst dancer anywhere.

This becomes rather

'(E$e_1$) (m  Enj  $e_1$, '⟨m,D,worst  dancer  anywhere⟩'  ·  ⟨m,D,worst dancer anywhere⟩$e_1$ )'.

Although 'duke' is replaceable by 'worst dancer anywhere', ' 'duke' ' as occurring in ' '⟨m,D,duke⟩' ' is not of course replaceable by ' 'worst dancer anywhere' '.

Consider next a compound such as

'I expected Maria to enjoy dancing with the Duke of Regalia'.

For this an *Art des Gegebenseins* within an *Art des Gegebenseins* is needed, thus:

'(E$e$) (*I* Expect $e$, '{$e'$ ₃(⟨m,D,duke⟩$e'$  ·  M Enj $e'$, '⟨m,D,duke⟩')}'')'.

Another example of a nested *Art des Gegebenseins* (one within another) is as follows.

'I am hunting for a bigger apartment than Maria is'

becomes

'(E$e$) *I* H  $e$, '{$e'$₃(Apt $e'$  ·  (E$e''$) (E$e'''$) (m H $e''$,$e'''$  ·  'Apt' $e'''$ · $e'$ Bigger $e''$)}'')'.

The $e'''$ is the *Art des Gegebenseins* of $e''$. And still another:

'Raoul is able to perform the Sonata more beautifully than Gina is'

becomes

'(E$e$)r Able $e$,' $\{e'\ni(\langle r,\text{Perf},\text{the Sonata}\rangle e'$ · $(e'')$ (g Able $e''$, '$\langle g,\text{Perf},\text{the Sonata}\rangle'$ $\supset e'$ MB $e'')$ ) $\}$ ' '.

Contrast this with

'Raoul is able to perform the Sonata more beautifully than Gina does',

which becomes

'(E$e$)r Able $e$,'$\{e'\ni(\langle r,\text{Perf},\text{the Sonata}\rangle e'$ · $(e'')$ $(\langle g,\text{Perf},\text{the Sonata}\rangle e''\supset e'$ MB $e'')$ )$\}$' '.

Ability seems to be like skill in requiring mention of the mode of description. In fact all disposition terms apparently require this.

'Salt is soluble'

becomes here

'(E$e$) salt Able $e$, '$\{e'\ni\langle\text{salt},\text{Dissolves},\text{water}\rangle e'\}$' ',

and this even if the salt is never immersed.

Let us reflect a little more now upon the problem of complex events.

Davidson has raised an interesting point as follows. "First, we should observe that we may easily know that an event is a pouring of poison without knowing that it is a killing [of a person, say a traveller], just as we may know that an event is the death of Scott without knowing that it is the death of the author of *Waverley*. To describe an event as a killing is to describe it as an event (here an action) that caused a death, and we are not apt to describe an action that caused a death until the death occurs; yet it may be such an action before the death occurs."[5]

Strictly we should not identify here the actual pouring of the wine with the killing, not even with the *intended* killing. "Two events are easy to distinguish here," Davidson writes, "my pouring of the poison, and the death of the traveller. One precedes the other, and causes it. But where does the event of my killing the traveller come in?" At least four events should be distinguished here: the intended killing, the means of doing so, the traveller's drinking the poison, and his dying. The actual killing is then a complex event, a sum event, of the means (the pouring of the poison), $e_1$, the traveller's drinking it, $e_2$, and his dying, $e_3$. Such a complex is a successive sum.[6] In addition there is the intention $e$ to kill the person. There is the intention to kill, perhaps by other means, before the means are chosen. The pouring is what might be referred to as the intended killing. There is the intended killing even if the person does not die. The actual killing here is thus the successive sum $(e_1 \cup e_2 \cup e_3)$ with $e$ as the intention to kill, where $e_1$ is before $e_2$ and $e_2$ is before or overlaps $e_3$. It is before if the person dies after he has stopped drinking the poison.

Events naturally range from the very smallest, point events, to the very greatest, the whole cosmos. Each event can be decomposed into its component point events, and longer events into shorter ones. Davidson's killing was so decomposed a moment back. But even the component events distinguished there, $e_1$, $e_2$, and $e_3$, may be further decomposed. Each in fact may be regarded as a succession of ultimate point events. Usually it is of no interest to decompose quite so far as this, but theoretically we may always do so if we wish. We see now why the calculus of individuals is of such interest in the

[5] D. Davidson, "The Individuation of Events," in *Essays in Honor of Carl G. Hempel* (Reidel, Dordrecht: 1969), p. 229. See also R. Chisholm, "States of Affairs Again," *Nous* 5 (1971): 179-189 and "Events and Propositions," *Nous* 4 (1970): 25-32, and D. Davidson, "Eternal vs. Ephemeral Events," *Nous* 5 (1971): 335-349.
[6] Cf. *Belief, Existence, and Meaning*, pp. 231 ff.

theory of complex events, in particular, in providing the notion of being a part of.

The problem of individuating events is closely related to the following. Given a complex event, a "whole four-dimensional material content," many predicates are often applied to it that properly should be applied only to certain *proper parts* of it, or the other way around. We might be tempted to say, to return to Davidson's example, that the pouring of the poison *is* the killing, in the sense of identity. Strictly, however, it is merely a proper part of the killing, as noted.

Consider Miss Anscombe's example. "Are we to say that the man who (intentionally) moves his arm $[e_1]$, operates the pump $[e_2]$, replenishes the water-supply $[e_3]$, poisons the inhabitants $[e_4]$, is performing *four* actions? Or only one?"[7] Let $e$ be the intention of doing $e_1$ under the appropriate description. Clearly $e_1$ is not the same as $e_2$ so that the intention $e$ of doing $e_1$ under the description is not the same as that of doing $e_2$. The complex action $e_3$ clearly consists of many more events, the flow of the water, and so on. Likewise $e_4$ contains as parts many actions on the part of the inhabitants who drink the water. Part of the complex action consisting of his poisoning the inhabitants is their drinking the water. There is no killing if the man does not die. So here, there is no poisoning if there is no drinking of the poisoned water. And so on. There are not just four actions here, but many more. Only four, however, have been singled out and put under the desired event-descriptive predicates.

Enough has been said to suggest that the structure of complex events may be fully analyzed within the vocabulary here of event logic.

Two or three examples of logical forms for sentences concerning knowing have already been given. The form '$e$ Knows $e_1,e_2$' was used to express that person $e$ knows $e_1$ under the linguistic description $e_2$. It seems likely that this form can be used to provide forms for all sentences containing 'knows' or its derivatives. And

---

[7] G.E.M. Anscome, *Intention* (Cornell University Press, Ithaca: 1957), p. 45.

similarly for analogous forms for believing, thinking, remembering, and so on.

A few further typical sentences concerning knowing may be handled as follows.

'Jones knows Smith to be rich'

becomes

'(E*e*) j Knows *e*, '⟨s,R⟩' '.

'Smith knows that Jones knows that he (Smith) is rich'

becomes

'(E*e*) s Knows *e*, '{*e'* ɜ(E*e''*) ⟨j,Knows,*e''*, '⟨s,R⟩'⟩*e'*}' '.

In general

'Everybody knows all ravens to be black'.

where 'Γ' is an event-descriptive predicate, presumably holds as a meaning postulate concerning 'Knows'. (Note that the corresponding principle would not hold concerning belief.) From both of these formulas it then follows, as it should, that Smith is rich.

Consider next

'Everybody knows all ravens to be black'

or

'All ravens are known by everyone to be black'.

These become

'(*e*) (*e'*) ( (Per *e'* · *e'* Knows *e*, 'Raven') ⊃ *e'* Knows *e*, 'Black')' or perhaps

'$(e)$ $(e')$ $((\text{Per } e' \cdot e' \text{ Knows } e, \text{'Raven'}) \supset e' \text{ Knows } e, \text{'Black'})$'.

In the interpretation of '$e$ Knows $e_1, e_2$', the $e_1$ is allowed to be anything at all, an object, a person, a state, act, process, and so on. The differentiation is made in the mode of description $e_2$. So here, in the formula just given, the first clause containing 'Knows' expresses that $e'$ knows the object $e$ under the description of being a raven.

Where '$e$ Blvs $e_1, e_2$' expresses that $e$ believes $e_1$ under the description $e_2$, a similar form emerges.

It is interesting to iterate 'Knows' and 'Blvs' in various ways.

'Everybody knows what he knows and what he believes, and what he doesn't'

can be "read" in several ways. The most immediate is perhaps as

'$(e)$ $(e_1)$ $(e_2)$ $(( e \text{ Knows } e_1, e_2 \supset (Ee_3) (Ee') (Ee'_1) (Ee'_2) (e'$ Des $e \cdot e'_1$ Des $e_1 \cdot e'_2$ Des $e_2 \cdot e$ Knows $e_3, \Gamma_1)) \cdot (e$ Blvs $e_1, e_2 \supset (Ee_3) (Ee') (Ee'_1) (Ee'_2) (e'$ Des $e \cdot e'_1$ Des $e_1 \cdot e'_2$ Des $e_2 \cdot e$ Knows $e_3, \Gamma_2)) \cdot (\sim e$ Knows $e_1, e_2 \supset (Ee_3) (Ee') (Ee'_1)$ $(Ee'_2)$ $(e'$ Des $e \cdot e'_1$ Des $e_1 \cdot e'_2$ Des $e_2 \cdot e$ Knows $e_3, \Gamma_3)) \cdot (\sim e$ Blvs $e_1, e_2 \supset (Ee_3) (Ee') (Ee'_1) (Ee'_2) (e'$ Des $e \cdot e'_1$ Des $e_1 \cdot e'_2$ Des $e_2 \cdot e$ Knows $e_3, \Gamma_4)))$',

where '$\Gamma_1$', '$\Gamma_2$', '$\Gamma_3$', and '$\Gamma_4$' are appropriate event-descriptive predicates. '$\Gamma_1$' for example is short for

$$\ulcorner \{ e'_3 \ni \langle e', \text{Knows}, e', e'_2 \rangle e'_3 \} \urcorner .$$

and similarly for the other '$\Gamma$'s *mutatis mutandis*. And similarly for any other readings.

Note that although Watson may know Mr. Hyde to be a

murderer, and Mr. Hyde = Dr. Jekyll, it does not follow that Watson knows Dr. Jekyll to be a murderer. This example is similar to the concerning Oedipus and Jocasta above. Clearly if

$$(Ee) (\langle h,M \rangle e \cdot w \text{ Knows } e, \text{'} \langle h,M \rangle \text{'})$$

and

$$h = j,$$

then

$$(Ee) (\langle j,M \rangle e \cdot w \text{ Knows } e, \text{'} \langle j,M \rangle \text{'}).$$

but not

$$(Ee) (\langle j,M \rangle e \cdot w \text{ Knows } e, \text{'} \langle h,M \rangle \text{'}),$$

Identity of objects may be handled as follows.

'Quine knows the dictator of Portugal to be Dr. Salazar'

becomes

'$(e)$ (q Knows $e$, '$\langle$Dict. of P.$\rangle$' $\equiv$ q Knows $e$, '$\langle s \rangle$')',

or simply

'q Knows Dict. of P., '$\{e \ni e = s\}$' '.

Note, incidentally, that a Quine-like reading of 'Knows' and 'Blvs' is quite in order. '$e$ Knows $e_1, e_2$' expresses after all that $e$ knows that $e_2$ is *true of* $e_1$. And similarly for 'Blvs'. Or, equally well, '$e$ Knows $e_1, e_2$' may be read as '$e$ knows that $e_2$ *denotes* $e_1$', taking 'denotes' here in the sense of multiple denotation as above.

Most of the foregoing sentences have been phrased without 'that'. Many sentences concerning knowing, believing, and the like, containing 'that' may be paraphrased into sentences not containing it. Perhaps sentences that cannot be paraphrased in this way can be handled in terms of the demonstrative 'that', somewhat in the manner suggested by Davidson as discussed in III.

A *subjunctive* is, according to the *O.E.D.,* an expression "designating a mood . . . . the forms of which are employed to denote an action or a state [italics added] *as conceived (and not as a fact)* and therefore used to express a wish, command, exhortation, or a contingent, hypothetical, or prospective event." The logic of subjectives might therefore reasonably be through to be a part of the logic of actions or states, in particular, of those that are "conceived" merely, or are "hypothetical" or "prospective" but are not "facts." Hypotheticals or conceivings may be viewed in terms of a suitable propositional attitude. Closely related with subjunctives are counterfactuals, semifactuals, counteridenticals, counterlegals, and the like. The proposal here is to attempt to handle all such sentences in terms of a suitable propositional attitude.

According to Nelson Goodman[8], "a counterfactual is true if a certain [lawlike] connection obtains between the antecedent and consequent." To try to spell out what that "connection" is in sufficiently clear-cut terms has turned out to be extremely difficult. According to the proposal here, a counterfactual is true if a certain connection is *regarded by the speaker* as holding between antecedent and consequent.

Let '*e* Sbjnct *e*'' express that person *e* takes a subjunctive attitude toward the sentential sign event *e'*, or takes it as "hypothetical" or "prospective" or something of the sort. And let us write

'*e* Subj $\Gamma$'    as short for    '(E*e'*) (*e* Subj *e'* $\cdot$ $\Gamma$ *e'*)',

where $\Gamma$ is a shape-descriptive predicate. Then

'If the piece of butter eaten yesterday and never heated had been heated to 150°F., then it would have melted'

becomes, where *sp* is the speaker,

[8] N. Goodman, *Fact, Fiction, and Forecast* (Athlone Press, London: 1954), p. 16.

'(b Bit butter · b Eaten *yesterday* · b was never heated · *sp* Sbjnct '(b was heated to 150° F. ⊃ b melted)')',

Consider next

(1) 'Even had that match been scratched, it still would not have lighted'

and

(2) 'Had the match been scratched, it would have lighted'.

Goodman regards the first as the "direct negation" of the second. In so doing, he presupposes a meaning to 'negation' as applied to subjunctives that has not been defined. According to the suggestion here, the first would become something like

'(~ Sm · ~ Lm · *sp* Sbjnct '(Sm ⊃ ~ Lm)')',

and the second,

'(~ Sm · ~ Lm · *sp* Sbjnct '(Sm ⊃ Lm)')'.

Clearly this is not the "direct negation" of the other. The presence of 'even' and 'still' has been disregarded here, but strictly should be taken account of.

To get at the logical form of subjunctives, one first spells out the immediate factual statements the subjunctive is supposed to have as logical consequences, and then puts the relevant conditional under the subjunctive attitude. Clearly a logical consequence of the first of the two foregoing forms is that ~ Sm, and also that ~ Lm, this circumstance mirroring that a supposed logical consequence of (1) is that that match had not been scratched and that it did not light. And similarly for the second form with respect to (2).

Goodman regards (1) as the "contrapositive" of

112

'Even if the match lighted, it still wasn't scratched'.

Again, he uses 'contrapositive', like 'negation', not in the usual sense. This sentence becomes rather

$$\text{'}(\sim Sm \cdot sp \text{ Sbjnct '}(Lm \supset \sim Sm)')\text{'}.$$

It is not clear that '$\sim Lm$' should be added here.

Consider next the "counteridenticals"

'If I were Julius Caesar, I wouldn't be alive in the twentieth century'

and

'If I were Julius Caesar, he would be alive in the twentieth century'.

The first becomes (somewhat simplified)

$$\text{'}(I \text{ L } 20thc. \cdot I \text{ Sbjnct '}(I = jc \supset \sim I \text{ L } 20thc.)')\text{'},$$

and the second,

$$\text{'}(\sim jc \text{ L } 20thc. \cdot I \text{ Sbjnct '}(I = jc \supset jc \text{ L } 20thc.)')\text{'}.[9]$$

Goodman comments that "although the antecedent in the two cases is a statement of the same identity, we attach two different consequents which, on the very assumption of that identity, are incompatible." This incompatibility holds only if the sentences are taken as indicative and not under the subjunctive attitude. When they are taken under the attitude by the speaker, both of these forms are true, because in fact he is (presumably) alive in the twentieth century and Julius Caesar is not.

[9] More properly, the first here becomes '($I$ L 20*thc.* $\cdot$ ($Ee$) ($Ee'$) ($I$ Ref $e,I,e'$ $\cdot$ $\ulcorner(e = $ jc $\supset \sim e$ L 20*thc.*)$\urcorner$ $e'$ $\cdot$ $I$ Subj $e'$)', and similarly for the second.

113

## EVENTS, REFERENCE, AND LOGICAL FORM

Enough has been shown to suggest that the approach outlined here towards counterfactuals, subjunctives, and the like, holds promise and should be worked out more fully.

One might urge against the foregoing account that 'Sbjnct' is taken as unanalyzed. Surely. To give the logical form for a sentence does not require that all the words in it be analyzed, or defined away in terms of primitives, as already noted. Davidson's policy here is a good one. We should distinguish the following tasks, he urges: "uncovering the logical grammar or form of sentences . . ., and analysis of individual words or expressions. . . . . I think it hard to exaggerate the advantage to philosophy of language of bearing in mind this distinction between questions of logical form or grammar, and the analysis of individual concepts."[10] Of course at some point we must make sure that these advantages are not those of theft over honest toil. Strategically, however, and this is Davidson's point, question of logical form are to be viewed as prior. Only after they have been settled, to some extent anyhow, is it fruitful to go on to analysis.

Questions, commands, exhortations, and the like, may be handled in somewhat similar vein.[11] Ordinary logic seems to have been framed primarily to accommodate the indicative mood. Each of the other moods therefore seems best handled by introducing a suitable pragmatical primitive, as here for subjunctives.

Let us review briefly now a miscellany of further forms, or types of forms, not explicitly included in the foregoing but of some interest on their own account.

Consider now 'cause'. Some construe causation as a dyadic relation between events.

$$(3) \qquad\qquad 'e_1 \ Cs \ e_2'$$

can, according to them, express that event $e_1$ causes event $e_2$. Here also, however, it would seem that the appropriate linguistic descriptions should be brought in as additional factors, as suggested in I.

[10] D. Davidson, "Truth and Meaning," p. 316.
[11] See *Belief, Existence,* and *Meaning,* pp. 260 ff.

Causation should perhaps thus be construed as a quadratic relation, so that

$$\langle e_1, e_2 \rangle \text{ Cs } \langle e_3, e_4 \rangle$$

can express that $e_1$ under the description $e_2$ causes $e_3$ under the description $e_4$, essentially as in I. Causal sentences should be linked with sentences of causal form. It might be thought that these latter are of the form

(4)    $(e) ((\text{----})e \supset (Ee') ((\langle \cdots \rangle)e' \cdot e \text{ Cs } e'))$,

with apropriate event-descriptive predicates filled in. Statements of this form would be to the effect that every event of such and such a kind causes an event of such and such another kind. What might be dubbed the covering-law model for causation is that behind every singular causal sentence of the form (3), there lurks a causal law of the form (4). However this may be, means are available here for expressing all manner of causal sentences, both singular and general.

The method of using the *Art des Gegebenseins* is ideally suited for handling hypothetical or fictitious objects of all kinds. Consider Peter Geach's delightful

'Hob thinks a witch has blighted Bob's mare, and Nob wonders whether she [the same witch] killed Cob's sow'.

Clearly this sentence is at least seven-way ambiguous, for Nob's wondering might be about the witch who did blight Bob's mare, or about the witch thought by Hob to have blighted Bob's mare, or about the witch thought by Nob to have done so, or about the witch thought by both Hob and Nob to have done so, or about the witch thought by Hob to have done so and who did so, or about the witch thought by Nob to have done so and who did so, or, finally, about the witch thought by both Hob and Nob to have done so and who did so. Let us consider only the first. Let 'h Th $e_1, e_2$' express that Hob thinks $e_2$ true of $e_1$ and 'n W $e_1, e_2$' express that Nob wonders whether $e_2$ is true of $e_1$. Geach's example then may take on the form

'(E$e$) (h Th $e$, '$\{e'$ə(E$e''$) (Witch $e'$ · Mare $e''$ · $e''$ Belongs Bob · $e'$ Blighted $e''$)$\}$ ' · n W $e$, '$\{e$ə(E$e''$) (E$e'''$) (Witch $e'$ · Mare $e''$ · $e''$ Belongs Bob · $e'$ blighted $e''$ · Sow $e'''$ · $e'''$ Belongs Cob · $e'$ Killed $e'''$ )$\}$ ' ) ).

If there are witches, this formula allows for such, If there are not, the $e$ here is null. Or, alternatively,

'( (E$e$)h Th $e$, '$\{e'$ə(E$e''$) (E$e'''$) (Witch $e''$ · Mare $(e'''$ · $e'''$ Belongs Bob · $\langle e''$,Blighted,$e''^1 \rangle e'$)$\}$ ' · (E$e$) m W $e$, '$\{e'$ə (E$e''$) (E$e'''$) (E$e''''$) (Witch $e''$ · Mare $e'''$ · $e'''$ Belongs Bob · $e''$ Blighted $e'''$ · Sow $e''''$ · $e''''$ Belongs Cob · $\langle e''$,Killed,$e'''' \rangle e'$)$\}$ ')'.
$e'$) $\}$ ' ) '.

Here the supposed actions of the witch are taken under the *Art des Gegebenseins,* not the supposed witch.

Consider the following, from the *Dhammapada*:

'An evil deed is better left undone, for a man repents of it afterwards; a good deed is better done, for having done it, one does not repent.'

Omitting for the moment 'for', we see that four component forms are involved here:

(5)  '($e$) ($e'$) ( ($e$ Does $e'$ · Evil $e'$) ⊃ (E$e''$)($e'$ B $e''$ · $\langle e$, Repents, $e' \rangle e''$) )',

(6)  '($e$) ($e'$) ($e''$) ( ($e$ Does $e'$ · Evil $e'$ · ~ $\langle e$,Does,$e' \rangle e''$) ⊃ $e''$ Better $e'$)',

(7)  '($e$) ($e'$) ( ($e$ Does $e'$ · Good $e'$) ⊃ ~ (E$e''$) ($e'$ B $e''$ · $\langle e$, Repents,$e \rangle e''$) )',

and

(8)   ‘$(e)\,(e')\,(e'')\,((e$ Does   $e'\,\cdot\,$ Good $e'\,\cdot\,\sim\,\langle e,$Does$,e'\rangle\,e'')\,\supset$ $e'$ Better $e'')$’.

Bringing in 'for', we note that what is stated is that (5) is taken by the speaker as the *reason* for (6), and (7) of (8). Let '$e$ Rsn $e_1,e_2$' express that person $e$ takes $e_1$ as the (or a) reason for $e_2$. Where $sp$ again is the speaker, our sentence then becomes

‘$(sp$ Rsn $(5),(6)\,\cdot\,sp$ Rsn $(7),(8))$’.

Let '$e_1$ Oblg$_c$ $e_2,e_3$' expresses that $e_1$ is obliged to do or bring about $e_2$ under the description $e_3$ on the basis of the moral code $c$.

'John does not intend to do all that he is obliged to'

then becomes

‘$\sim\,(e)\,(e')\,(j$ Oblg$_c$ $e,e'\,\supset\,j$ Intd $e,e')$’.

'John does not intend to do anything that he is obliged to'

becomes rather

‘$(e)\,(e')\,(j$ Oblg$_c$ $e,e'\,\supset\,\sim\,j$ Intd $e,e')$’,

Similarly,

'I persuaded John that he is obliged to leave'

can be handled as

‘$(Ee)\,I$ Prsd j$,e,$ ‘$\{e'\ni(j$ Oblg$_c$ $e',$ ‘$\langle j,L\rangle$’$)\}$’ ’.

To some ears

'There is something the theory says exists, namely, universals' seems ill formed. The paraphrase, obviously intended,

'There are things the theory says exist, namely, universals',

however, may be handled as follows. Let '*th* Says *e,e*', express that
the theory says *e'* of *e*. Then we have

'(E*e*) (*th* Says *e*, ' { *e'*ɘ Exists *e'* } ' · Univ *e*)'.

The grammar of the constituent notions here needs looking at, of
course, just as those in any other logical form do.

A few additional forms concerning knowing are as follows.

'Everything known to Jones he knows to be self-identical'

becomes

'(*e*) (*e'*) (j Knows *e,e'* ⊃ j Knows *e*, ' { *e'*ɘ*e'* = *e'* } ')',

whereas

'Everything is known by Jones to be self-identical'

is rather

'(*e*)j Knows *e*, ' { *e'*ɘ*e'* = *e'* } ' '.

Again,

'Jones knows that he knows that everything is self-identical'

becomes

'j K j, ' { *e*ɘ(Per *e* · (*e'*)*e* Knows *e'*, '{ *e''*ɘ*e''* = *e''* }')} ' ',

or

118

'(Ee)j Knows $e$, '$\{e'\ni(e'')\ \langle j, \text{Knows}, e''$, '$\{e'''\ni e''' = e'''\}$'$\rangle\}\ e'\}$' '.

Clearly all manner of examples of this kind can be handled here.
Also

'There is someone whom we believe to be the murderer, but we do not know anything more about him'

becomes

'(Ee) (Per $e$ • we Blv $e$, 'M' • $\sim$ (Ee') ($\sim$ 'M' $e'$ • we Know $e,e'$))',

whereas

'We believe there is someone who is the murderer but we do not know anything more about him'

becomes rather

'(Ee) (we Blv $e$, '$\{e'\ni(\text{Per } e' \cdot \text{Me}')\}$' • $\sim$ (Ee'') ($\sim$'$\{e'\ni$ (Per $e'$ • Me')$\}$'$e''$ • we Know $e,e''$))'.

Here the $e$ might be the null event, whereas in the former case the $e$ is of course a person.

The following is of interest in combining numerosity words with 'true'.

'Half of what Jones writes is true, but half of it is false'

becomes

'(Ee$_1$) (Ee$_2$) (Ee$_3$) ($e_1$ Num $\{e'\ni(\text{Sent } e' \cdot j \text{ W } e' \cdot \text{Tr } e')\}$ • $e_2$ Num $\{e'\ni(\text{Sent } e' \cdot j \text{ W } e')\}$ • $(2 \times e_1) = e_2$ • $e_3$ Num $\{e'\ni$

$$(\text{Sent } e' \cdot \text{j W } e' \cdot \sim \text{Tr } e')\} \cdot (2 \times e_3) = e_2)'.$$

Most of the foregoing examples will be recognized as having been under discussion somewhere or other in the recent literature.

No one of the foregoing forms is claimed to provide a final rendition of its parent English sentence. On the contrary, many are merely tentative first approximations, put forward as a basis for further study. Some are no doubt too simple and perhaps fail to catch the full subtlety of the English original. All that is claimed is that the underlying framework provides all the materials needed, that is, all the notation, for a fairly comprehensive system of deep structure, perhaps the most comprehensive that has yet been suggested.

For the present, the logical forms are arrived at merely by translating the English original into logical notation. Here the intuitions and language habits of being a native speaker help us, as well as some skill in handling the logical symbols. Eventually, of course, exact rules are to be framed leading from the English original to its logical form.

# VI

# ON HOW
# SOME ADVERBS WORK

*"Si quid novisti rectius istis,
Candidus imperti; si non, his utere mecum."*

In his valuable "Notes on what it would take to understand how one adverb works"[1] George Lakoff, one of the most able of the younger linguists, urges (p. 328) that "you can't understand one [linguistic] phenomenon adequately without studying a great many other related phenomena, and the way they fit together in terms of the linguistic system as a whole." He complains that "much of the discussion of natural language in the philosophical and logical literature is based on a very small sampling of data that is skewed in nontrivial ways." He thinks that "now that philosophers and logicians are turning to more detailed studies of natural language phenomena, it is perhaps the right time to suggest that philosophical and logical training be expanded to include the study of natural languages as entire systems."

Now of course logic *par excellence* is concerned with systems as a whole and the time is no doubt ripe also for linguists to turn to a more detailed study of logic. Although it is true that much philosophic attention has been confined to details, the whole surely

---

[1] In *The Monist* 57 (1973) 328-343.

121

has not been lost sight of. And where attention has been confined to a detail, this is usually done surely with no intent of skewing the data in essential ways. What is needed now is a good deal of cooperative work on the part of linguists, logicians, and philosophers with the aim of constructing a system of deep structure both logically serious and materially adequate for the "representation" of as many sentences of natural language as possible. The deep structure of a sentence is regarded here merely as its logical form, an identification, it seems, that is more and more becoming an accepted one. The system will be "logically serious" if it meets certain minimal requirements of rigor, simplicity, economy, and so on — preferably as a simple, applied, functional calculus of first order in the sense of Church. As to material adequacy, the impossible should not be expected of so young a science. No empirical science is ever quite adequate to all its data, even the most mature. Even so, the aim should be to make the system as comprehensive as is feasible at the present stage of research.

Let us reflect now upon the various sentences containing adverbs considered by Lakoff, and attempt to provide suitable deep structures for them within the extended system of event logic outlined in the preceding papers.

Lakoff thinks the logical form of

(1)                     'John walked slowly,'

should be couched in terms of rates of change over time in order to bring out similarity with

(2a)          'This country changes slowly,'
(2b)     'The rate at which this country changes is slow,'
(2c)          'Change in this country is slow.'

(2b) is a paraphrase of (2a) and (2c) and "means the same as" whatever they mean. Lakoff seems to think that any paraphrase of a sentence must have the same logical form. This would seem doubtful. Paraphrase and logical form, rather, should be sharply distinguished.

122

It might turn out, of course, after investigation that the logical forms of paraphrases are in fact equivalent, in view of commonly accepted meaning or other postulates concerning key words or phrases. Indeed, it seems likely that this might be the case, as will be seen in a moment with some examples. But even so, the logical form of a paraphrase is not to be identified *ab initio* with the logical form of the original sentence. Thus the logical form of (2b) need not be the logical form of (2a) and (2c), even though the three form a paraphrastic set. Some essential reference to a rate of change will occur in the logical form of (2b) but not in those of (2a) and (2c).

No attempt to define 'the logical form of sentence $a$' is made by Lakoff. For the present let it be required at least that the basic non-logical (as opposed to logical or auxiliary) words of $a$' will be "represented" by words that must occur in the logical form. Further, given any two logical forms of the same sentence, they are to be L-equivalent in essentially Carnap's sense.

Adverbs are to be handled here in a certain way as adjectival of events.[2] Some adjectives admit of positive, comparative, and superlative degrees in a most fundamental way. Given the comparative relation *slower-than* as between events, let

$$\text{'Low}(e,\text{Slower-than},F)\text{'}$$

express that $e$ is low in the scale of events graded slow to fast as confined to members of the virtual class $F$. Every comparative relation of this kind carries along with it a rough and ready scale of comparison, usually without numerical degrees attached. 'Low' here serves merely to indicate a rather vague position in the scale. And similarly for 'High', 'Middling', 'Very low', 'Very high', and so on. Many adjectives, it seems, can be handled in this way in terms of a rough and ready scale of comparison.

More specifically, where $R$ is a non-intentional comparative relation available in the system, let

---

[2] Cf. John Wallace, "Positive, Comparative, Superlative," *The Journal of Philosophy* 69 (1972): 773-782.

# EVENTS, REFERENCE, AND LOGICAL FORM

'VLow$(e,R,F)$',
'Low$(e,R,F)$',
'Mid$(e,R,F)$',
'High$(e,R,F)$',

and

'VHigh$(e,R,F)$'

be available primitively to express that $e$ is very low, low, middling, high, or very high in the $R$-scale as confined to members of $F$. These five forms are chosen merely for illustrative purposes, the full theory of adjectives requiring many more gradations.

To simplify the handling of tense, '*now*' is used in effect as above as a demonstrative for the present time, either a long or short span, however the speaker wishes.

For the moment, let (1) above be given the deep structure

(1'). '$(Ee)$ $(\langle j,W\rangle e \cdot e$ B *now* $\cdot$ Low$(e,$Slower-than,$\{e' \ni (Ep)$ (Per $p$ $\cdot \langle p,W \rangle e')\}))$' '

with the obvious symbolization. (1') reads roughly: there is a process of John's walking that bears the before-than relation to *now* and is low in the Slower-than scale as confined to walkings by human persons.

On the other hand the more specific sentence, suggested by Harman[3],

(α)        'John walks slowly for a man of his age,'

may be given the form

'$(Ee)$ $(\langle j,W\rangle e \cdot$ Low$(e,$Slower-than, $\{e' \ni (Ep)$ (Per $p$ $\cdot \langle p,W \rangle e'$ $\cdot p$ Same-Age j)$\})$)'.

---

[3] Gilbert Harman, "Logical Form," Princeton mimeo, 1971.

124

(2) is by no means a paraphrase of (1), nor indeed should it have the same logical form.

Consider now the sentences (2a), (2b), and (2c). (2a) seems to become

(2a′)   '(E$e$) ($e$ = Fu'$\{$ $e'$ $\ni$ ⟨this Country,Changes⟩ $e'$ $\}$ · Low($e$, Slower-than, $\{$ $e'$ $\ni$ (E$x$) (Country $x$ · $e'$ = Fu'$\{$ $e''$ $\ni$ ⟨$x$,Changes⟩ $e''$ $\}$ ) $\}$ ) ) )',

and (2c) becomes

(2c′)   '(E$e$) ($e$ = Fu'$\{$ $e'$ $\ni$ (Change $e$ · $e$ In this Country) $\}$ · Low($e$,Slower-than, $\{$ $e'$ $\ni$ (E$x$)(Country $x$ · $e'$ = Fu'$\{$ $e''$ $\ni$ (Change $e''$ · $e''$ In $x$) $\}$ ) $\}$ ) ) )'.

But (2a′) and (2c) are very likely equivalent in view of some general principles concerning 'Change' and 'In'. (2b), on the other hand, it would seem, has a quite different form.

Let

(1″)                               'rate($e$) = $r$'

express that the rate of the process $e$ is $r$ units where $r$ is a rational number (the units being miles per hour or whatever). To say that the rate of $e$ is slow for members of $F$,

Sl (rate($e$),$F$),

is presumably to say that $r$ < some fixed $r_0(F)$, where $r_0$ is the cut-off point between slow and not slow for members of $F$. Then

($\beta$)                     'The rate of John's walking is slow,'

is represented by

# EVENTS, REFERENCE, AND LOGICAL FORM

'(E$r$) (E$e$) ($\langle$j,W$\rangle$  $e$  $\cdot$  rate($e$) = $r$  $\cdot$  Sl(rate($e$), {$e'$ $\ni$ (E$p$) (Per $p$ $\cdot$ $\langle p$,W$\rangle e'$)}) )'.

It is interesting to note, however, that the following equivalences presumably obtain,

($\gamma$)    Low($e$,Slower-than,$F$)  $\equiv$  Sl (rate($e$),$F$)  $\equiv$  (E$r$) (rate($e$) $r$  $\cdot$ $r < r_0$ ($F$) ),

so that the deep structures of

($\delta$)                              'John walks slowly,'

and of ($\beta$) are presumably equivalent. And similarly for the deep structures of (2a) or (2c) and (2b).

Note that the quantifier '(E$r$)' is the existential quantifier over rational numbers, available within event logic. Lakoff thinks that such quantifiers raise problems, for Davidson and Harman anyhow, for they commit us to having rates of change as values for variables. Note, however, that the quantifier here merely covers a rational number, not some mysterious entity of which the rational number is the measure. So no difficulty over ontological commitment need arise here.

Another difficulty Lakoff finds with speaking of rates of change is (p. 331) that "*slow* and *slowly* involve rate change with respect to time, and any adequate analysis must show how time is involved." Here Lakoff seems to be mistaking giving an *analysis* of a term with giving a logical form for a context in which the term occurs, quite different enterprises surely.

Note incidentally that the equivalences ($\gamma$) involve interrelating a *comparative* notion Slower-than with *quantitative* ones *rate* and $r_0$($F$), relative of course to the same reference class $F$. The full logic of measurement for such notions should be spelled out more fully perhaps than seems to have been done.

Lakoff seems to think that the use of variables over events, in the fashion of Reichenbach, Davidson, and the foregoing, simply will not do. His reason, however, seems like a chaff of wheat in a haystack. He regards

(3)                     \*'That event was slow'

as nonsensical. But event variables include in their range acts, states, processes, and the like, and

'That process was slow,'
'That act was slow,'

are surely meaningful. Thus 'slow' or 'slowly' may significantly be attributed to some of the entities within the range of the event variables. Thus by no means do examples such as (3) "show the inadequacy of the Harman and Davidson analysis in terms of events."

Consider again ($\delta$) or (1). ($\delta$) is a little simpler, no past tense being involved. Should ($\delta$) be given a form similar to (1'), that is,

($\delta'$)   '$(Ee)\ (\langle j,W\rangle e\ \cdot\ Low(e,\text{Slower-than}, \{e'\ \ni\ (Ep)\ (\text{Per}\ p\ \cdot\ \langle p,W\rangle\ e')\})$'?

This states in effect that at least one of John's walkings is low in the Slower-than scale for human walkings. Actually ($\delta$) is ambiguous. It might be construed as ($\delta'$). But consider also

'John always walks slowly,'
'John usually walks slowly,'

and

'John is walking slowly,'

Each of these might be taken as a paraphrase of ($\delta$) and each has its own deep structure, no two of them equivalent. These deep structures may be construed respectively as

127

$(\delta'')$   '$(e) (\langle j,W \rangle e \supset$ Low$(e,$Slower-than, $\{ e' \ni (Ep)$ (Per $p \cdot \langle p,W \rangle e') \} ) )$',

$(\delta''')$   'Few $\{ e \ni (\langle j,W \rangle e \cdot \sim$ Low$(e,$Slower-than, $\{ e' \ni (Ep)($Per $p \cdot \langle p,W \rangle e') \} ) \} )$',

$(\delta'''')$ '$(Ee) (j,W) e \cdot e$ During *now* $\cdot$ Low$(e,$Slower-than,$\{ e' \ni (Ep)$ (Per $p \cdot \langle p,W \rangle e') \} )$'.

Lakoff's "syllogism," if such it be,

(4a)        'John does everything that requires effort slowly,

(4b)                Running requires effort,

(4c)             Therefore, John runs slowly,'

is at best an enthymeme. Perhaps it may be analyzed as follows. Let '$e$ Like $e'''$ express that $e$ is *like* $e'$ in the sense of being of the same general kind. (4a), (4b), and (4c) (construed in the sense of $(\delta'')$ *mut. mat.*) then become

(4a') '$(e) ( (j$ Does $e \cdot e$ Requires-effort) $\supset$ Low$(e,$Slower-than, $\{ e' \ni (Ep)$ (Per $p \cdot e'$ Like $e \cdot p$ Does $e') \} ) ) )$',

(4b') '$(e) (p) ( ($Per $p \cdot \langle p,R \rangle e) \supset e$ Requires-effort)',

(4c') '$(e) (\langle j,R \rangle e \supset$ Low$(e,$Slower-than, $\{ e' \ni (Ep)$ (Per $p \cdot \langle p,R \rangle e') \} ) )$'.

In addition the following premises are needed.

(4d')    '$(e) (\langle j,R \rangle e \supset j$ Does $e)$',

(4e')    'Per $j$',

(4f')    '$(e) ( ( (Ep) ($Per $p \cdot \langle p,R \rangle e) \cdot$ Low$(e,$Slower-than, $\{ e' \ni (Ep)$ (Per $p \cdot e'$ Like $e \cdot p$ Does $e) \} ) ) \supset$ Low$(e,$Slower-than,$\{ e' \ni (Ep)$ (Per $p \cdot \langle p,R \rangle e') \} ) )$',

to the effect that if $e$ is an event of John's running, John does $e$; John is a person; and that if $e$ is an event of some human's running and $e$ is slow for the reference class of all human doings like $e$, then $e$ is slow for the reference class of all human runnings. Only with such

128

additional premisses can (4c′) be said to follow from (4a′) and (4b′), and hence (4c) from (4a) and (4b).

Another Lakoffian "syllogism" is

(5a)   'Men of John's age typically walk a mile in twenty minutes,
(5b)   John walked that mile in ten minutes,
(5c)   Therefore, for a man of his age, John did not walk slowly in walking that mile.'

Let $F$ be the reference class

$$\{e \ni (Ep)\,(Ex)\,(\text{Per } p \cdot p \text{ Same-Age } j \cdot \text{Segment } x \cdot \text{length}(x) = 1 \text{ mile} \cdot e \text{ Typical } p \cdot \langle p, W, x \rangle e)\}.$$

Then (5a) may be represented as

(5a′)                    '$r_0(F) = 1/20$',

and (5b) as

(5b′)   '$(Ee)\,(e \text{ B } now \cdot \text{rate}(e) = 1/10 \cdot \langle J, W, \text{that Mile}\rangle e)$'.

And (5c) becomes

(5c′) '$(Ee)\,(\langle j, W, \text{that Mile}\rangle e \cdot e \text{ B } now \cdot \sim \text{Low}(e, \text{Slower-than}, F))$'.

(5c′) may be seen to be a logical consequence of (5a′) and (5b′), by using the following principles.

(5d′)   '$(r_0(F) = 1/20 \cdot Fe \cdot r(e) = 1/10) \supset \sim \text{Low}(e, \text{Slower-than}, F)$',
(5e′)   '$(Ex)\,(\text{that Mile} = x \cdot \text{Segment } x \cdot \text{length}(x) = 1)$',
(5f′)   'Per $j \cdot j$ Same-Age $j$',

and

(5g')                           '⟨j,W,that Mile⟩ $e$ ⊃ $Fe$'.

There seems to be nothing new here in principle not previously encountered, except in the use of the demonstrative phrase.

Lakoff thinks that "still more problems" arise in connection with the following.

(6a)                'The stew is cooking slowly,'
(6b)                'Sam thinks slowly,'
(6c)      'Teddy arrived at that decision slowly,'
(6d)           The earth developed slowly,'

Again, Lakoff thinks the deep structures of these sentences should be given in terms of rates of change. The view here, on the contrary, as noted, is rather that the deep structures should contain mention of a suitable reference class, and that rates of change come in only in suitable principles of equivalence. Thus (6a) becomes here

(6a')   '(E$e$) (⟨this Stew,Cooks⟩ $e$ ・ $e$ During $now$ ・ Low($e$, Slower-than,$\{e'$ ə (E$x$) (Stew $x$ ・ ⟨$x$,Cooks⟩$e'$)$\}$) )'.

(6b) becomes

(6b')    '($e$) (⟨s,Thinks⟩ $e$ ⊃ Low($e$,Slower-than, $\{e'$ ə (E$p$) (Per $p$ ・ ⟨$p$,Thinks⟩ $e'$)$\}$ ) )'.

(Note however that

                    'Sam is thinking slowly'

becomes rather

   '(E$e$) (⟨s,Thinks⟩ $e$ ・ $e$ During $now$ ・ Low($e$, Slower-than, $\{e'$ə (E$p$) (Per $p$ ・ ⟨$p$,Thinks⟩ $e'$)$\}$ ) )'.

130

Finally (6d) becomes

(6d′)  '(E$e$) ($e$ = Fu '$\{$ $e'$ ϶ (⟨the Earth,Develops⟩ $e'$ • $e'$ B *now*) • Low($e$,Slower-than, $\{e'$ ϶ (E$x$) (Planet $x$ [or Star $x$] • $e'$ = Fu '$\{e''$ ϶ ⟨$x$, Develops⟩ $e''$ $\}$ ) $\}$ ) )'.

Again, nothing essentially new emerges here.

If rates of change are brought in, as Lakoff thinks they should be, some complications arise, but nothing in principle that cannot be handled by extensions of the methods above, in particular by suitable instances of the principle (γ). Lakoff thinks (p. 333) that "the logical form of (6a) would have to contain something like a function . . . indicating rate of change with respect to degree of doneness with respect to time," and his "guess is that in order to account for what is changing in (6a), one would probably need to have variables over degrees of doneness, and since there is no such real-world entity as a degree of doneness, so much the worse for Quine's views on ontological commitment." If rates of change are handled as above, however, there is no need of hypostatizing degrees of doneness, and Quine's criterion of ontological commitment may be kept intact. That criterion is more important than Lakoff realizes and is not to be given up too lightly.

"The question of what changes with respect to time [p. 333] is thornier in (6b)." Indeed it is, and a good deal of empirical research on the measurement of mental processes would be needed before very much of a reliable kind could be said about it. And in any case, questions of logical form are not to be burdened with such considerations. "In (6d)," Lakoff writes, "the physical state of the earth is changing over a very long period of time. There is no conceivable way of analyzing (6d) in terms of a single event." But of course there is, namely, in terms of the fusion of events referred to in the reference class of (6d′). Lakoff fails to avail himself of the resources of the calculus of individuals and to recognize that any two individuals may be summed.

The logical form of (6c) must contain a demonstrative phrase for 'that decision'.

131

(6c′)　'($Ee$) (⟨Teddy,Arrives-at,that Decision⟩ $e$ · $e$ B *now* · Low ($e$,Slower-than,{$e'$ ϶ ($Ep$) ($Ea$) (Per $p$ · Decision $a$ · ⟨$p$,Arrives-at, $a$⟩ $e'$)}) )'.

A "decision" here is taken merely as some sentence expressing the results of some act or process of deciding, and 'that decision' is taken as referential of some such sentence. Again, Lakoff thinks that an "understanding of what *slowly* modifies in (6c) requires an understanding of just what is changing when one is reaching a decision." The job of understanding is not to be identified with that of giving a logical form. The theory of the rates of change needed here would belong rather to depth psychology than to deep grammar.

　　Lakoff thinks there is additional difficulty with the following.

(7a)　　　　　　　'John left the party slowly,'
(7b)　　　　　　　'The guests left the party slowly.'

(7a) is clear enough, but (7b) is ambiguous. (7a) becomes here

(7a′)　'($Ee$) (⟨j,Leaves,the Party⟩ $e$ · $e$ B *now* · Low($e$,Slower-than, {$e'$ ϶ ($Ep$) ($Ee''$) (Per $p$ · Party $e''$ · ⟨$p$,Leaves,$e''$⟩$e'$) }) )'.

But (7b) might become

(7b′)　'($p$) ($p$ Guest the Party ⊃ ($Ee$) (⟨Leaves,the Party⟩ $e$ · $e$ B *now* · Low($e$,Slower-than,{$e'$ ϶ ($Ep$) ($Ee''$) (Per $p$ · Party $e''$ · ⟨$p$,Leaves,$e''$⟩ $e'$)}) ) )',

or

(7b″)　'($Ee$) ($e$ = Fu '{$e'$ ϶ ($Ep$) ($p$ Guest the Party · $e'$ B *now* · ⟨$p$,Leaves, the Party⟩ $e'$)}· Low($e$,Slower-than,{$e'$ ϶ ($e'$ = Fu' {$e''$ ϶ ($Ep$) ($Ee'''$) (Per $p$ · Party $e'''$ · ⟨$p$,Leaves,$e'''$⟩ $e''$) )}) )'.

132

"To account for the ambiguity of (7b)," Lakoff says, "one must provide two different logical forms specifying just what it is that is changing in each case." In (7b'), it is John's leaving the party. In (7b''), it is the fusion of the processes of the various guests' leaving the party.

Again

| (8) | 'John answers questions slowly,' |
| (9) | 'John is slow to answer questions,' |
| (10a) | 'John reacts slowly when you throw something at him,' |
| (10b) | 'John is slow to react when you throw something at him,' |

raise interesting problems concerning the differences between *slowly* and *slow to* or *slow to do*. (8) seems ambiguous. In one rendering (9) is its paraphrase. (9) has the deep form

(9')   '$(e)$ $(a)$ ( ($\langle j, Answer, a \rangle$ $e$ · Question $a$) & j Slow-to-Do $e$)'.

In the other reading (8) would become

(8')   '$(e)$ $(a)$ ( ($\langle j, Answer, a \rangle e$ · Question $a$) $\supset$ Low($e$,Slower-than, $\{ e' \ni (Ep) (Ea) (Per \ p$ · $\langle p, Answer, a \rangle$ $e'$ · Question $a) \} ) )$'.

(10a) has a similar ambiguity and in one rendering has (10b) as a paraphrase.

"This seems to suggest," Lakoff notes (pp. 334-335), "that there are two senses of *slow*" — "normal slow — involves rate of change over time during process" and "slow to — involves amount of time before process starts. Obviously, these two senses of *slow* are not unrelated and one would like to understand the relation between them. . . .Hopefully there should be a single concept *slow* that will cover both cases, but I have no idea at present what it might be." Well, let us unpack *slow to do* as *slow to start to do*. (9') then would become

(9'')   '$(e)$ $(a)$ ( ($\langle j, Anwser, a \rangle$ $e$ · Question $a$) $\supset$ (E$e'$) ($\langle j, Starts, e \rangle$

$e'$ · Low($e'$,Slower-than,$\{e''$ ∍ (E$p$) (E$b$) (E$e'''$) (Per $p$ · Question $b$ · ⟨$p$,Start,$e'''$⟩$e''$ · ⟨$p$,Answer,$b$⟩ $e'''$)$\}$) )'.

In (8') and (9') there is the same rendering of *slow* except for the differences in the reference class. In this way a single rendering for *slow* is provided to justify Lakoff's hope.

The foregoing are concerned exclusively (p. 335) with "the sorts of problems with *slowly* that philosophers and logicians have not looked at," Lakoff writes — an oversight herewith hopefully rectified. We go on now to matters that philosophers have been concerned with. From

(12a)               'John ran slowly,'
(12b)               'John ran'

follows logically. Consider also

(13a)               'John didn't run slowly,'
(13b)               'Did John run slowly?',
(13c)               'John may have run slowly.'

Now (12b) is a logical consequence of (12a) and also of each of the sentences of (13). Lakoff follows Davidson and others in noting that (12b) follows from (12a), or rather

(14b)           '(E$e$) (⟨j,Runs⟩ $e$ · $e$ B *now*)'

from

(14a) '(E$e$) (⟨j,Runs⟩ $e$ · $e$ B *now* · Low($e$,Slower-than, $\{ e'$ ∍ (E$p$) (Per $p$ · ⟨$p$,Runs⟩ $e'$)$\}$) )',

by first-order logic. "Unfortunately [p. 335] for . . .[Davidson's] proposal, the inferences from the sentences of (13) to (12b) cannot be accounted for in this way. Indeed the presuppositional nature of the relationship between (12a) and (12b) is inconsistent with a

134

Davidson-style analysis, since presuppositions cannot be accounted for by conjunctions." On the contrary, they can be if the sentences of (13) are rendered as follows.

(13a')  '(E$e$) (⟨j,Runs⟩ $e$ · $e$ B *now* · ~ Low($e$,Slower-than, { $e'$ ∋ (E$p$) (Per $p$ · ⟨$p$,Runs⟩ $e'$)}) )',

(13b')  '(E$e$) (E$a$) (⟨j,Runs⟩ $e$ · $e$ B *now* · *sp* Qstn $a$ · (E$b$) ($b$ Des $e$ · ⌜Low($b$,Slower-than, { $e'$ ∋ (E$p$) (Per $p$ · ⟨$p$,Runs⟩ $e'$)} )⌝ $a$) )',

(13c')  '(E$e$) (E$a$) (⟨j,Runs⟩ $e$ · $e$ B *now* · *sp* Subj $a$ · (E$b$) [etc., as in (13b')] '.

From each of these, (14b) follows by first-order logic, contrary to Lakoff's contention. And note that the renderings (13a'), (13b'), and (13c') are eminently reasonable. In (13a) it is not John's running that is denied, but only its slowness. In (13b), it is not John's running that is questioned, but only its slowness. In (13c), it is not John's running that is subjunctivized, but only its slowness. Similar comments hold of the paraphrases of the sentences of (14) involving rates of change.

Another argument for not adopting a Davidson-style analysis, according to Lakoff (in agreement with Terence Parsons), is that the following sentences (p. 336) "should, on the Davidson analysis, have the same logical form, though they mean very different things and have different entailments."

(16a)      'John wrote painstakingly and slowly.'
(16b)      'John painstakingly wrote slowly.'

"(16a) entails that John wrote painstakingly while (16b) does not," Lakoff writes. "The Davidson analysis can handle cases like (16a) but not cases like (16b)." But clearly now (16a) can be rendered in a first approximation as

(16a')  '(E$e$) (⟨j,Writes⟩ $e$ · $e$ B *now* · High($e$,Less-Painstaking-than, { $e'$ ∋ (E$p$) (Per $p$ · ⟨$p$,Writes⟩$e'$) } · Low($e$, Slower-than, { $e'$

135

϶ (E$p$) (Per $p$ · ⟨$p$,Writes⟩ $e'$) } )',

whereas (16b) would be rendered rather as

(16b')  '(E$e$) (E$e'$) (⟨j,Takes-Pains,$e'$⟩ $e$ · $e$ B *now* · ⟨j,Writes⟩
$e'$ · Low($e'$,Slower-than,{ $e''$ ϶(E$p$) (Per $p$ · ⟨$p$,Writes⟩ $e''$ ) } ) )'.

(16b') is to the effect that John took pains to write slowly, and this
does not of course entail that John wrote painstakingly. Better
renditions will be given in a moment.

Lakoff carries on a running critique also against the Montague-
Parsons handling of adverbs in terms of functions, which according
to some condemns itself philosophically anyhow on the grounds of
ontic extravagance.[4] No more need be said concerning that method
here.

Consider next

(25a)  'John ran a mile slowly and climbed a mountain slowly and
did ten pushups slowly,'
(25b)  'John ran a mile, climbed a mountain, and did ten pushups
slowly.'

"(25a) does not entail (25b)" nor conversely and this circumstance
should be provided for in the logical forms. Clearly it may be, for
(25a) becomes

(25a')  '(E$e_1$) (E$e_2$) (E$e_3$) (⟨j,Runs a Mile⟩ $e_1$ · $e_1$ B *now* ·
Low($e_1$,Slower-than, { $e'$ ϶ (E$p$) (Per $p$ · ⟨$p$,Runs, a Mile⟩$e'$) }) · ⟨j,
Climbs a Mountain⟩ $e_2$ · $e_2$ B *now* · Low($e_2$,Slower-than, { $e'$ ϶
(E$p$) (Per $p$ · ⟨$p$,Climbs a Mountain⟩ $e'$) } ) · ⟨j,Does Ten Push-
ups⟩ $e_3$ · $e_3$ B *now* · Low($e_3$,Slower-than, { $e'$ ϶(E$p$) (Per $p$ · ⟨$p$,
Does Ten Pushups⟩ $e'$) } ) )',

[4] See the author's "Pragmatics, the Metatheory of Science, and Subjective Intensions,"
in *Logic and Art, Essays in Honor of Nelson Goodman*, ed. by R. Rudner and I. Scheffler
(The Bobbs-Merrill Co., Indianapolis and New York: 1972).

whereas (25b) becomes

(25b')    '(E$e$) (E$e_1$) (E$e_2$) (E$e_3$) (⟨j,Runs a Mile⟩ $e_1$ · $e_1$ B *now* · ⟨j,Climbs a Mountain⟩ $e_2$ · $e_2$ B now · ⟨j,Does Ten Pushups⟩ $e_3$ · $e_3$ B *now* · $e$ = Fu '$\{e_1,e_2,e_3\}$· Low($e$,Slower-than, $\{$ $e'$ ϶ (E$p$) (E$e_4$) (E$e_5$) (E$e_6$) (Per $p$ · ⟨$p$,Runs a Mile⟩ $e_4$ · ⟨$p$,Climbs a Mountain⟩ $e_5$ · ⟨$p$,Does Ten Pushups⟩ $e_6$ · $e'$ = Fu '$\{e_4,e_5, e_6\}$) $\}$ ) ) )'.

Clearly (25a') and (25b') bring out the different structures of (25a) and (25b) in terms of fusions and the different reference classes.

The handling of adverbs throughout has been in terms of location within a scale of low to high with respect to a given relation and a given reference class. The reference class in effect provides for the fact that 'slow' is a relative word. The phrase 'slow for a ———' becomes 'slow for a member of the class of all $x$'s such that ——$x$——' Thus

(30a)         'McGovern is honest for a politician'

becomes something like

(30a')    'High (McG, Less-honest-than, $\{$ $x$ ϶ (Per $x$ · Politician $x$) $\}$ )',

and

(30b)                  'Kate is smart for a woman'

becomes

(30b')    'High (k, Less-Smart-than, $\{x$ ϶(Per $x$ · Fem $x$) $\}$ )'.

(30a) and (30b) "respectively entail that politicians are not expected to be particularly honest and that women are not expected to be particularly smart," Lakoff observes, following Fillmore. But they

137

are "pragmatical" entailments and not logical ones and hence presumably should not be forthcoming from considerations concerning logical form alone.

Consider another context containing 'for a',

(34a)     'Harvey knows a lot of facts for a philosopher,'

Let us say that person $p$ knows less factually than person $q$ now in the special sense that $q$ knows all factual truths that $p$ does but not conversely. Let '$p$ Kn $a$' where $a$ is a sentence express that $p$ knows $a$. Also let

'$p$ Knows-Less-Factually-than $q$' abbreviate '($\{a_{\ni}(FTr\ a \cdot p$ Kn $a)\} \subset \{a_{\ni}(FTr\ a \cdot q$ Kn $a)\} \cdot \sim \{a_{\ni}(FTr\ a \cdot q$ Kn $a)\} \subset \{a_{\ni}(FTr\ a \cdot p$ Kn $a)\}$ )',

where '$\subset$' is the symbol for virtual-class inclusion, 'FTr $a$' expresses that a is a *factual* truth is essentially Carnap's sense, and Kn is the relation of knowing. (34a) may then perhaps be rendered as

(34a')   'High(h,Knows-Less-Factually-than, $\{p_{\ni}(Per\ p \cdot Phil\ p)\}$ )',

where Phil is the virtual class of philosophers.

Consider now *very* in

'Kate is very smart for a woman.'

This serves to indicate that Kate is very high in the scale of Less-Smart-than in the reference class of women. This becomes

'VHigh(k, Less-Smart-than, $\{p_{\ni}(Per\ p \cdot Fem\ p)\}$ )'.

The *rather* in

'Kate is rather smart for a woman'

138

would seem to indicate that Kate is just below the middle in the smarter-than scale for women.

'Kate is moderately smart for a woman'

would seem to say about the same. In a similar way other adverbs of like character may presumably be handled.

Lakoff thinks (p. 342) that because "relative attributes are fuzzy concepts" and "can be modified by hedges such as *rather, sort of, very,* etc.," it follows that "they cannot be dealt with in two-valued logic. Rather they require a continuous-valued logic and a semantics with distribution functions." If the suggestions of the preceding paragraph are feasible, however, this is not the case. The hedge-words may be handled by suitable location within the relevant scale for the given reference class.

The present discussion has covered only certain kinds of adjectives and hence only certain kinds of adverbs. There are of course many others. In particular, intentional adjectives are to be presumed handled by means of certain intentional relations, with an *Art des Gegebenseins* as additional argument. Consider the intentional adjective 'expert'. In place of, say,

'Low($e$,Slower-than,$F$)',

we have

'Low($p$,Less-Expert-than,$a$,$F$)',

where $a$ is the intentional relatum of the relation Less-Expert-than. And similarly for 'High' and so on.

Let $a$ have the shape

'$\{ e' \ni (Ep) (Ee'') (\text{Per } p \cdot \langle p,\text{Plays},e'' \rangle e' \cdot \text{ChessGame } e'') \}$'.

Then

'High(h,Less-Expert-than,*a*,Phil)'

expresses that Harvey is high in the Less-Expert-than scale of chess-playing as confined to philosophers. Often the reference class and the virtual class designated by the intentional relatum will coincide, but not always, as this example shows, Note that h here is a member of Phil and stands in the intentional relation. For significance, only members of the reference class can stand in the intentional relation. (*a* here is the *Art des Gegebenseins*.)

Perhaps even 'slowly' and its ilk should be treated more intentionally. It might be argued that the reference class itself should be intentionalized. If so, in place of

'Low(*e*,Slower-than,*F*)'

and so on, we could now write

'Low(*e*,Slower-than,*F*,*a*)'

and so on, where *a* is a one-place predicate, the *Art des Gegebenseins* of *F.* Such an intentional handling is needed for some adjectives and adverbs, but perhaps not for all. This is a matter that may be left open for the present, pending some criterion whereby intentional relations are distinguished from non-intentional ones.

A few further examples of deep structure may be given as follows.

Consider the first commandment,

'Thou shalt love the Lord thy God with all thy heart and with all thy soul and with all thy mind.'

As in V above, essentially anyhow, let

$$'p \text{ Oblg}_c \ e,a'$$

express that $p$ is obliged to do $e$ under the description $a$ on the basis of the moral code $c$. The first commandment then becomes approximately

'(Ee) ($You_s$ Oblg$_{NT}$ $e$, '{$e'$ Э ( $You_s$,Love,the Lord) $e'$ · the Lord = ($\imath e_1$) ($e_1$ = God · $e_1$ Of $You_s$) · Highest($e'$, Less-Loving-than, $e'''$ Э $You_s$ Able $e''$, '{$e_2$ Э(Ee$_3$) (⟨$You_s$, Love,$e_3$⟩ $e_2$ · $e_2$ With ($\imath e_1$) (Heart $e_1$ · $e_1$ Of $You_s$) ) } ' } ) · Highest($e'$,Less-Loving-than, {$e''$Э⟨$You_s$ Able $e''$, '{$e_2$Э(Ee$_3$) (⟨$You_s$,Love,$e_3$⟩ $e_2$ · $e_2$ With ($\imath e_1$) (Soul $e_1$ · $e_1$ Of $You_s$ ))}'}) · Highest($e'$,Less-Loving-than, {$e''$ Э ⟨$You_s$ Able $e''$, ' {$e_2$ Э (Ee$_3$) (⟨$You_s$,Love,$e_3$⟩$e_2$ · $e_2$ With { ($\imath e_1$) (Mind $e_1$ · $e_1$ Of $You_s$)) }'}))}' · ($e'$) ($e'$ During $You_s$ ⊃ $e$ During $e'$) )'.

Most of the notation here is already familiar. NT is the virtual class of principles determinative of the moral code of the New Testament. The clause concerning 'During' assures that the obligation is continuous throughout one's life span. To simplify, '$You_s$' here is handled as an individual constant. And of course 'Heart', 'Soul', and 'Mind' are presumed forthcoming as predicates.

There may be a scale of obligation, in which case

$$'p \text{ More-Obliged-than}_c \ q,e,a,e',b'$$

would express that $p$ is more obliged to do $e$ under the description $a$ than $q$ is obliged to do $e'$ under the description $b$ on the basis of the moral code $c$.

Next let us reflect upon the famous pair of sentences

'John is easy to please'

and

EVENTS, REFERENCE, AND LOGICAL FORM

'John is eager to please'.

The first becomes something like

'$(e)\,(a)\,(x)\,(\langle x,\text{Pl},j,a\rangle e \supset \text{High}(e,\text{Less-Easy-than},a,\{\,e'\ni(Ey)\,(Eb)\,\langle y,\text{Pl},j,b\rangle e'\})\,)$',

to the effect that all pleasings of John under a description are high in the Less-Easy-than scale relative to that description and relative to all pleasings of John whatsoever. The other sentence is to the effect that John is eager to do some $e$ under the description of its being a pleasing of some person or other. Thus

'$(Ee)j\ \text{Eager-to-Do}\ e, \text{`}\{\,e'\ni(Ee_1)\,(Ea)\,(\text{Per}\ e_1\cdot\langle j,\text{Pl},e_1,a\rangle\,e')\}\text{''}$'.

Another example involving fusions is of interest. Contrast

'He slowly tested each bulbs'

with

'He slowly tested all the bulbs'.

The bulbs referred to here are of course not all bulbs in the cosmos but just those, say, that are proper parts of some fusion $x_0$ of bulbs. The first then becomes

'$(e)\,(\,(\text{Bulb}\ e\cdot e\ \text{P}\ x_0\cdot\sim x_0\ \text{P}\ e)\supset(Ee')\,(e'\ \text{B}\ now\cdot\langle he,\text{Tests},e\rangle\,e'\cdot\text{Low}(e',\text{Slower-than},\{\,e_1\ni(Ep)\,(Ee_2)\,(\text{Per}\ p\cdot\text{Bulb}\ e_2\cdot\langle p,\text{Test},e_2\rangle\,e_1)\,\})\,)\,)$'.

The second, however, seems to become something like

142

'$(Ee'') (e'' =$ Fu ' $\{e' \ni (Ee)$ (Bulb $e \cdot e$ P $x_0 \cdot \sim x_0$ P $e \cdot \langle he, \text{Tests}, e \rangle e' \cdot e'$ B $now)\} \cdot$ Low$(e'', \text{Slower-than}, \{e_1 \ni (Ey) (e_1 =$ Fu ' $\{e_2 \ni (Ep) (Ee_3)$ (Per $p \cdot$ Bulb $e_3 \cdot \langle p, \text{Test}, e_3 \rangle e_2 \cdot e_3$ P $y \cdot \sim y$ P $e_3) \} \cdot (Ea) (p$ Crrlt $a, x_0, \text{Bulb} \cdot p$ Crrlt $a, y, \text{Bulb}) \cdot (e_4) (e_5) ( ($Bulb $e_4 \cdot e_4$ P $y \cdot$ Bulb $e_5 \cdot e_5$ P $x_0) \supset e_4$ Like $e_5) ) \} ) )$'.

This is to the effect that the fusion of his past testings of the bulbs that are proper parts of $x_0$ is low in the Slower-than scale relative to the virtual class of fusions of human testings of bulbs like those of $x_0$ and which are proper parts of some $y$, where $y$ contains the same number of bulbs as proper parts that $x_0$ does.

Finally, consider an example of a quite different kind, due to Hiż,

'Mary did her homework, and so did John'.

This becomes

'$(Ee) (Ee')$ $(e$ B $now \cdot e'$ B $now \cdot \{ qe'' \ni \langle q, \text{Does}, q$'s homework$\rangle e'' \}$ me $\cdot \{ qe'' \ni \langle q, \text{Does}, q$'s homework$\rangle e'' \}$ je$')$',

the use of 'so' being accommodated by means of the special relational abstract.

The use of the variables '$p$' and so on for persons, '$x$' and so on for physical objects, and '$a$' and '$b$' and so on for sign events here, as in IV also, is arbitrary. Event variables could have been used here exclusively equally well.

Again, here as in V above, no one of the forms given is intended to be a final deep-grammatical rendering of the given English sentence. Only enough structure has been uncovered as seems relevant, but to draw the exact line here is not easy. Some of the subtlety of the original sentences may not have been captured.

## EVENTS, REFERENCE, AND LOGICAL FORM

Again, it is not always clear just how much nuance or innuendo should be captured in the deep structure. Concerning this opinions may well differ. The only contention here is that nothing seems to have been left out that cannot be accommodated within the event-logical framework presupposed.

Lakoff's final paragraph (pp. 342-343) is an eloquent and timely plea for an attitude that is at once holistic, systematic, and empirical. "I think it should be clear that none of the proposed analyses of adverbs [he considered] . . . has come close to a full understanding of an adverb like *slowly*, which I chose only because it has been widely discussed. My guess is that any other arbitrarily chosen adverb would lead one into the study of at least as many seemingly unrelated phenomena . . . . This experience should make one wary of studying small fragments or just looking at a handful of sentences, as many philosophers have a tendency to do. Studying a single phenomenon, or even a single word, in a natural language is like fooling with a giant delicately balanced mobile. Touch one piece and the whole thing moves." Quite, as the foregoing has tried to show. The delicate balance must be that of a logical system for deep structures, however, as both linguists and philosophers must sooner or later come to recognize.

# VII

# ON HIŻ'S
# ALETHEIC SEMANTICS AND
# NON-TRANSLATIONALITY

*"Hanc personam induisti, agenda est."*

Most semantical metalanguages contain the object language as a part, either directly or at least in translation. Hence metalanguages of this kind can be conveniently referred to as *translational.* The Tarski metalanguages, those of Carnap, those of model theorists, and those of the foregoing essays, all share this one crucial feature. In a paper presented at the International Congress in 1953, and later incorporated and expanded in *Truth and Denotation,* a sketch of a semantical metalanguage was presented that lacked this crucial feature.[1] Such metalanguages are *non-translational.* In non-translational semantics something is sacrificed no doubt, but much less than might appear. Non-translational semantics can be made surprisingly powerful and in fact can do pretty much everything one wants a semantics to do.

In an important recent paper Hiż has sketched what he calls an "aletheic semantic theory" that is non-translational in character.[2] Hiż develops the theory as primarily applicable to natural languages as object languages whereas the object languages of the 1953 paper

---

[1] Chapters VIII, IX, and XIII.
[2] *The Philosophical Forum* 1 (1969): 438-451. All quotations are from this paper.

145

were applied first-order language systems. The sole semantical primitive for Hiż is presumably the semantical truth predicate itself applicable to sentences, whereas that of the 1953 paper was a relational predicate for *comprehension* as a relation between one-place predicate constants. Finally, Hiż assumes by way of logical substructure all manner of sets, classes, and relations as provided by a suitable set or type theory, whereas the semantics of the 1953 paper was itself formalized as a first-order system without using such powerful additional devices.

The point of the present paper is to show that what Hiż purports to achieve in his aletheic theory can apparently be achieved equally well in the much simpler kind of theory of the 1953 paper. In addition some philosophical comments are given concerning both the details and general character of Hiż's semantics.

"Truth [or rather, a predicate for it (?)] being the basic primitive term of the semantic theory, the spirit with which the theory is built may be called *aletheism* from ἀλήθεια, truth," Hiż notes (p. 443). More particularly, of course, his is a non-translational aletheic theory. Translational metalanguages may also be aletheic. There is nothing sacrosanct about taking the truth predicate as a primitive, however, the crucial feature of Hiż's theory being its non-transla-tionality. The predicate for truth is easily definable in terms of 'Cmprh' for comprehension, and conversely. And there are of course other possible primitives to consider here also.

In taking a truth-predicate as a primitive one must have tagging along with it the notion of being a *sentence* of the object language, the truth predicate being applicable to sentences and sentences only. Thus Hiż's theory is syntactically very strong. Let 'Sent *a*' as above express that *a* is a sentence of the object language, which for Hiż is a natural language. 'Sent' or some equivalent must then be taken as a primitive, no satisfactory definition of it for a natural language having ever been given. In fact, much of linguistics may be described as being devoted to gaining a satisfactory definition of this notion for given languages. Hiż's employment of 'Sent' as a primitive is thus very bold, a kind of theft, as it were.

If 'Cmprh' for comprehension is taken as a primitive in place of the truth predicate, no theft is required. 'Cmprh' has as its arguments one-place predicates and only such, and hence the notion 'Sent' need not be presupposed. Thus 'Cmprh' actually seems more appropriate than the truth predicate when the object language is a natural language, provided one has available for it a general notion of *one-place predicate*. But such a notion is much simpler than that of being a sentence and presumably more readily available for natural languages.

Hiż makes much of the notion of a *truth model*. "A truth model [p. 440] may be thought of as a set of sentences one believes to be true, or a set of sentences each two of which are paraphrases of each other, or a set of sentences which must be accepted as the content of a mythology . . . . . Or a truth model may be an infinite set of sentences of a book." In any case "no two contradictory sentences should belong to the same set." The notion of a truth model is thus relative to a notion of *negation* in terms of which 'contradictory' is to be construed.

More precisely, Hiż states (pp. 441-442) that a "set $\Gamma_i$ of sentences . . . in [language or sub-language] M is a truth model in M if and only if there is an operation $O_i$ on sentences of M and resulting in sentences of M . . . such that for every $\alpha$ in $\Gamma_i$, $O_i(\alpha)$ is in M or $\alpha = O_i(\beta)$ where $\beta$ is in M, and for no $\alpha$ both $\alpha$ and $O_i(\alpha)$ are in $\Gamma_i$," the $O_i$ being "the sort of negation appropriate to this particular $\Gamma_i$." Is this sentence intended to provide a definition of 'truth model in M [relative to $O_i$]'? It seems so. Yet note that the truth predicate does not occur explicitly in the definiens. The notion of a truth model seems, as thus defined, quite independent of the semantical notion of truth. The notion of a truth model, as thus defined, is in fact merely a notion of syntax.

"The concept of truth which is here fundamental receives a twist which may look 'relativistic,' " Hiz writes (p. 442). "There are many truth models, and a sentence may be a member of one and not of another of them; another truth model may contain its negation." The question arises as to what notion of truth is being referred to here. If none is referred to in the definiens of the definition of 'truth model', it is not clear that any concept of truth at all is being

147

employed, whether as "fundamental" or derivative, "relativistic" or not.

It might be replied that a semantic notion of truth is needed to characterize the negation $O_i$. "The essential point [p. 440] . . . is that a member of a truth model should be in principle true or false, should be evaluable with respect to truth." Hiż does not explain, however, how negation is supposed to be related to truth and falsehood. Is any $O_i$ such that, for any $\alpha$, either $\alpha$ is true or $O_i(\alpha)$ is true? Also, for any $O_i$ and any $\alpha$, it is not the case that both $\alpha$ and $O_i(\alpha)$ are true? In any event, Hiż's definition of 'truth model' as it stands seems inadequate and needs supplementation. There may be many truth models, but a sentence $\alpha$ cannot, it would seem, be a member of one $\Gamma_i$ and $O_i(\alpha)$ a member of another $\Gamma_j$. Of course $O_j(\alpha)$ might be a member of $\Gamma_j$, but this is a very different matter.

Another point is that a given set of sentences $\Gamma_i$ might be inconsistent even if no sentence together with its negation occurs therein explicitly. Thus much spelling out of the theory of negation and of contradiction seems needed for Hiż's account to work.

Further, it is by no means clear that the notion of a truth model should be relative only to negation. How about conjunction, disjunction, and so on, to say nothing of the quantifiers? If a truth model contains a conjunctive sentence, this conjunction must presumably have the property of being true if and only if both conjuncts are. Hence the truth model $\Gamma_i$ should be relative to a conjunction operator $C_i$ having suitable properties.

Actually Hiż needs as a primitive not a one-place predicate for truth, but a two-place *relational* predicate in accord with which one can say that a sentence $\alpha$ is *true in* a given set of sentences $\Gamma_i$. Only in terms of such a two-place predicate, it would seem, can the theory accomplish what it is intended to. To the definiens of the definition of '$\Gamma_i$ is a truth model in M (relative to $O_i$)' above one would add a conjunct to the effect that *every member of $\Gamma_i$ is true in $\Gamma_i$*.

Incidentally it may be noticed that this reconstituted definition can be given within the first-order version, that essentially of the 1953 paper, by speaking of $\Gamma_i$ as a virtual class of sentences and construing 'Cmprh' as a triadic relation with $\Gamma_i$ as another argument.

Thus a one-place predicate may be said to comprehend another in a given virtual class of sentences $\Gamma_i$. For this "relativistic" notion of course the notion of being a sentence is presupposed. Alternatively one could perhaps take $\Gamma_i$ as merely a virtual class of *expressions*, but choose it always in such a fashion that in fact all its members are sentences. (Perhaps Hiż could avoid using the notion of sentence in full generality in a similar way. But see below, for a more pragmatical account.)

Hiż goes on to define a number of interesting notions concerned with *interpretation in a truth model under a given assignment.* "Though interpretation is a semantical concept, as it uses truth in its definiens, it is a relation between sequences of phrases and sentences," Hiż notes (p. 445). The definition embodies an adaptation of Tarski's use of infinite sequences. It is not clear, however, how "it uses truth in its definiens." In an assignment some phrases are replaced by others in the same "grammatical category." Here too, it would seem, a crucial clause concerning being true in a given set of sentences $\Gamma_i$ is left out.

Especially interesting, Hiż thinks, are truth models closed with respect to paraphrase. The relation of being a paraphrase of is not defined, however. Perhaps (p. 446) "paraphrase is [logical] consequence both ways; two texts are paraphrases of each other just when either of them is a consequence of the other." Hiż notes, however, that "it is much easier to test empirically paraphrases than consequences. Linguists often hesitate to enter work on consequences." Thus apparently a symbol for paraphrase is taken as an additional primitive.

If paraphrase is taken as mutual consequence, it is of course a notion quite different from synonymy. Paraphrase is presumably a necessary condition for synonymy but not a sufficient one. Mutual consequence or L-equivalence is surely a most significant semantical relation, but for paraphrase some deeper structural similarity seems needed. Thus sentence $\alpha$ is a paraphrase of a sentence $\beta$ if and only if $\alpha$ and $\beta$ are mutual consequences of each other and $\alpha$ and $\beta$ are structurally interrelated in a very intimate way.[3] Unfortunately Hiż

[3] See *Belief, Existence, and Meaning,* Chapter VII, and recall III above.

tells us little about the inner structure of paraphrase, so to speak, either here or elsewhere. It is difficult to see how by means of this notion, there is much advance over earlier discussions of synonymy and the like.

Note that for Hiż paraphrase is a semantical relation, not a pragmatical one. For some purposes, however, it might be of interest to regard it as the latter. It is persons who paraphrase, and different persons in quite different ways. And even one and the same person, quite differently at different times. The important notion here would perhaps best be expressed by 'person $p$ paraphrases sentence (or phrase) $\alpha$ as sentence (or phrase) $\beta$ at time $t$', essentially as in III above. Here is a suitable locution with which to capture the "empirical" character of paraphrase. The results of all empirical tests concerning paraphrase could no doubt be couched in terms of it.

The only point at which Hiż needs set theory, more particularly, a quantifier over a set of sentences, is in his reference to essentially Tarski's definition "that $\alpha$ is a consequence of $\beta$ if and only if every model of $\beta$ is also a model of $\alpha$. Therefore, $\alpha$ is a paraphrase of $\beta$ if and only if, for every $\Gamma_k$ (maximally consistent with respect to $O_k$), $a$ is in $\Gamma_k$ if and only if $\beta$ is in $\Gamma_k$." This definition, however, Hiż does not adopt, the notion of paraphrase embodied in the definiendum being, according to him, not sufficiently testable empirically. All other uses of sets or quantifiers over them in Hiż's paper can easily be accommodated in terms of virtual classes. Accordingly the set theory may be dropped.

The point is an important one. In some circles it is thought that model theory provides the logic needed for all philosophic, linguistic, and methodological problems. Its adherents claim this with an almost fanatical enthusiasm. The fact is, however, that model theory is primarily of mathematical interest and its use elsewhere has not served to illuminate where simpler methods fail to do so. Surely in lingustics there is no evidence that model-theoretic methods are needed, all the results of hard empirical and theoretical toil being expressible in a more restricted vocabulary.

As an aside, Hiż comments (p. 445) "that the alethetic semantics based on truth models can be applied to the standard treatments of model theory in the foundations of mathematics, so that most of the standard model theory becomes, *mutatis mutandis,* a particular case of the aletheic semantic theory." The resulting model theory is of course a non-translational one. The lack of a translation of the object language is in effect compensated for by variables and quantifiers over all manner of sets. This is not very surprising. Given any individuals or *Urelemente,* if a vast domain of sets, of sets of sets, and so on, is admitted with sufficiently strong axioms, one can of course easily develop mathematics. The linguistic expressions of the object language can be regarded as the *Urelemente.* Hiż seems to think that there is a "difficulty with non-denumerable models (say a model with real numbers)." But real numbers can easily be constructed in the usual way in aletheic semantics based on set theory. In a first-order aletheic theory, however, the matter is quite different. There, Hiż's suggestion of expressing a Dedekind cut in terms of interpretations is of interest. The details may be omitted. Hiż says that he defines "the set of rational numerals which is a suitable synonym for the real numeral '$\sqrt{2}$'," but he actually defines only 'a phrase $\alpha$ is in the set $\Delta_{\sqrt{2}}$ of rational numerals', a very different matter. A similar restriction occurs in most attempts to build up the reals from the integers with variables and quantifiers only over the latter. It is very doubtful that Hiż can provide in this way very much of the full arithmetic of real numbers.

What now is to be made of Hiż's relativism? He tell us (p. 440) that "in Greek mythology *Zeus was often angry* is generally accepted" and hence may be regarded as true in a suitable truth model for Greek mythology. But it would be false in a model for atomic physics or Greek history. All manner of sentences can be "believed to be true" or "accepted as the content of a mythology" or taken as paraphrases of each other, without thereby being true. The kind of relativity Hiż has in mind has less to do with truth than with belief, acceptance, paraphrase (in the pragmatic sense suggested above), and the like. With only slight changes in wording Hiż's entire theory could thus be restated in pragmatical terms. In place of 'true in a set (or virtual class) $\Gamma_i$' one could read 'accepted at time $t$ and in $\Gamma_i$' or 'believed at time $t$ and in $\Gamma_i$' or something of the sort. That Hiż

151

has these pragmatical notions in mind anyhow is evident from the informal explanations. The empirical character of Hiż's theory is thus accommodated, but no longer as merely a semantics.

What happens then to truth? Is it no longer needed? Does it play no role in linguistics? None in the philosophy of science? What role should 'true', as opposed to 'accepted at $t$ and in $\Gamma_i$', play in linguistics and elsewhere? There is no doubt but that a great deal can be done with only the latter and without the former. Hiż's paper attests to this. Nonetheless something seems left out. One can never say in Hiż's theory that a sentence is true *simpliciter*, true in our world, true once and for all *sans phrase*. No, instead, one must always specify the set of sentences *in* which it is true. Truths of logic itself seem as relative as any other. A tautology 'Jones is tall if and only if Jones is tall' may be true in some $\Gamma_i$, but nothing seems to prevent its being false in some other $\Gamma_k$. One could not even say thus that this tautology is true in *all* $\Gamma_i$, for it might well not be accepted or believed to be true by everyone. And similarly for the presumed "truths" of mathematics, sciences, and daily life. Something very significant has been left out in Hiż's semantics. Some one truth model must be picked out as standard or paradigmatic in some fashion to capture the notion of *true in this world* or simply *true actually*. Hiż's theory does not account for this, and as he notes, apparently cannot be extended to include it lest semantical antinomies result. "The set of all true sentences of a language is neither very natural . . . nor desirable," he notes. "It is not desirable because it may lead to well-known semantic antinomies." Yet without an account of *true actually* one cannot give a deep structure for many English sentences containing 'true' nor can one provide for the key paradigmatic use of it that has been of such interest to philosophers since at least the time of Aristotle. Hiz's aletheic semantics is in fact like a performance of "Hamlet" without the key character.

The mention of Aristotle leads at once to the Aristotle-Tarski "paradigm"

(A)　　To say of what is that it is or of what is not that it is not is true, or, in more modern terms and somewhat more generally, essentially as in III above,

$$(T) \qquad\qquad \mathrm{Tr}\, a \equiv \text{-----},$$

where in place of '-----' a sentence is inserted and in place of '$a$' its shape- or structural-descriptive name. That (T) holds for all sentences of the language is essential for adequacy. In Hiż's semantics, not only can (T) not be stated, it does not even hold. What condition of adequancy is there for his 'true in $\Gamma_i$'? None is given. Yet some condition here is surely essential if Hiż's 'true in $\Gamma_i$' is even remotely to capture some of what is contained in 'true'.

Note that in the non-translational semantics of the 1953 paper, although (T) cannot be stated, the theory is clearly constructed in accord with it. A semantics which accords with (T) may be said to be *genuine,* for within such a semantics the real content of 'true' is captured.

Hiż no doubt thinks it is a merit of his theory that within it the barriers between syntax and semantics, and between semantics and pragmatics, are ostensibly broken down. Non-translational semantics, of whatever kind, can be viewed as a kind of extended syntax, only linguistic expressions being values for variables. If his 'true in $\Gamma_i$' is taken as primitive, no genuine semantics results, as noted. If in place of 'true in $\Gamma_i$' the locution 'believed at $t$ and in $\Gamma_i$' or 'accepted at $t$ and in $\Gamma_i$' is used, no genuine semantics emerges, but rather something that borders on a pragmatics. Only if variables over *users* of the language are brought in do we have a genuine pragmatics. It seems then that Hiż has not succeeded in breaking down these barriers but has rather trespassed upon them illicitly. Let us be clear about our boundaries, and let us bring to light explicitly the character of each theory being dealt with. If pragmatic or epistemic notions such as *accepts* or *believes* are used, let us bring them out clearly and with the "natural" arguments they take. *Human beings* accept or believe, and thus they are taken as natural values for variables in pragmatics.

# EVENTS, REFERENCE, AND LOGICAL FORM

If Hiż's theory is reconstructed by using a pragmatical 'accepts' in place of 'true in $\Gamma_i$', the notions of sentence and of paraphrase should perhaps be pragmatized as well. Thus the full notion of being a sentence in the natural language is dropped in favor of $\alpha$'s being *taken as a sentence* by person $X$ at time $t$, where $\alpha$ is in $\Gamma_i$. And similarly, in place of the notion of paraphrase, one would now use the locution 'person $X$ paraphrases $\alpha$ as $\beta$ at $t$, where both $\alpha$ and $\beta$ are in $\Gamma_i$'.

Semantics is a normative discipline, to some extent anyhow, whereas Hiż has tried to turn it into an empirical one. A theory built upon 'person $X$ accepts $\alpha$ at $t$ where $\alpha$ is in $\Gamma_i$', 'person $X$ takes $\alpha$ as a sentence at $t$ where $\alpha$ is in $\Gamma_i$', and 'person $X$ paraphrases $\alpha$ as $\beta$ at $t$, where $\alpha$ and $\beta$ are both in $\Gamma_i$' would be properly empirical and "testable" and would enable us to achieve non-translationally, and on the basis of a first-order logic only, everything that Hiż attempts to do. Perhaps in fact these are the very notions he has in mind. In any case, no harm can arise from bringing in the additional arguments or factors, for they can always be handled as parameters if not needed in a given context.

Even if it could be worked out successfully, however, it is doubtful that Hiż's aletheic semantics or the reconstruction of it just suggested can accomplish for linguistics all that is expected of it. It is remarkable and interesting that so much can be done non-translationally in connection with natural language. However, this approach neglects the key topic of logical form. It is this that has interested logicians of language since the time of Mill, Peirce, and Frege. Presumably the deep structure of a sentence is its logical form, as suggested above, or at any event is to be gotten at by means of it. How does Hiż's semantics help in the study of logical form? How does it help in constructing a viable theory of the parts of speech? How does it help in formulating rules concerning how the parts of speech are combinable into longer locutions? How does it help to gain an adequate theory of adverbs, or of adjectives for that matter, or of prepositions? For answers to these and similar questions one must presumably build an object language $L$ of very great expressive power and then study how words, phrases, and sentences of a natural

154

language can best be correlated with corresponding expressions of $L$. This is a task of enormous difficulty that aletheic semantics merely tries to avoid.

Such an object language is of course of philosophic interest also, throwing light on fundamental problems of ontology, of how our natural language is related to the world, of the logical structure of fundamental epistemic notions such as 'believes', 'knows', and so on, and of their interrelations. It paves the way for analyses of the deontic notions, for handling values, human acts, and the like. And so on. Hiż's semantics, on the other hand, is of little interest in connection with any of these topics. It merely takes language as it finds it and leaves it there. The alternative approach suggested also takes language as it finds it, does not "regiment" it or make it behave in any other way than is customary, but seeks to give as exact an account as possible of all relevant logical forms. In short, logical form is the fundamental notion that we should seek to explicate, every English sentence being, in the phrase of Mill, "a lesson in logic."

Hiż's paper is obviously an important one. It is interesting that in dealing with natural language a non-translational semantics may be helpful. Hiż's specific suggestions concerning 'synonymy' and 'meaning' are of interest, although given 'true' and 'logically true' or 'analytically true' it is no longer surprising that suitable definitions of these notions are forthcoming. And, above all, the use of modern semantics or pragmatics in the study of natural language is to be welcomed most warmly, scarcely anything really serious along this line having yet been achieved, in spite of valuable steps forward here and there. Hiż's paper is thus the kind of paper that one must agree with and do likewise, or disagree with and not. The various points raised above give grounds for the disagreement and, in part, for the not.

# VIII

## ON CARNAP'S SEMANTICS, HIŻ'S NOTION OF CONSEQUENCE, AND DEEP STRUCTURE*

*"Si volet usus*
*Quem penes arbitrium est, et jus, et norma loquendi."*

I come to praise Carnap and not to bury him. He was one of the first — along with Frege and Tarski — to have recognized the very central role that semantical considerations must play in analytical philosophy, particularly in the methodology of science and the philosophy of language. He was one of the first to realize that these disciplines must themselves become increasingly scientific and that the philosophy of the future will make use more and more, in the phrase of Peirce, of an "immense technical vocabulary."

Let us recall first the remarkable passage in *The Logical Syntax of Language* (1934) to the effect that logical syntax — which even then Carnap treated so widely that it embraced a good deal of what later came to be called 'semantics' — will help in "the analysis of the incredibly complicated word-languages. The direct analysis of these,

*This paper was presented at a meeting in honor of Rudolf Carnap of the Conference on Methods in Philosophy and the Sciences at the New School for Social Research, New York City, on February 18, 1973.

157

# EVENTS, REFERENCE, AND LOGICAL FORM

which has been prevalent hitherto" — and is still prevalent in such remote places as the Massachusetts Institute of Technology — "must inevitably fail, just as a physicist would be frustrated were he from the outset to attempt to relate his laws to natural things — trees, stones, and so on. In the first place, the physicist relates his laws to the simplest of constructed forms; to a thin straight lever, to a simple pendulum, to punctiform masses, etc. Then, with the help of the laws relating to these constructed forms, he is later in a position to analyze into suitable elements the complicated behavior of real bodies, and thus to control them. One more comparison: the complicated configurations of mountain chains, rivers, frontiers, and the like are most easily represented and investigated by the help of geographical coordinates — or, in other words, by constructed lines not given in nature. In the same way, the syntactical [and semantical] properties of a particular word-language, such as English, . . . , are best represented and investigated by comparison with such a constructed language which serves as a frame of reference."[1]

To be sure, this famous passage has been criticized by certain linguists, who, however, it seems, have failed to understand properly the aims and methods of logical syntax and hence of course could not succeed in using those methods in any effective way in linguistics. Now, 40 years after it was written, this passage may be assessed anew. First, however, let us reflect a little upon logical syntax and semantics themselves, which help to make possible a theory of deep structure sufficiently broad to be linguistically interesting.

Carnap learned much from his study of Tarski's *Der Wahrheitsbegriff in den formalisierten Sprachen*[2] and was always most generous in acknowledging his indebtedness to it. In fact, he was the first to recognize the significance for philosophy of Tarski's work. However, Carnap went about building up semantics in a quite different way by attaching primary importance to semantical relations of *designation*.[3]

---

[1] *Logical Syntax of Language* (Routledge and Kegan Paul, London: 1934), p. 8.
[2] In *Logic, Semantics, Metamathematics*, VIII.
[3] See especially *Introduction to Semantics* (Harvard University Press, Cambridge: 1942), pp. 49 ff. and recall III above.

There is not just one relation of designation, there are several. If the object language be one of first order with some primitive non-logical individual and predicate constants, it is appropriate to consider separately the designation of individuals, the designation of classes or properties or attributes, the designation of relations, and perhaps even the designation of propositions. Carnap first uses 'designation' in a technically self-conscious way, in his monograph *Foundations of Logic and Mathematics* in the *Encyclopedia of Unified Science* (1939).[4] There in effect is given the first systematic definition of 'true' in terms of 'designation' taken as a semantical primitive. The definition, however, is far from being technically correct and leaves much to be desired. Nor is the matter ever put to rights later. In *Introduction to Semantics* (1942) the definitions are for the most part informal and the systems considered are extremely weak. However, these matters may be remedied, and a technically correct and materially adequate definition of 'true' in terms of 'designation' may be given if a higher order logic in the metalanguage is presupposed.

The most controversial of Carnap's relations of designation is DesProp, that of propositions regarded as extra-linguistic intensional entities of some kind or another. Carnap thought "there is no danger in speaking of propositions and classes of propositions provided it is done in a cautious way .... However, there are advantages of avoiding propositions altogether and speaking instead about the sentences or classes of sentences expressing them, whenever this is possible. First, we avoid a discussion of the controversial question whether the use of the concept of proposition would involve us in a kind of Platonic metaphysics and would violate the principles of empiricism. Second, there is the technical advantage that for this method a metalanguage of simpler structure sufficies."[5] Although Carnap vacillated back and forth on this point, there is no need here to review the various issues involved. Even so, he is one of the first to have emphasized the significance for semantics of purely extensionalist procedures and their philosophical advantages. This does not

---

[4] (University of Chicago Press, Chicago: 1939), pp. 9-10.
[5] *Logical Foundations of Probability,* p. 71.

require that intensionalist procedures be eschewed, but that they should be shown to be forthcoming by definition from an extensionalist or at least "neutral" base.[6]

Designation of individuals, already mentioned in III above, and of classes and relations remain, it seems, as important relations, providing in fact some of the semantical roots of reference. Another is denotation, also mentioned above, in the sense in which a one-place predicate applies severally to the individuals that fall under it. If 'denotes' is taken as fundamental, the various relations of designation are forthcoming by definition.[7]

Tarski emphasized rather a very complex relation of *satisfaction*, in accord with which an infinite sequence of objects is said to satisfy a sentential function containing any arbitrary number of free variables. A *sentence*, that is, sentential function containing no free variables, is then shown to be satisfied either by all sequences or by none. A *true* sentence is one by definition satisfied by all sequences, a false sentence by none. To achieve the effect of this definition, however, one may equally well use only finite sequences, as noted by Popper. And in fact, one can go still further, and use a much simpler satisfaction relation in accord with which an object is said to satisfy a sentential function of just one variable. A suitable definition of truth, both technically correct and materially adequate, is forthcoming on the basis of such a relation.

Another interesting semantical relation, first studied by Carnap, is that of *determination*, a relation between a sentential function of one variable and a class. Thus, for example, the sentential function '$x$ is red and $x$ is a rose' may be said to determine the class of red roses. Determination likewise may be taken as a basis for semantics, and of course these various relations (designation, denotation, satisfaction, and determination) are under appropriate circumstances interdefinable.

Carnap was also one of the first to call attention to the usefulness of introducing into semantics a parameter for the human user of

---

[6] *Meaning and Necessity,* 2nd ed. (University of Chicago Press, Chicago: 1956), pp. 145 ff.

[7] See *Truth and Denotation,* Chapter VII.

language, in other words, of introducing pragmatics. "There is an urgent need for a system of theoretical pragmatics," he wrote in 1955, "not only for psychology *and linguistics* (italics added), but also for analytic philosophy."[8] The extent to which pragmatics is needed in methodological and linguistic discussions is controversial, but Carnap was clear that the adjunction of pragmatics to semantics might prove to be helpful in all manner of ways.

Carnap's semantical writings did not meet with much approval in the philosophic world. In fact they were greeted by many with open hostility, especially in reviews by Nagel and Ryle.[9] In spite of these infelicitous reviews, however, Carnap's technical semantics lives on to bury its undertakers. If the real roots of reference are to be found in semantics, as it seems they should be, then the subject might be approached somewhat *de novo* as follows.

Let

(Ref)                     '$p$ Ref $a,x,b$'

express that person $p$ uses the sign event $a$ (as occurring in the sentence $b$) to refer to the entity $x$, as in III. In terms of 'Ref' taken as a primitive, it will be recalled that 'truth' as applicable to occasion sentences — in Quine's sense — may be defined. Thus, for example, 'He opened the door' is a true occasion sentence if the predicate 'opened the door' denotes or is true of the person referred to by the speaker.

To illustrate further, consider an example like those of Hiż of a supposedly valid inference in natural language involving an occasion sentence.[10]

(1)                     'John went home.'
(2)                     'He opened the door.'
(3)                     'John opened the door.'

[8] *Meaning and Necessity*, p. 250.
[9] See the reviews by E. Nagel, *The Journal of Philosophy* 39 (1942): 468-473 and G. Ryle, *Philosophy* 24 (1949): 69-76. See also the author's "On Some Criticisms of Carnap's Early Semantics: Nagel and Ryle," *Philosophia* 2 (1972): 55-73.
[10] See his "On the Rules of Consequence for a Natural Language," *The Monist* 57 (1973): 312-327.

# EVENTS, REFERENCE, AND LOGICAL FORM

Hiż would contend that the inference from (1) and (2) to (3) is valid in natural language. But is it? If the 'He' of (2) is taken to refer to John, then presumably yes, although *the exact form of the inference must be spelled out.* But we are not compelled to regard the 'He' of (2) as referential of John. Suppose John and his pet retriever are side by side. Wherever John goes his pet retriever is sure to follow. In the context John is referred to by his name, but his pet retriever is referred to by a low-keyed, prolonged, tremulous 'He-e-e.' Then it by no means follows from 'John went home' and 'He-e-e opened the door', that John opened the door. Still more clearly, interchange the order of (1) and (2). From 'He opened the door' and 'John went home' it by no means follows logically that John opened the door. The point is obvious enough, namely, that a good deal must be spelled out concerning the reference of 'He' in (2) before the validity of the inference from (1) and (2) (or from (2) and (1)) to (3) may be established. It is far from clear that this can be done without bringing in a parameter for the speaker or user of language. Of this, more in a moment.

Carnap suggested, it will be recalled, that it would be useful for linguistics to introduce the speaker explicitly. Hiż denies this. "The relation between premises and consequence is an objective fact," Hiż writes (p. 326). "If $\ulcorner \alpha \supset \beta \urcorner$ and $\alpha$ are true sentences, so is $\beta$. It is misleading to formulate *modus ponens* or any other rule of consequence (or any other rule of language (?)), by saying that if you (or one) has accepted $\ulcorner (\alpha \supset \beta) \urcorner$ and $\alpha$, you (or he) may accept $\beta$. If such a reading is taken seriously, metalogic (and grammar) would be a peculiar theory about (or about somebody) asserting your (his) possibilities of action. But neither metalogic nor grammar are about you. They are about sentences and their semantic relations . . . . Anyone may choose to use metalogic or grammar, just as he may choose to use physics. A grammatical or metalogical rule is not to be read as an instruction or program. It is rather an assertion that a sentence is true if another sentence is true. It is perhaps better not to use the term *rule.* For, misreading what rules say, some people may conclude, as it were, that man is a rule-obeying animal when using language and not when falling off the roof. The rules of grammar are essentially not different from the rules of physics. As man obeys the rules of grammar in speaking, so an electron obeys the rules of mechanics in circling the nucleus.''

Several comments are in order, in defense of Carnap's position as over and against Hiż's. In the first place 'modus ponens' is a highly ambiguous phrase, standing *inter alia* now for a logical law of the object language,

$$`(x)\,(y)\,((\mathrm{P}x \cdot (\mathrm{P}x \supset \mathrm{Q}y))\supset \mathrm{Q}y)',$$

now for a law of syntax,

$$`(a)\,(b)\,((\mathrm{Thm}\,a \cdot \mathrm{Thm}\,(a\ hrsh\ b))\supset \mathrm{Thm}\,b)',$$

now for a law of semantics,

$$`(a)\,(b)\,((\mathrm{Tr}\,a \cdot \mathrm{Tr}\,(a\ hrsh\ b))\supset \mathrm{Tr}\,b)',$$

and now for a statement in the pragmatics of acceptance,

$$`(p)\,(a)\,(b)\,((p\ \mathrm{Acpt}\ a \cdot p\ \mathrm{Acpt}\,(a\ hrsh\ b))\supset p\ \mathrm{Acpt}\ b)',$$

and so on.[11] No one formulation is any more "misleading" than any other. They are merely different, but closely interrelated laws. Surely the pragmatical forms are to be taken "seriously," but pragmatics need not therewith become a "peculiar theory about you" or me, but a theory nonetheless. Such a theory is needed, as already suggested, to accommodate Hiż's validation of the inference from (1) and (2) to (3).

"Anyone may choose to use metalogic or grammar, just as he may choose to use physics," he writes, but the intent of this contention is not too clear. The use of 'use' here is vague. Clearly one has no choice — if he wishes to speak correctly — when it comes to

[11] 'Thm *a*' here expresses that *a* is a theorem, 'Tr *a*', that *a* is true, '*p* Acpt *a*' that person *p* accepts *a*, and '*hrsh*' is the structural-descriptive name of ' ' within non-inscriptional syntax. Cf. *Truth and Denotation*, Chapter III. In some subsequent papers also, a non-inscriptional or classical semantics will occasionally be used or mentioned.

obeying the rules of the grammar of the language he uses, nor of course does he have any choice in obeying the laws of physics. But there is an important difference nonetheless. The study of language is human oriented in a way in which physics is not. The language of physics contains no special names or variables for human beings — except perhaps in the case of reference to the observer in relativity theory. Reference to the speaker, especially the fluent or native speaker, is essential in some areas at least of linguistics. You and I are no doubt flattered in being values for the physicists' variables too, but along with much else. In linguistics the only values for variables are (presumably) human persons together with those of his artifacts that constitute items of language. To leave out the human person would be like leaving out the nucleus in quantum mechanics. One could not formulate laws concerning circling the nucleus unless 'circling' and 'nucleus' were words of the language. Hiż, however, would have us formulate all rules of grammar for speaking, and indeed for the whole of linguistics, but never admit the word 'speaking' itself nor any reference to who is speaking.

Hiż attaches more importance to reference than most current linguists, and in this respect is a follower of Carnap. He does not admit a form such as (Ref) above, however, but rather uses what is essentially Jespersen's notion of a *referential*.

Hiż uses 'referential' in such a way (p. 315) that "if $\alpha$ is a referential for $\beta$, then $\alpha$ and $\beta$ are occurrences of phrases in the text."[12] Evidently then 'referential' is a word within a non-translational semantics. The semantics employed, moreover ("Referentials", p. 147), "is based on paraphrase and consequence as primitives, and those in turn can be reduced to truth. Truth is a property of sentences, and more generally, of texts." If definitions of 'consequence' and 'paraphrase' were to be given in terms of 'truth', it is natural to think that a higher-order logic or set theory would be presupposed. Hiż gives no such definitions, however, and we may thus take him at his word that 'paraphrase' and 'consequence' are the primitive semantical notions, and that we are presumably free to

---

[12] Cf. also his "Referentials," *Semiotica* I (1969): 136-166.

employ wherever needed or desired notions of a higher-order logic or set theory. To employ such, however, is suspect if the semantics be non-translational. There is not much point of insisting upon non-translationality if the ontological economy thereof is tossed to the winds in admitting as values for variables all manner of sets of, and relations between or among, the basic linguistic expressions.

Note that if $\alpha$ is a referential for $\beta$, both $\alpha$ and $\beta$ are for Hiż *occurrences* of phrases, occurrences being taken as inscriptions (sign events) rather than shapes (sign designs). An inscriptional syntax is thus apparently presupposed. The language of the "text" is a fragment of natural language. In addition to structural-descriptive predicates for the letters of the alphabet of the language of the text, a predicate for a *pause* or *caesura* is presumably needed as well as predicates for the various punctuation marks, comma, period, semicolon, and so on. Only thus could the structural description of an entire text be given. No doubt all of this can easily be characterized by a straightforward extension of known syntactical axioms for concatenation as applied to inscriptions.

Concerning 'consequence' and 'paraphrase' certain rules must be presumed given in the metalanguage. (Note that rules of consequence and of paraphrase are thus themselves metalinguistic statements, a point that will be significant in a moment.) We can imagine what these rules would be like — Hiż does not state them — by reflection upon the rules of truth needed within an inscriptional, non-translational semantics.

The key theoretical innovation of Hiz's paper ("Referentials," p. 145) is the purported definition (4.14) of 'an occurence $\alpha_1$ of a phrase $\alpha$ (in a text $\beta$) is a referential for an occurrence $\gamma_1$ of a phrase $\gamma$ . . . with respect to a rule R'. The definiens uses in effect the locution 'rule R is applied to the text $\beta$ in a way preserving the occurrence $\alpha_1$ in $\beta$' in a most fundamental way. This locution is defined in turn by (4.13), in the definiens of which we find as one clause 'R is stated in such a way that it speaks about a string. . . .' This latter clause is surely clear enough. The difficulty is that it is *not a clause in the metalanguage*. It concerns the way in which a metalinguistic sentence R is formulated, and all such discussion must, in the context at hand, be metametalinguistic. Definitions (4.13) and (4.14) are thus, as they stand, not definitions within Hiż's semantics but within its (syntactical or semantical (?)) metalanguage, a significant lapse of rigor and contrary no doubt to the intention.

Hiż speaks of

$$(4.2) \qquad\qquad S_1 \cdot S_2 \rightarrow S_2$$

as a "rule of consequence" in accord with which (3) is correctly inferred from (1) and (2). Presumably then we are to construe (4.2) as

$$(4.2') \qquad\qquad \{S_1, S_2\} \rightarrow S_2$$

where '$\rightarrow$' is a metalinguistic sign read 'has as a logical consequence'. (1) and (2) consist of two sentences, not one, and thus the rule should concern $\{S_1, S_2\}$ not the conjunctive sentence $\ulcorner(S_1 \cdot S_2)\urcorner$. The difference may seem unimportant. Hiż has equated the '$\cdot$' of conjunction with the caesura, or rather with the period followed by the caesura, of (1) and (2) taken together. Often this equating can be made but not always. Nor do all English uses of 'or' go over into 'v', of 'not' into '$\sim$', and so on. To equate these too readily is the source of much confusion in the study of the exact relations between constructed logical systems and natural languages.

However this may be, a notion closely akin to the Jespersen-Hiż notion of a *referential*, or *cross*-referential, with the user explicitly brought in, may be defined in terms of 'Ref' as follows.

(Def.) '$p$ CoRefntl $a,b,c,d$' abbreviates '(Sent $b$ $\cdot$ Sent $d$ $\cdot$ $a$ Occ $b$ $\cdot$ $c$ Occ $d$ $\cdot$ (E$x$)($p$ Ref $a,x,b$ $\cdot$ $p$ Ref $c,x,d$))'.

In terms of 'Ref', let us explore a little more deeply now the inference of (3) from (1) and (2). This is to be done by "representing" — the word is Carnap's, recall, and it is interesting to note that it is creeping back in the technical literature on deep structure — these sentences within a constructed system as a frame of comparison. Let (1) and (2) be represented by

(1')                                'Wjh'

and

(2')                                'O*he*d'.

Then

(3')                                'Ojd'

represents (3). Let '*sp*' refer to the speaker, or whatever. Let e be the inscription of (2') and e' of (3') uttered by the speaker. And let $e_1$ be the inscription of '*he*' occurring in e and $e_2$ of 'j' in e'. Consider now the following pertinent statements or principles.

(4)   '(*sp* Utt e · 'O*he*d' e · '*he*' $e_1$ · $e_1$ Occ e · *sp* Utt e' · 'Ojd' e' · 'j' $e_2$ · $e_2$ Occ e')',
(5)   'sp Ref $e_1$,j,e',
(6)   '(*sp* Ref $e_1$,j,e · *sp* Utt e) ⊃ TrOcsnSent e,j,*sp*',
(7)   '(TrOcsnSent e,j,*sp* · sp Ref $e_1$,j,e · *sp* Ref $e_2$,j,e' ) ⊃ TrEtSent e',
(8)   '*sp* Ref $e_1$,j,e'',
(9)   'TrEtSent e' ≡ Ojd'.

From (4), (5), and (6)

(10)                          'TrOcsnSent e,j,*sp*'

follows. And from (11) and (9), (3') itself follows.

Of these principles (4) and (5) are empirical assumptions or boundary conditions. (6) follows from (2') using the definition of 'TrOcsnSent'. (7) is an instance of a general principle connecting reference with truth. (8) is a principle of reference — recall *RefR3* of III — and (9) is an instance of the Tarski paradigm or Adequacy Condition for the truth of eternal sentences within inscriptional semantics.

Can we conclude now that (3) is a logical consequence of (1)? Certainly not. First, it should be observed that at best the inference is enthymematic. Statements (4) through (9) are required to carry out the inference. And secondly, (1)-(3) are sentences of English, whereas (1')-(3'), and (4)-(11), are formulae within a formalized theory of reference. The only meaning for 'logical consequence of' admitted here is the standard one for logical systems of first order. What then does 'logical consequence of' in English mean? Clearly we should say that sentence $\alpha$ is a logical consequence in English of sentences $\beta$ and $\gamma$ if and only if the (or a) deep-structure representative of $\alpha$ is a logical consequence of the (or a) deep-structural representatives of $\beta$ and $\gamma$. In this sense of course, (3) may be regarded as an enthymematic consequence of (1) and (2) in English.

Note incidentally that in the derivation of (3') from (1') and (2') via (4)-(11), no use was made of (1'). In fact (3') was obtained from (2') alone. This might be thought a defect of the foregoing. To rectify this the supposition (5) may be replaced by the following, where e'' is the relevant inscription of (1') and $e_3$ the inscription of 'j' occurring in e''.

(5')   '($sp$ Ref $e_3$,j,e'' $\cdot$ 'Wjh'e'' $\cdot$ 'j'$e_3$ $\cdot$ $e_3$ Occ e'')',
(5'')   '$sp$ CoRefntl $e_3$,e'',$e_1$,e'.

From these, however, (5) itself is forthcoming using the principle of reference that

(12)        '($sp$ Ref $e_3$,j,e'' $\cdot$ $sp$ Ref $e_3$,x,e'') $\supset$ j = x'.

Putting the assumptions (5') and (5'') here in place of (5) is no doubt the better procedure. Even so, it is interesting to note that (1') need not be regarded as asserted. It may be commanded, questioned, or exclaimed, or whatever. Nor need it even be uttered, which is more surprizing yet. It may merely hover vaguely in the speaker's consciousness. Its role in the inference here is merely to supply a basis for the cross-referentiality.

It is by no means clear now Hiż can justify the inference of (3) from (1) and (2), however, even non-enthymematically. Nor does there seem to be any way for Hiż to supply the missing premisses within the semantics he allows himself. He lacks any way of speaking of the objects to which expressions are supposed to refer, in view of non-translationality. So even if he were to allow the premiss (5″), it is not clear what he could do with it. Further, of course, Hiż has no way of establishing (9), an instance of the Adequacy Condition for 'Tr'. The reason, again, is his use of a non-translational truth predicate.

In the foregoing, there has been no discussion of tense nor of the descriptive phrases 'home' and 'the door', which are irrelevant for present considerations. However, these should be looked at separately, for they raise interesting problems on their own.

Hiż is concerned with the "rules of consequence" for a natural language. Strictly, however, if the foregoing is correct, there are no such rules. There are rules of consequence for logical systems in which sentences of natural language may be "represented," but this is something quite different. In seeking to enunciate rules of consequence for natural language, Hiż seems to be using the direct approach disparaged by Carnap.

Incidentally, Hiż is not friendly to deep-structure linguists. "I suspect the hypothesis of deep structure to be implausible," he writes ("Rules of Consequence," p. 320, footnote 4), "at least if the structures allowed are of the sort used by Chomsky and others in practice and if the structures are assigned to sentences only, and not to longer utterances." Quite. The real defect of the M.I.T. deep structures is that they are not very deep after all, and that the "theory" governing them is far from being anything of the kind that a logician would be willing to call 'a theory'. Referential considerations such as those above must be brought in explicitly, it would seem, as well as various notions from event logic and the theory of intentionality.

# IX

# ON FITCH'S PROPOSITIONS
# AND STATES OF AFFAIRS

*"Ficta voluptatis causa sunt proxima veris."*

In his valuable and intriguing "Propositions as the Only Realities" Fitch has sketched a kind of unified logico-metaphysical scheme in which it is claimed that everything that is may be accommodated.[1] The most important types of things are, according to this account, persons, physical objects, events, facts, classes, and relations. Accordingly, each of these types of entities is "reduced" to propositions. The first step is to show that classes of propositions and relations between or among them can themselves be treated as propositions *simpliciter*. Facts are handled as *true* propositions and events as facts that are given *spatio-temporal location*. Finally, then, persons and physical objects are handled as *classes* of events or as *relations* between or among events.

It has frequently been claimed that propositions are an obscure kind of entity crying for analysis in terms of other more fundamental, clearer types of entities.[2] Fitch thinks, on the contrary, that the notion of a proposition is presumably as clear as any notion ever is.

[1] The *Journal of Philosophy* 66 (1969): 781-782 (Abstract) and *American Philosophical Quarterly* 8 (1971): 99-103.
[2] See especially *Belief, Existence, and Meaning, passim*.

# EVENTS, REFERENCE, AND LOGICAL FORM

And even if they are obscure *ab initio,* he proposes to analyze them implicitly, as it were, by constructing a broad theory concerning them. Propositions are then, roughly, the objects satisfying that theory. To be clear about propositions and what they are is then to be clear about the theory concerning them; nothing more, nothing less. An implicit characterization of propositions within an overall system is then all that is needed. One must be sure, before being convinced by this argument, however, that the overall system is itself acceptable and beyond suspicion.

The first items we must be clear about in Fitch's account are the primitives. In the reduction of classes of propositions to propositions *simpliciter,* two primitives play a crucial role, identity and various substitution relations $S_n$. The identity relation between propositions need not be cavilled. Presumably it obeys adaptations of the two Hilbert-Bernays conditions for identity.[3] These adaptations are, where '$p$' and '$q$' are propositional variables,

$$`(p)\ p = p'$$

and

$$`(p)\ (q)\ (p = q \supset ( (\cdots p \cdots) \supset (\cdots q \cdots) ) )',$$

where '$(\cdots p \cdots)$' is any sentence containing '$p$' as a free variable and '$(\cdots q \cdots)$' differs from it appropriately. Among the sentences here are included of course intensional ones such as 'so and so believes $p$', 'so and so desires $p$', and so on.

How now are the $S_n$-relations, one for each positive, finite value of '$n$' to be understood? It is stated that any sentence of the form

(1) $$`S_n p q_1 \cdots q_n r_1 \cdots r_n s'$$

is an axiom "provided that the sentence '$p$' results from substituting the sentences '$q_1$', $\cdots$ , '$q_n$' respectively for the sentences '$r_1$', $\cdots$ ,

---

[3] See D. Hilbert und P. Bernays, *Grundlagen der Mathematik,* Vol. I (Springer, Berlin: 1939), pp. 164 ff. Cf. *IdR1-IdR2* in II above.

172

'$r_n$' in the sentence '$s$'." This condition needs spelling out. What is meant is presumably the following: provided that some sentence $a$ of the system is put in in place of '$s$', '$r_1$', $\cdots$ , '$r_n$' are propositional variables, a sentence $b_i$ of the system is put in in place of '$q_i$' ($1 \leq i \leq n$), and the sentence that results from $a$ by the simultaneous substitution of $b_1, \cdots , b_n$ for '$r_1$', $\cdots$ , '$r_n$' respectively is put in in place of '$p$'. Thus any formula of the form

$$\text{'}S_n(\text{---}q_1,\cdots,q_n\text{---})q_1\cdots q_n r_1 \cdots r_n (\text{---}r_1 , \cdots,r_n \text{---})\text{'}$$

is an axiom, where (etc., as needed).

It should be noted that an infinity of primitives ($n$ = 1,2,$\cdots$), each of a very considerable complexity, is being employed. Ordinarily substitution is regarded as an operation on *sentences* resulting in sentences. In fact, this seems to be the only clear way of handling substitution that there is, as an operation on linguistic expressions yielding linguistic expressions. All the extant accounts of it attest to this.[4] The $S_i$'s might thus be regarded as syntactical relations. Fitch takes them otherwise, however, as object-linguistic relations among propositions, and propositions are a non-linguistic kind of entity. It is difficult to see, nonetheless, how the '$S_i$'s are to be interpreted other than in terms of substitution on *expressions*. A proposition is an abstract Platonic unit or indivisible whole of some kind and not a linguistic expression.

What then can '$S_1 pqrs$' mean? (To simplify let $n$ = 1.) One might try to give a semantical rule stating the conditions under which sentences of this form are true. But '$r$' here must be a *variable*. Hence there cannot be in the object language instances of '$S_1 pqrs$' that could be said to be *true* — for presumably only sentences or statements (containing no free variables) are true. One can only conclude that the $S_i$'s are an obscure kind of relation not suitable for the logico-metaphysical purposes intended. Like propositions them-

---

[4] See, for example, *inter alia* A. Tarski, *Logic, Semantics, Metamathematics,* p. 180, R. Carnap, *The Logical Syntax of Language,* pp. 22, 90 f., and 191 f., and W. V. Quine, *Mathematical Logic,* pp. 301 f.

selves they cry for analysis in clear-cut terms in which the distinction between use and mention is meticulously maintained.

In using a form such as '$S_1 pqrs$' is there in fact violation between use and mention? There is if the $S_i$'s are construed in terms of substitution. The system, however, does not demand that one do so. One might seek another interpretation for them, in terms of 'about'. Propositions are "about" things, in particular about propositions. Suppose '$S_1 pqrs$' were to be read as 'proposition $p$ is about proposition $q$ in the same way that proposition $s$ is about $r$' or 'proposition $p$ expresses or says of proposition $q$ whatever it is that proposition $s$ expresses or says about $r$'. Some such readings as these would not violate the use-mention distinction but would involve obscurities of their own. 'About' is notoriously sticky and difficult to characterize, as is 'expresses'.[5]

The question also arises as to how 'truth' is to be handled. Perhaps Fitch wishes it to be handled as a primitive predicate of propositions. Thus 'Tr $p$' might express primitively that the proposition $p$ is true. 'Tr' in this sense would provide Carnap's absolute concept of truth, not the semantical one. The difficulty with this absolute notion is that it is extremely limited, enabling nothing to be accomplished with it that cannot be done without it, as has frequently been noted.[6] Perhaps Fitch has in mind some other way of handling 'Tr'. In any case, it must be handled *within* the object language in order that *facts* may be accommodated therein as true propositions. To handle truth within the object language is of course dangerous, lest semantical antinomies arise therefrom.

In a full presentation of Fitch's theory of propositions, it would be shown in detail precisely how some (but not all) propositions are given a spatio-temporal ordering. This would be accomplished presumably in terms of a primitive before-than relation. '$p$ B $q$' could express that $p$ is before $q$ in the ordering. Not all propositions partake of this ordering, however, only some. Precisely which ones?

---

[5] On 'about' see especially N. Goodman, "About," in *Problems and Projects* (Bobbs-Merrill, Indianapolis: 1972).

[6] See, for example, the author's "Truth and Its Illicit Surrogates," *Neue Hefte für Philosophie*, 2/3.

And why should some partake of this ordering but not all? The answer to these questions would differentiate precisely between events and facts. It might seem doubtful *ab initio* whether any clear and natural line of demarcation could be drawn here within an object language in Fitch's terms. Events are real goings-on in the world, facts are intensional constructs handled in terms of the semantical notion of *factual truth,* so that a really clear line of demarcation can be drawn, but only in a metalanguage.

Another puzzling feature of Fitch's treatment, also about 'about', is the following. Propositions are presumably "about" something other than just themselves. Some propositions might be about themselves, some about other propositions. But some ultimate atomic propositions, it would seem, ought to be about something other than a proposition. For the whole system of propositions to have content, some proposition or propositions would presumably have to be about something other than themselves. Propositions regarded as the ultimate realities cannot, it would seem, be merely about other propositions, and these in turn about others, and so *ad inf.* The whole system would have to get started in some way, so to speak, with at least one proposition that would not be about either itself or another one.

A closely related point is the following. Atomic propositions are presumably whatever are "expressed" by atomic sentences, just as molecular propositions are "expressed" by molecular sentences. Molecular propositions are thus given a kind of structure in terms of their components. What structure do atomic propositions have? For Fitch, atomic propositions must presumably be indivisible wholes, not further decomposable. Atomic *sentences* are of course decomposable into terms and class and relation words. It would seem reasonable then to decompose atomic propositions also in terms somehow of the constituents of the atomic sentences that express them. It is not clear how this could be done in Fitch's system, if at all, containing as it does propositions and propositions only. Whatever the constituents of atomic propositions are, they cannot be just other propositions.

Fitch's system, like all systems, is described syntactically within a syntactical metalanguage and given an interpretation within a semantical metalanguage. If propositions are the sole realities, then of course the very expressions of the language themselves must be handled as propositions. There are only two possibilities here. Expressions are handled either as sign designs or shapes or as sign events or inscriptions. Fitch apparently regards them as the latter, in other words, as propositions with spatio-temporal location. Just what form the semantics for Fitch's system takes, as based on inscriptions, however, is by no means obvious. In fact, the only semantics based on inscriptions that seems yet to have been formulated — other than that of II and III above — is that of the metalanguage ISM$_L$ of *Truth and Denotation.*[7] To fit it to Fitch's system would require a very considerable modification, with a sacrifice of some of its most desirable features.

In any case, the structure of syntax and semantics, in short, of metalogic, remains to be explored on Fitch's basis. It is by no means clear that this can be done simply or with any advantages over the more usual modes of treatment. And it is above all recent advances in metalogic that have made out of modern logic the tremendously powerful tool for philosophic analysis that it has become. Modal logic and its ilk, deontic logics and so on, have not been of help where metalogic has failed to be. On the contrary, modal and deontic logics, it seems, receive their clearest formulation only within suitable metalanguages.[8] Thus at some point, all the problems concerned with designation, denotation, satisfaction, the L-concepts, analytic truth, and so on, must be clearly faced by proponents of propositions.[9]

Fitch seems to think that only propositions can be taken as the sole "realities" and thus that no other type of entity could be made to suffice. This is not the case. Presumably by suitable technical maneuvres everything could be regarded as a *property.* Paraphrasing Fitch's own reductions, individuals could be regarded as unit

---

[7] Chapter XI.
[8] See *Belief, Existence, and Meaning, passim.*
[9] As even Alan Anderson has pointed out in his "On Professor Martin's Beliefs," *The Journal of Philosophy* 59 (1962): 600-607.

properties. Relations are then properties of ordered couples of unit properties, and atomic (subject-predicate) proposition are ordered pairs of properties with unit properties. Atomic relational propositions may be handled similarly. An atomic proposition involving a dyadic relation would then be an ordered pair of that dyadic relation with an ordered pair of two unit properties. (It is assumed here that inhomogeneous pairs may be suitably introduced.) And so on for events and facts, perhaps in Fitch's manner. By similar technical devices, dyadic relations could be taken as the sole realities also.

A variant of Fitch's method, or at least a closely related one, is that of Chisholm, in which, however, *states of affairs* are regarded as the one and only fundamental type of entity, in addition to "concrete individual things and their properties."[10] Propositions, events, and facts are then introduced by definition. Chisholm needs also a model operator for *necessarily true*. It is good to come into touch again with concrete individual things, after Fitch's solo flight into the lofty realm of propositions. The suspicion is, however, that Chisholm does not need *both* states of affairs and properties (and presumably relations) in addition. By technical devices like those used in the paragraph above, expressions for one could be defined no doubt in terms of the other. Chisholm's suggestions provide an interesting alternative, the details of which remain to be formulated.

All of these methods are objectionable, however, to one who wishes to analyze out all intensional ingredients in terms of items already available in semantics.

The methods of Fitch and Chisholm owe such cogency as they possess only at the neglect of the various delicate distinctions that semantics enjoins. Once these are all spelled out, together with suitable and natural extensions into pragmatics, the theory of action, and epistemics, all need for such entities as unanalyzed propositions or states of affairs *sui generis* is seen to disappear.

If one is to eschew all unanalyzed intensions *sui generis, events* (taken in extension) seem to be the most natural kind of entity to regard as the sole realities. In I-III above a wholesale and integrated

---

[10] Roderick M. Chisholm, "The Identity of Events and States of Affairs," one of the Arthur Young Lectures given at New York University, December, 1969.

logico-metaphysical theory was suggested in which events and events only are taken as the values of variables. The theory there is closely tied not only to physical science but to the logical study of language as well. The talk of propositions in the Fitch-Chisholm methods seems so remote from actual language as to shed little light upon the intricacies of its logical structure.

If one is sensitive to matters of ontic commitment, the underlying logic ought to be neutral as to what there is. The conception of logic as subject-matter neutral, as it were, has dominated much of the history of the subject. One is then free to *apply* logic to the theory of any specified domain of objects whatsoever. If logic is developed right at the very beginning in terms of propositions, however, this neutrality is violated straightaway. Proposition logic weds basic logic to a kind of entity that is not necessitated by the nature of the subject. Then result is a *mésalliance.* One should do basic logic first neutrally, then apply it wherever one will. Not to do so is to build into one's logic a metaphysical view, to close the door to alternatives, and to block the road to inquiry in favor of some one metaphysics. This is precisely what logic should not do. On the netural view of logic, one is free to explore alternative metaphysical views and their interconnections, each being formulated upon the basis of a neutral logic, preferably of first order.

Chisholm used states-of-affairs logic as a basis for the discussion of good and evil, in his Presidential Address.[11] "The things that are intrinsically good and the things that are intrinsically bad are, all of them, states of affairs," he contends (pp. 22-23). "We may also put this point by saying that states of affairs are the bearers of intrinsic value." This contention seems rather arbitrary, however, and events may equally well serve here. The logic of 'intrinsically better' and of other ethical terms may be developed more simply in terms of events. 'Intrinsically better' is handled by means of a relation, anyhow, in Chisholm's treatment, and that the relata be states of affairs is only an incidental requirement.[12]

[11] "The Defeat of Good and Evil," in *Proceedings and Addresses of the American Philosophical Association* 42 (1968-69): 21-38.
[12] See Chisholm and E. Sosa, "On the Logic of 'Intrinsically better'," *American Philosophical Quarterly* 3 (1966): 244-249.

Fitch thinks his system is closely related to the cosmological scheme of Whitehead's *Process and Reality.* The system based on events seems a more likely candidate here, however, "Actual entities" or "actual occasions" are for Whitehead "the final real things of which the world is made up. There is no going behind actual entities to find anything more real."[13] All else are constructs in terms of actual occasions. Whatever actual occasions are, they are not propositions; these latter in turn are rather constructs, no doubt of an intensional kind, in terms of them. Actual occasions are like the events in the theory mentioned, everything being regarded as either an event, or a complex of such, or some construct.

Let there be no misunderstanding. There are always interesting logico-metaphysical alternatives to be formulated in an open-minded and exploratory vein. Each alternative usually has some advantages to offer. All of the alternatives discussed in this paper are at the present stage mere programs crying for a fuller and more exact characterization. Only when they and their metalanguages are fully formulated in exact detail will we be able to decide which is the most worthy of rational admiration. "Everyone is at liberty to build up his own logic, i.e., his own form of language, as he wishes. All that is required of him is that, if he wishes to discuss it, he must state his methods clearly, and give [exact] syntactical [and semantical] rules . . ."[14] Even then, philosophical disagreement will remain concerning the form and acceptability of the rules.

---

[13] *Process and Reality,* p. 24.
[14] R. Carnap, *Syntax,* p. 52.

# X

# ON QUINE'S *PHILOSOPHY OF LOGIC*

*"Animum curis nunc huc nunc dividet illuc."*

In many respects Quine's philosophy of logic is admirable and the most adequate we have.[1] In fact it recommends itself so strongly that it is a pity that we must face up to its lack of unity and coherency. In this paper some of its basic features will be discussed critically but with the sympathetic aim of smoothing out difficulties along the way. The net result is the kind of philosophy of logic that Quine, on his own grounds, should have been putting forward all along.

The notion of truth has played an increasingly important role in Quine's thought over the years. It is the truth predicate that (p. 35) "preserves his [the logician's] contact with the world, where his heart is." Mere grammar is not sufficient for this. By "semantic ascent" we arise to the apprehension, more specifically, to the definition, of the truth predicate. This predicate is not to be defined piecemeal, however, step by step, as applied only to individual sentences *seriatim.* Such definitions would be simple enough, but would result only in the no-truth or "disappearance" theory of

---

[1] W. V. Quine, *Philosophy of Logic* (Prentice-Hall, Englewood Cliffs, N.J.: 1970).

truth.[2] Instead, the predicate 'Tr' must be defined in context 'Tr *a*' *for variable 'a'*. Here is the essential reason for semantic ascent in the first place, the need for variable '*a*'. It is very important to understand this reason, lest the purport of semantic ascent be lost sight of.

Quine does not limit his discussion to language systems *L* of the kinds studied by Carnap and others. No, his concern rather is with natural language as "regimented" in such ways as first-order logic demands. By 'sentence' or 'statement' Quine means, unless otherwise limited, a sentence or statement of natural language. Further, although he often writes as though he regarded sentences, and linguistic expressions in general, as shapes or sign designs, here he comes down rather in favor of regarding some sentences at least as tokens or inscriptions or sign events. "What are best regarded [p. 14] as true or false are not propositions but sentence tokens, or sentences if they are eternal," an eternal sentence being one "whose tokens all have the same truth value."

A curious mixed view results in which some sentences are regarded as shapes, while others are tokens. Not all sentences are then of the same logical type. This seems awkward and an unnecessary complication. It would be more in keeping with the spirit of Quine's comments here if all sentences were to be regarded either as one or the other. Sentence shapes are presumably of one type higher than that of sentence tokens. Since he wishes to regard occasion or non-eternal sentences as tokens, eternal sentences could be regarded as virtual classes of all sufficiently similar sentence tokens having the same truth value.

On the previous page (p. 13), Quine commented that "what are best seen as primarily true or false are not sentences, but events of utterance. If a man utters the words 'It is raining' in the rain, or the words 'I am hungry' while hungry, his verbal performance counts as true. Obviously one utterance of a sentence [shape] may be true and another of the same sentence be false." It is surely of interest to define the truth predicate as applicable to acts of utterance, as in III

---

[2] See again "Truth and Its Illicit Surrogates."

above. Quine, however, nowhere does this. Acts of utterance are not merely tokens or inscriptions over again, however, so that the two ways of construing the truth predicate are not the same. It is thus not clear how Quine can regard both of them as "best." (More will be said about tokens in a moment.)

Quine's object language consists then of a "regimented" natural language, for which he needs at least three truth predicates, one applicable to its eternal-sentence shapes, another to its occasion-sentence tokens, and a third to acts of utterance. Presumably if we have the second of these we could easily get the other two. What is worrisome at the moment rather is that Quine proposes to provide a truth predicate applicable to natural language without contradiction. Tarski has warned us forcefully — in italics — on this matter. *"The attempt to set up a structural definition of the term 'true sentence' applicable to colloquial* [natural] *language is confronted with insuperable difficulties"* and *"the very possibility of a consistent use of the expression 'true sentence' which is in harmony with the laws of logic and the spirit of everyday language seems to be very questionable, and consequently the same doubt attaches to the possibility of constructing a correct definition of this expression."*[3] Quine can reply that after all his object language is regimented. However, he has not shown us that this is done so as to avoid all the difficulties that might ensue were we to assume a truth predicate available applicable to all its sentence shapes, sentence tokens, or acts of utterance. Regimentation consists only in telling us that variables are available, together with some one-place and two-place predicates (perhaps some three-place predicates, and so on), in addition to the usual connectives and quantifiers, perhaps identity also. Clearly, however, this is not sufficient. We must also be assured that the predicates are not of the kind giving rise to any of Tarski's "insuperable difficulties." The point is of the highest importance, and thoroughly trained linguists have spent long hours worrying as to how such difficulties and doubts here might be alleviated.

If natural language is regimented too narrowly, the possibility of

---

[3] Tarski, *loc. cit.*, pp. 164-165.

these difficulties is likely to increase. If it is overregimented, the result might no longer be recognizable as a natural language. The safest procedure here no doubt is to introduce piecemeal specific primitive predicates by enumeration as needed.[4] If we do this, however, we are no long dealing with natural language at all, but rather with specific first-order language systems $L$.

Quine does not distinguish the object-language predicates that are to be taken as primitive from those that are not. Some no doubt are to be primitive, and the lexicon then presumably supplies the rest. Quine does not quite say this, however. Perhaps the lexicon for him is not that of the logician, where all non-primitive expressions are defined non-circularly in terms of preceding expressions, which in turn are defined ultimately in terms of the primitives. (Clearly he does not regard all the predicates as primitives, for in this event there would be no need of a lexicon at all.) In any case Quine seems to overlook the need for axioms or rules governing the predicates taken as primitives. Their behavior is left indeterminate, however, if such axioms or rules are not given. Of course the moment one seeks to specify such axioms one has parted from pure logic, in the strict first-order (with perhaps identity) sense.

To convince us that a regimented natural language is suitable to be taken as an object language, its primitives should be exhibited together with the axioms upon them. It should then be shown that an adequate predicate for truth for that language is not therein definable. It is not enough merely to go through the ritual of semantic ascent to a general definition of 'satisfies' in a metalanguage. It must be provided that no such definition is forthcoming prior to such ascent. No one would dream of taking a set theory as object language without telling us what its axioms are. Why should a regimented natural language be different in this respect? In unregimented natural language, it might be contended, no axioms are needed. Regimentation consists in part, however, in making various terms behave in a logically acceptable way. One would have thought that the specification of axioms would be essential for this.

[4] Cf. *Truth and Denotation,* Chapter I.

That there is need for semantic ascent has been established beyond all doubt by Tarski, Carnap, and others. That such ascent must be carried out via set theory, however, as Quine seems to contend, is by no means the case. It may be, but it need not be, and the price for so doing is high.

Quine, following Tarski, makes much of the relation of satisfaction, in the general form by use of which infinite sequences of objects are said to satisfy a sentential function containing any arbitrary number of free variables.[5] To define explicitly an expression for this relation, an elaborate set-theoretic machinery is required, and thus semantic ascent becomes indissolubly linked up with set theory. (Even a type theory is now almost always regarded as a set theory in some kind of disguise.) This linkage has been well advertised in recent years by almost all writers on the subject, and Quine here merely follows suit.

In *Truth and Denotation*[6] it was show beyond a shadow of a doubt that such linkage is not essential. The truth predicate for first order *L*'s may readily be defined by taking instead a suitable semantical relation as primitive. Note that on all methods some notions must be taken as primitives in the metalanguage that do not occur, either as primitives or as defined, in the object language. Quine takes '$\epsilon$' for the relation of set membership plus structural-descriptive names or predicates and concatenation. And governing all of these, of course, are assumed the axioms of some set theory plus those of syntax. (The method of Gödel numbers may, as with Quine, be disregarded here for the moment.) The staggering wealth of deductive consequences of such an axiom set should be noted —— also its dubiousness. In terms of this extraordinary array of doubtful notions and principles, the definition of 'Tr' may be given, and the fundamental principles concerning it may be proved. Friends of set theory think this a triumph. Its foes, however —— Quine himself is sometimes one —— may well object that the price paid is exhorbitant. The alternative method, as based on denotation, needs no set theory at all. In place of the very powerful axioms of set theory, two

[5] Tarski, *loc. cit.*, pp. 193 ff.
[6] Chapters IV and V.

Rules of Denotation are assumed that provide all the deductive power that is needed.

Arguments against sets are legion. Sets are never needed in mathematics, if one takes a suitable constructive or quasi-constructive approach to it. To use set theory to explicate so essentially simple a notion as truth is like using a huge computer to multiply 2 by 3. Further, it is to explicate a simple notion in terms of something much more obscure. Quine himself has frequently berated explaining the *obscurum per obscurius* in other contexts. The simplicity of the semantic truth notion is as nothing as compared to the complexities of set theory. Further, the very *definition* of 'Tr' in terms of satisfaction is very much more complicated than that in terms of the alternative method.

Note that it will not do to defend the set-theoretic approach on the grounds that after all the notions of satisfaction and truth are defined within it, whereas in the alternative 'Den' for denotation is taken as a primitive. In the set-theoretic approach it is '$\epsilon$' that is the primitive. It is '$\epsilon$' versus 'Den' that is at issue here, not having definitions available for truth and satisfaction versus taking 'Den' as a primitive.

Quine himself has argued cogently and forcefully against admitting obscure intensional objects such as propositions (in the sense of the meanings of sentences), attributes, Fregean senses, and the like, as values for variables. His objections to these (p. 3) are three-fold. One is on grounds of parsimony, "from a desire to dream of no more things in heaven and earth than need be." Another is from the point of view of particularism, "a disapproval of intangible or abstract entities." The third is the difficulty over synonymy.

How seriously is Quine's particularism to be taken? The answer is: as seriously as possible, provided a workable view can be made of it. The tragedy of Quine's philosophy is that he does not take it seriously enough. When doing set theory he forgets it. A fundamental cleavage thus emerges, an incoherency, a Monday-Wednesday-Friday Tuesday-Thursday-Saturday dichotomy, all right perhaps on Sundays or if you like dichotomies but otherwise not. Quine is not fond of the cleavage between analytic and factual truth, and has urged a somewhat holistic view toward that between theoretical and observational truth. By parity of dislike and to preserve holism, that between particularism and set theory should not be tolerated either.

Quine's ontology ends up then as rather mixed. At heart he seems to condone only physical objects. "We might think of a *physical object,*" he writes (p. 30), "as simply the whole four-dimensional material content, however sporadic and heterogeneous, of some portion of space-time. Then if such an object happens to be fairly firm and coherent internally but coheres only rather slightly and irregularly with its spatio-temporal surroundings, we are apt to call it a body. Other physical objects may be spoken of more naturally as processes, happenings, events. Still others invite no distinctive epithet." Physical objects are to be the only values for variables, then, together with sets where and when needed.

Quine clearly regards "processes, happenings, events" as physical objects also. He nowhere seeks to characterize what is distinctive about such entities, however, or in any way to delineate their inner structure. It might well be that such entities may be regarded as constructs in terms of physical objects, but this is not to regard them as physical objects *simpliciter.* In fact, whatever "processes, happenings, events" are, they are not just species of physical objects. More cogent, it would seem, is the converse view, that physical objects constitute a species of events. In any case, Quine needs to tell us a great deal more about the inner structure of processes, happenings, and so on, before convincing us that his ontology is acceptable.

Quine does not claim (p. 31) that his "austere little standard grammar," his object language, "is adequate to all purposes of cognitive discourse: that everything can be said in a language comprising just these constructions and variables and a finite lexicon of predicates." In particular, he worries about adverbs and expressions for the propositional attitudes and for the modalities. He recognizes that the matter of adverbs is linked with the ontology of events. Adverbs may be handled in terms of events, it may be maintained, if the suggestions put forward in VI above are sound.

Quine considers here four ways of handling the propositional attitudes (thinking, believing, wishing, knowing, intending, and the like), but rejects all of them. Curiously he does not mention a fifth, which seems the most promising, the most Quinean in spirit and in letter, to which he has called attention elsewhere. This fifth method involves semantic ascent. We can let, as above,

$$\text{'}p \ \text{Blvs} \ x,a\text{'}$$

express that person $p$ believes the virtual class expression $a$ to be true of the object $x$. Similarly for knowing, thinking, and so on. In *Word and Object*, it will be recalled, similar forms were discussed and not rejected. It has been urged, above and elsewhere,[7] that they seem to hold the best promise of turning out to be the most satisfactory. Semantic ascent and the device of quotation (via structural descriptions) are needed anyhow, so that we may as well use them here.

Quine has never been a friend of handling the modalities in an object language in the manner of modal logic, and he does not become one here. Curiously, however, he does not comment upon the method of handling the modalities via semantic ascent. If by 'necessary' is meant *logically necessary*, it may be handled in terms of the semantical predicate for logical truth. If by 'necessary' is meant something else —— physical necessity —— it may be handled in terms of some other suitable metalinguistic predicate. Let $\Gamma$ be a virtual class of the fundamental laws of physics. For a sentence to be physically necessary is then for it to be a logical consequence of this class. And so on. Again, the clearest and most promising treatment of the various uses of the modal words, Quine does not here so much as mention. So deeply has he become embroiled with his critique of Aristotelian essentialism in one form or another, that he has neglected to recall some of his own best insights.

Quine claims (pp. 33-34) that "we would be within our rights in holding that no formulation of any part of science is definitive so long as it remains couched in idioms of propositional attitude or modality. But to claim this is more modest than to claim that our standard logical grammar is enough grammar for science. Such good

---

[7] In *Belief, Existence, and Meaning*, Chapters IV and V.

uses as the modalities are ever put to can probably be served in ways that are clearer and already known; but the idioms of propositional attitude have uses in which they are not easily supplanted. Let us by all means strive for clearer devices adequate to those purposes; but meanwhile we have no assurance that the new devices, once found, will fit the elegant grammar that we are calling standard." The methods just suggested do, it should be noted, fit a suitable extension of the elegant standard grammar if not that grammar itself. The use of idioms such as (1) for handling the propositional attitudes, and handling the modalities via semantic ascent, however, introduce nothing foreign either in letter or spirit.

Quine's standard grammar may be adequate for science, but this is not to say that it is adequate for natural language. There are more linguistic idioms in the latter than are needed for the "cognitive" parts of the former. We are not told how questions and commands are to be handled, for example, nor the deontic notions. Once suitable forms for these are given we still have scarcely begun. The difficult problem of showing precisely how logical forms are to be arrived at from the corresponding sentences of a natural language still remains. Logic may "chase truth up the tree of grammar," as Quine puts it, but the rules of the chase remain explicitly to be formulated. Logical forms are on the one hand and the multifarious sentences of a natural language on the other. It is of little use to equate them *ex cathedra* without the kind of help that empirical and structural linguistics can offer. Conversely, of course, the study of logical form should be of help to the linguist also in his search for deep structure.

Quine is brilliant (p. 79) in contending that "the rewards of staying within the bounds of standard grammar are great." The first is that of extensionality, no mean desideratum and to be given up only at one's peril. Not only should the object language be extensional in a suitable sense, the metalanguage should be also. If we can handle the propositional attitudes, modalities, questions, commands, the deontic notions, and so on, within such a metalanguage, we are making progress indeed.

There is also, Quine remarks, "the efficiency and elegance of the logic of truth functions and quantification. There is its completeness" — and also its consistency. Of course similar claims can be made by proponents of deviant logic or metalogic, so that too much importance should not be attached to these. On the other hand, Quine is surely right that the standard classical logic (p. 85) "is a paragon of clarity, elegance and efficiency." "The paradoxes emerge only with set theory and semantics," he continues. "Let us then try to resolve them within set theory and semantics, and not lay fairer fields waste." Better yet, let us eschew set theory altogether, dubious at best. Then let us develop a consistent semantics *ad hoc* rather than as a branch of set theory, and then go on to make more of constructivistic procedures in mathmatics itself and develop them within a broadly conceived event logic.

There is also the "maxim of minimum mutilation," the principle of conservation. Although in principle logic is open to revision just as any empirical science is, in practice "revisions are seldom proposed that cut so deep" as to justify altering it. In practice, in judging the validity of arguments in either natural language or in the sciences, it is almost always to the standard logic that appeal is made.[8]

Quine speaks only of deviant logic, not of deviant semantics. Although recently there has been some talk of the latter, usually logicians accept semantics of only the standard (even if set-theoretic) type. Where the object language is itself deviant, it is usually required, and desired, that its semantics be standard. It is thought a great victory if a deviant system can be given an interpretation within a standard semantics. It is the latter than then becomes important, however, and the original deviancy may be forgiven. Also, at the very heart of the deviant system some conceptual or technical confusion or other can usually be found, often that of use and mention. Here are two more arguments on behalf of the standard, classical point of view.

It is curious that Quine makes no mention of the calculus of individuals as contributing to regimentation. The far-reaching philosophical usefulness of this is now beyond dispute, one would have thought, and its adjunction to standard logic a matter of course.

[8] Cf. *Belief, Existence, and Meaning*, pp. 24 ff.

It is curious also, if linguistic expressions are construed as tokens or inscriptions rather than as shapes, that Quine does not emphasize more first-order inscriptional syntax and the first-order semantics based on it. These are in accord with his general view, his parsimony, and his particularism. To construct on the groundwork of inscriptional syntax a veritable skyscraper of a set theory results in a top-heavy edifice. The one is finitist, or at least neutral as between assuming a finite or an infinite number of expressions, the other out and out infinitist in the domain of the abstract. Again, an odd mixed view results, penny wise but pound foolish. Why require parsimony on the one hand, only to have its advantages squandered in profligacy on the other?

Another aspect of Quine's thought, the doctrine of gradualism, also ill accords with his use of set theory. "I am concerned to urge [p. 100] the empirical character of logic and mathematics no more than the unempirical character of theorectical physics; it is rather their kinship that I am urging, and a doctrine of gradualism." The point is surely, however, that no gradualism is possible between set theory and empirical science. Between the two there is a gap as wide as possible. Set theory is *sui generis* in its admission as values for variables entities of a kind altogether different from those considered in empirical science.

*Extrapolation* is the procedure whereby one goes from observation to theory in the sciences, and indeed in geometry as well.[9] Extrapolation from empirical science to set theory, however, seems impossible. Here Quine wants his set theory and gradualism too, but the two do not accord with each other either in spirit or in letter.

Quine makes much of the supposition that his views help to make procedures of learning intelligible. We should (p. 101) "think in terms . . . of how a child actually acquires his language and all those truths or beliefs, or whatever kind, that he acquires along with it." Some of these truths are truths about truths. Quine's account of truth via set theory, however, again, ill accords with the way in which such truths are learned. They are not learned by first

[9] See the author's "Steps towards a Pragmatic Protogeometry," *Diálogos* 23 (1973).

191

encountering set theory and then the theory of satisfaction, but rather ultimately by confrontation of word with object. The account of truth and logical truth in terms of denotation, which relates a one-place predicate with an object to which it applies, then, seems much better suited as a basis for a theory of learning than the alternatives.

The net result of these reflections is that we cannot live with Quine's philosophy of logic. But we cannot do without it either. We must all absorb with gratitude the lessons it has taught us. They are not casually thought out but deeply grounded on sound and well worked-out views concerning what logic is and what logic is not. However, Quine has not been true to his own best insights and we cannot rest content with just what he has told us. We must move on to a more unified and coherent view, in which neither parsimony nor particularism nor gradualism nor extensionality is lost sight of. Once these are suitably arranged for, synonymy, analytic truth, intensional semantics, and the study of intentionality will take care of themselves.

# XI

# ON POPPER'S THIRD WORLD OF OBJECTIVE SPIRIT

*"Qui a nuce nucleum vult, frangat nucem."*

Let $S_1$ be some "world" or domain of objects or entities so that '$S_1 x$' expresses that $x$ is an object of that world. Let $S_2$ be some second world so that '$S_2 x$' expresses that $x$ is an object of it. Then clearly, of course '$(S_1 x \lor S_2 x)$' can be abbreviated as '$(S_1 \cup S_2)x$', using the sign '$\cup$' of *22.03 of *Principia Mathematica*. The predicate '$(S_1 \cup S_2)$' stands in effect for a unified world consisting of both $S_1$ and $S_2$. In this way any two worlds may be unified. And similarly, any "third world" may be unified with it. Thus, no matter how many worlds one wishes to distinguish *ab initio,* they may always be unified in this way.

There are of course other trivial ways of unification. One is by means of the Löwenheim-Skolem theorem. Let all worlds be unified as in the preceding paragraph, and let the theory of that one unified world be formulated as a first-order system. Then by that theorem there exists another "model" for the axioms of that theory within the world of the positive integers. In this way the positive integers may be made to serve as the only objects of the one unified world.

Everything might instead be regarded as a set. In place of individuals, speak of the sets whose only members are those individuals, as, for example, in Quine's *Set Theory and Its Logic.*

Then in place of an individual constant 'Socrates' we would have some set predicate, say 'Socratizes', designating the set whose only member is Socrates. There are numerous other ways in which sets might be regarded as the only individuals. And similarly for relations, functions, and the like.

More important ways of integrating the objects of various worlds arise by formulating a logico-metaphysical system in which everything can, in an interesting and non-trivial way, be regarded as a special case of the one kind of object taken as basic. One such way is by means of Fitch's propositions. Another is by means of events. There may be still others, but no theory concerning them seems to have been worked out in any logical detail.

These various comments show that any supposition of two worlds is suspect, let alone of three or more. Once two are admitted, there seems little reason to stop at any assigned finite number. Popper[1] distinguishes (p. 333) first "the world of physical objects or physical states," then "the world of states of consciousness, or of mental states, or perhaps of behavioural dispositions to act," and finally the "third world," that of *objective contents of thought,* especially of scientific and poetic thoughts and of works of art." Popper does not contend that these worlds cannot be unified in the various ways mentioned, and perhaps in others, but only that "we may distinguish" them in order to call attention especially to the importance of the third, and its multifarious contents.

The "third world" has much in common, we are told, with Plato's theory of forms, with Hegel's objective spirit, with Bolzano's universe of propositions in themselves, but "resembles most closely the universe of Frege's objective contents of thought." Let us examine some of the fascinating things Popper has to say about this third world in order to sharpen some of them in the light of syntax, semantics, pragmatics, and event logic. All inhabitants of the third world, it will be contended, as well as of the first and second, have

---

[1] See especially Sir Karl Popper, "Epistemology without a Knowing Subject," *Proceedings of the Third International Congress for Logic, Methodology, and Philosophy of Science* (North-Holland Publishing Co., Amsterdam: 1968), pp. 333-373, and also "On the Theory of the Objective Mind," *Akten des XIV. Internationalen Kongresses für Philosophie* (Herder, Wien: 1968), Vol. I, pp. 25-53.

their rightful place in the ontology of the latter. Some critical comments will be made along the way, but there will be much underlying agreement nonetheless.

Popper hopes to provoke those whom he calls 'belief philosophers' who (p. 334) "are interested in our subjective beliefs, and their basis or origin. Against these belief philosophers," he urges, "our problem is to find better and bolder theories; and that *critical preference* counts, but *not belief*." But can one not be interested both in subjective beliefs and in better and bolder theories? Critical preference surely counts but so also does belief. Further, one can believe a bolder theory, and critically prefer it to some other. Belief can perhaps be handled in terms of *acceptance*, and critical preference is essentially *cognitive preference*.

Popper comes down firmly against "epistemic logic," concerned with formulae such as 'person $p$ knows $a$', 'person $p$ believes $a$', and the like. Such formulae, he thinks, have nothing to do with scientific knowledge: . . . the scientist . . . does neither know nor believe." But of course he does. He believes as other mortals do, and knows *per excellence* if anyone does. And in the second place, he knows and believes on better evidence often than other mortals do, so far at least as concerns items in his special science. However, the scientist $S$ also, as Popper contends (p. 364), does much more. "What does he do? I will give a very brief list [with a minor notational change] :

'$S$ tries to understand $a$',
'$S$ tries to think of alternatives to $a$',
'$S$ tries to think of criticisms to $a$',
'$S$ proposes an experimental test for $a$',
'$S$ tries to axiomatize $a$',
'$S$ tries to derive $a$ from $b$',
'$S$ tries to show that $a$ is not derivable from $b$',
'$S$ proposes a new problem $x$ arising out of $a$',
'$S$ proposes a new solution of the problem $x$ arising out of $a$',
'$S$ criticizes his latest solution of the problem $x$'.

This list could be extended at some length. It is miles removed in character from '$S$ knows $a$' or '$S$ believes $a$' or even '$S$ mistakenly believes $a$' or '$S$ doubts $a$'." Certainly; the miles of removal, however, afford no ground for thinking that they cannot be successfully traversed. Epistemic logic is in its infancy and only very simple forms have yet been studied in any detail.

Attention has been called elsewhere and above, to such forms as '$S$ accepts $a$', '$S$ cognitively prefers $a$ to $b$', '$S$ utters $a$', '$S$ asserts $a$', '$S$ apprehends $a$', '$S$ rejects $a$', '$S$ tests $a$, '$S$ asks $a$', '$S$ commands $a$', and so on.[2] If these are added to the forms of epistemic logic, the step from them to the forms suggested by Popper seems not very great. To become really clear about any of these forms, however, is a difficult business. Just what properties is each supposed to have? Some are surely definable in terms of others. Just how? What are the fundamental ones in terms of which the others may all be defined? Only in terms of such forms and with suitable answers to these questions, it is thought, may the pragmatics of scientific procedure, method, discovery, and the like, be systematically studied with any precision.

Popper's list, it might be thought, is concerned too much with trying, proposing, and the like. Sometimes the scientist really does succeed, to some extent anyhow, in doing the things he tries. He may really think up alternatives to $a$. He may succeed in devising an experimental test for $a$. He may actually show that $a$ is derivable or not from $b$. And so on. The forms concerning what the scientist really does are perhaps more useful than those concerned merely with what he tries to do. Even so, Popper's forms need not be rejected, and some of them might well take their rightful place in a complete list of the forms needed.

Important inmates of the third world, it is claimed, are theoretical systems, problems, problem situations, critical arguments, states of a discussion, states of a critical argument, and so on. Popper thinks that one cannot relegate all these entities to the second world of mental states, dispositions, and the like. He thinks that the third world is independent of the second. He does not claim, however, that

---

[2] See especially *Logic, Language, and Metaphysics,* Chapter I.

it is independent of the first. In fact, the "objective" character of the objects of the third world can perhaps best be accommodated in terms of linguistic objects regarded as items in the first world together with certain relations that human persons bear to them.

Let us regard the items in the third world as actual sign events or inscriptions in the physical cosmos. A well-developed syntax and semantics is at hand for sign events that will be of use here.[3] It is especially important that semantical truth predicates be available, essentially as in III. Sign events of certain kinds may be said to be true; others false. It is curious that Popper frequently mentions the Tarski truth concept approvingly, but makes nothing of the painstaking methods and notions whereby and wherewith it was arrived at — structural-descriptive names of expressions, concatenation, syntax generally, the semantical relation of satisfaction, and so on, perhaps even designation and denotation.

Let us note that Popper's standard arguments for the independent existence of the third world relative to the second do not establish its independence of the first. We are asked to imagine the situation (pp. 334-335) wherein "all our machines and tools are destroyed, all our subjective learning, including our subjective knowledge of machines and tools, and how to use them. But *libraries and our capacity to learn from them* survive. Clearly, after much suffering, our world may get going again." Next, imagine that "*all libraries are destroyed also,* so that our capacity to learn from books becomes useless." In this second case, "there will be no re-emergence of our civilization for many millenia." Even so, of course, the physical environment, human beings, and many artifacts remain to help man get started again. Popper does not seem to take memory into account here, and his second argument seems to require that at the moment of destruction a total amnesia sets in. Otherwise, even though all machines and tools are destroyed, all subjective learning and so on, still the memory of our experiences remains. We may remember what a wheel is like, for example, even if all wheels are destroyed. Further, even if all memory is taken away, still the

[3] See *Truth and Denotation,* Chapters XI and XII, or II and III above.

presence of some artifacts in the human enivronment would help clever people decide what to do with them. Popper perhaps underestimates human ingenuity here and man's capacity to learn and discover independent of what is contained in libraries.

Even with all this universal destruction, however, the third world remains *in toto*. Language remains in the form of inscriptions or sign events in space-time, irrespective of whether they are ever exhibited, seen, or heard. Also human beings survive and stand in certain pragmatic relations to items of language, such as acceptance, critical preference, trying to understand, trying to think of alternatives, and so on. Even if a person does not know the language, he still may be regarded as standing in certain relations to linguistic expressions. It is *we* who might say this of him, not he. A mouse's fear of a cat may be described as his fearing true a certain English sentence even though he knows no English.[4]

More important than all this, however, is that *truth* survives. A given sign event of appropriate shape is true or false quite irrespective of a man's subjective learning, machines, tools, memory, and libraries. Truth here, note, is taken as adjectival of inscriptions or sign events, and these in turn are regarded as physical objects or processes or states in the first world. *Truth, however,* it is thought, *is the foremost denizen of the third world.* Thus truth vanishes only with the supposition of the total destruction of the first world itself.

Popper need not disagree with any of these contentions. He seems not to note here, however, how central the notion of truth is for the delineation of the world of "objective spirit," including scientific knowledge. Also it is essential to his view concerning the logic of discovery — for without truth there is presumably nothing to discover. Men might invent or create various artifacts, but not truth. Truth is there to be discovered, not to be invented or created.

Popper berates traditional "subjectivist" epistemology for its lack of interest in the theory of objective scientific knowledge. "*Knowledge or thought in an objective sense*" consists (p. 335) of problems, theories, and arguments as such. Knowledge in this objective sense is

---

[4] This example is Quine's in *Word and Object*.

totally independent of anybody's claim to know; . . . . Knowledge in the objective sense is *knowledge without a* knower; it is *knowledge without a knowing subject.*" Problems, theories, and arguments, in the objective sense, are always concerned with *truth.* A problem can always be regarded as a problem as to whether such and such a sentence or statement is true. A theory is a set of closely interrelated statements that purport to be true. An argument, in the objective sense, is a sequence of statements purporting to establish or to help establish that a given statement is true. Traditional epistemology has no doubt been hampered in lacking the clear-cut, semantical notion of truth, and even up to the moment few epistemologists seem to take sufficient note of it.

It is most important to distinguish between 'true' and 'known to be true' or 'taken to be true', and so on, as Popper in effect urges. Failure to make this distinction, and other related ones, has resulted in putting forward many illicit surrogates for truth.

Popper thinks that the semantic notion of truth "is a simple elucidation of the idea of *correspondence with the fact.*"[5] The point is somewhat more controversial than he admits, however. He first decides "explicitly to take 'truth' as a synonym for 'correspondence with the facts' and then *proceed to define the idea of 'correspondence with the facts'.*" All one would get out of such a procedure, however, is a definition of the complex phrase 'correspondence-with-the-facts' as an indivisible phrase. One gets no elucidation concerning correspondence with such and such a fact, more specifically, with fact $f_1$, fact $f_2$, and so on. An adequate definition of 'correspondence', in the sense of the traditional correspondence theory, would seem to require a definition of '$a$ corresponds with $f$', for variable '$a$' and *variable* '$f$'. There is no difficulty about the expressional variable '$a$'. The difficulty is to know what kind of "objects" facts are for the variable '$f$' to range over. Also there are the difficulties concerning the existence of negative, conjunctive, disjunctive, implicational, and general facts.

[5] See K. R. Popper, *Conjectures and Refutations* (Routledge and Kegan Paul, London: 1963), p. 224.

# EVENTS, REFERENCE, AND LOGICAL FORM

Popper notes that

> The statement, or the assertion, 'Snow is white' corresponds to the facts if, and only if, snow is, indeed, white.

This is in effect an instance of the Tarski "paradigm" of adequacy for any truth definition. In Popper's formulation, it concerns only 'corresponds to the facts' as an indivisible linguistic phrase. Note that Popper does *not* contend, and indeed quite properly so, that

> The statement 'Snow is white' corresponds to the fact that snow is white,

nor does he regard this as an instance of some paradigm for any definition of 'corresponds'.

Popper speaks of the semantic notion of truth as the "objective" or "absolute" notion. Strictly, however, the "absolute" notion is something quite different, as noted above and in "Truth and Its Illicit Surrogates."

Popper thinks that the view that the semantic notion of truth (*C. & R.*, pp. 223-224) "is applicable only to formalized languages is . . . mistaken. It is applicable to any consistent and — more or less — 'natural' language. So we must try to learn from Tarski's analysis how to dodge its inconsistencies; which means, admittedly, the introduction of a certain amount of 'artificiality' — or caution — in its use." To dodge inconsistencies is easier said than done, however, and as soon as a certain amount of artificiality is introduced, one is of course well on the way to a formalization. Structural linguists who take the truth concept seriously seem to have had considerable difficulty on this point. (Recall VII above.)

For truth to play the role in objective knowledge that it does in Popper's view, some degree of formalization of the object language must thus, it would seem, be presupposed. This object language furthermore must be a very broad, inclusive one in which all scientific knowledge may presumably be expressed. It need not be required that such a language system be available in full detail; its main features must be given, however, so that a full formalization could be given if desired. It is not clear from Popper's writings just what this system would consist of. One can speak of "science as an axiomatized deductive system" only rather loosely, and much more needs to be said concerning its exact structure. As a matter of historical fact, only a very few axiomatized deductive systems have been formulated for specific empirical sciences, and of these still fewer — if any — in adequate fashion. None, however, it would seem, has heretofore been formulated sufficiently comprehensive to contain all of science. The view here is of course that it is in event logic that one finds a "non-conventional," natural kind of language system of very great expressive power of the kind essential for Popper's discussion of objective knowledge and the third world.

It is contended that "the method of constructing artificial model languages is incapable of tackling the problems of the growth of our knowledge; and it is even less able to do so than the method of analysing ordinary languages, simply because these model languages are poorer than ordinary languages. It is a result of their poverty that they yield only the most crude and the most misleading model of the growth of knowledge—the model of an accumulating heap of observation statements."[6] On the contrary, the view here is that it is only within a model language, or rather metalanguage, that "the problem" of the growth of knowledge can even be formulated. Further, only in model metalanguages do we find clear-cut logical forms, such as those in Popper's list above. And thirdly, there is no intrinsic link between model languages and the accumulation of heaps of observation statements. The use of model languages is by no means the exclusive privilege of the logical positivists. Their use is quite as appropriate for the study of growth, change, development, and so on, as for any other subject matter.

Popper frequently (for example, in *C. & R.*, p. 246) introduces a "table" of "ideas" with 'Designations of Terms or Concepts', 'Words', 'Meaningful', 'Meaning', 'Definitions', and 'Undefined Concepts' in a left column, and 'Statements or Propositions or Theories',

---

[6] K. R. Popper, *The Logic of Scientific Discovery* (Hutchinson, London: 1959), p. 21.

# EVENTS, REFERENCE, AND LOGICAL FORM

'Assertions', 'True', 'Truth', 'Derivations', and 'Primitive Propositions', respectively, on the right. He contends that "the left side of this table is unimportant" and that "what should interest us are theories, truth, argument." Of course theories and truth should interest us, but so also should the items out of which they are composed. If truth interests us, then surely the semantic definition of it, so extolled by Popper, should also. But this definition, more particularly, in its definiens, makes fundamental reference to the terms, words, formulae, sentences, and primitive notions of the object language. Further, the terms, words, formulae, sentences, definitions, and primitive notions of the metalanguage in which the definition of 'true' is given are obviously of "importance" for the formulation of the definition. In short, the items of the right column presuppose, or require for their analysis, the items of the left column. If the items in the right column interest us, the ones in the left surely should also.

Frege's *thoughts* are *par excellence,* according to Popper, members of the third world. But these, it is contended here, may be handled as objects taken in intension or under given modes of linguistic description, within event logic.[7]

The third world is "autonomous, even though we constantly act upon it and are acted upon by it," in the sense in which language itself is autonomous. Language is a human product in the sense that human beings use certain physical sign events for certain purposes, but also "it creates, in its turn, as do other animal products, its own *domain of autonomy*."

Popper's schema

(P)                    $'P_1 \rightarrow TT \rightarrow EE \rightarrow P_2'$

contains the germ of the "logic of discovery." In order to solve a *problem* $P_1$, a *tentative theory TT* is constructed, then subjected to *error elimination EE,* which in turn may give rise to a *new problem* $P_2$, and so on. Whatever the merits of this schema, the question arises

---

[7] Recall I above and *Logic, Language, and Metaphysics,* Chapter II.

as to how it may be accommodated within a unified theory such as that provided by event logic. A problem $P_1$ may be regarded as a *question* as to whether a given sentence is true. The scientist $S$ asks himself whether $a$ holds or not. He then formulates a set of sentences $\Gamma$ either including $a$ or having $a$ as a logical consequence. $\Gamma$ itself is merely tentative. (It may perhaps best be regarded merely as hypothetical in essentially the sense in which the Axiom of Infinity and the Multiplicative Axiom were in *Principia Mathematica,* as we shall see.) Some undesirable consequences may ensue, some consequences that do not accord with the results of experimental test, and so on. Another problem $P_2$ then arises as to which is or are the undesirable members of $\Gamma$, how it or they can be improved, tested, and so on. The vocabulary of event logic is sufficiently extensive to enable us to express here whatever is needed.

Popper's view that all science and philosophy are really cosmology has its echo in the metaphysical character of event logic. In fact, the latter is a kind of cosmological metaphysics or "speculative philosophy" in essentially Whitehead's sense. The axioms of event logic, however, are not strictly statements of science, as we shall see. What role do scientific theories play within such a metaphysical scheme?

Let $\Gamma_1$ be a thoery of some science. This may be handled as a set of sentences of event logic closed with respect to logical consequence. Or instead the theory may be regarded as merely a set of sentences taken as axioms. The axioms determine the theory uniquely. It would not be appropriate to regard them as metaphysical axioms, and hence we would not wish to add them outright. Russell's device of taking them as hypotheses, already mentioned above, is useful here. Let $\Gamma_1$ contain only a finite number of sentences and let '$\gamma_1$' abbreviate their conjunction. Then

$$'\gamma_1 \supset \text{-----}'$$

is appropriately significant. Popper's schema (T) may then be sharpened little as follows. $S$ may *tentatively accept* $\gamma_1$ as a result of having asked some problem $P_1$. He then may question some constituent of $\gamma_1$ or submit it to empirical *test*. He may try some alternative to some constituent of $\gamma_1$. Various problems may arise here, in answer to which he formulates a $\Gamma_2$. And so on.

Popper's "model" for the growth of science is then a sequence of theories $\Gamma_1$, $\Gamma_2$, and so on, each with greater "verisimilitude" than its precedessor. For this model to be significant, as already suggested, a total language in which $\Gamma_1$, $\Gamma_2$, and so on, may all be expressed must be available—a total language for unified science. And for this language the truth concept must be available, as well as a precise notion of verisimilitude. (Note that only a *comparative* notion of verisimilitude is needed, not a quantitative one. One need not speak here of the *degree* of verisimilitude, but only of the verisimilitude of one theory as *greater* than that of another.)

The question now arises as to just how the schema (P) or some refined version of it, is to be understood. Is it intended as a description of how scientists sometimes proceed? Or always? Is it supposed to be taken as in some sense prescriptive? Is it supposed to contain explicit rules of scientific procedure? Or merely rules of thumb? Above all, what kind of a "logic" is the logic of discovery? What is its vocabulary? What are its axioms and rules of inference? How are they related to principles of induction and probability? To answer these questions adequately would be difficult indeed. We are just at the stage here of some problems without a tentative theory in terms of which they could be handled. In constructing a tenative theory there are first syntactical problems to be faced in its formulation, and then semantical ones. The basic sentential forms of a tentative theory here could perhaps be taken as some of the logical forms suggested above. Each of these, however, requires a careful looking at and semantical characterization. Enormous difficulties are here to be faced. Until a tentative theory is formulated, however, one cannot reasonably claim that the logic of the growth of science has as yet grown very much.

Sufficient unto the philosophy of science are the difficulties thereof. The task of the philosophic logician is rather different from that of the philosopher of science. That of the former is to provide a suitable vocabulary; that of the latter, to use it wisely for his purposes. The logician provides the mathematician with suitable linguistic tools but he does not therewith do mathematics. So the logician of the philosophy of science need not quā logician do philosophy of science. It is enough that he merely clears the way by providing a suitable vocabulary and linguistic format.

Space does not permit considering some of Popper's intriguing and valuable comments concerning such topics as mathematical intuitionism, the connection between evolution and scientific growth, and the logic of the *Geisteswissenschaften*. Under this latter are included foundational studies concerned with the human being's use of language, his reactions to language, his actions and behavior (especially in connection with his reactions to and use of language), and such more special topics as concern his mental, volitional, valuational, and social activities. Much recent work in analytical philosophy has been devoted to these topics. The discussions, however, have tended to be piecemeal and fragmental, with no secure logical underpinning or basic of the kind provided by systematic pragmatics and event logic.

Not all work in the logic of the humanities need concern itself directly with human beings, in the sense of having them as values for variables. Theories concerning particular topics in the arts, for example, can often profitably abstract from specific reference to or mention of the human being. Thus in music theory, having to do with pitch-classes and their chordal and temporal interconnections, no mention of the human being need enter explicitly.[8] And similarly no doubt for other areas in aesthetics and the theory of the arts. The interesting fact is that when we move into areas where human beings do figure fundamentally — and it is such areas after all that are covered by the term 'pragmatics' — the same logical underpinning is applicable, but now with human beings explicitly admitted as values for variables.

Research in the *Geisteswissenschaften* on the basis of a unified pragmatics and event logic should contribute greatly to our under-

[8] See the author's "On the Prototheory of Musical Structure," *Perspectives of New Music* 9 (1970): 68-73.

standing of the nature and interrelations of the humanistic disciplines. For one thing, their foundations can be explored more deeply than heretofore seems to have been possible, as already noted. Secondly, they are all seen to be branches of the same tree, growing out in various directions from a common trunk. Methodologically also, they are seen to constitute a unified whole. It will not do to claim that methods applicable to or in one are inapplicable to or in another, although of course the form these methods take may vary considerably from one to another. We are all making inferences in our daily speech and writing. The particular forms, usually highly elliptical, that these inferences take in humanistic research, seem never to have been explored very deeply.

Logic is one of the great building forces of our modern world and civilization. It "meddles with all subjects," in Peirce's phrase, and justifiably so, unifying them and giving them shape, consistency, and coherence. Without it all rationality would crumble. Now that the subject has developed so tremendously, its applicability to areas heretofore thought intransigent to its methods should be explored.

# XII

# SOME REMARKS ON
# THE LANGUAGE OF
# MATHEMATICAL INTUITIONISM

*"Solvitur ambulando."*

In his "Some Remarks on Intuitionism,"[1] Heyting urges the distinction between what he calls 'theories of the constructible' and 'constructive theories'. "In a theory of the constructible," he writes (p. 69), "a certain class of mathematical objects is defined as that of constructible objects. Three points are essential here: (i) a mathematical theory is presupposed in which the class of constructible objects can be defined; (ii) the notion of constructibility is a defined notion, not a primitive notion; (iii) there is some liberty in the choice of a definition of the constructible, provided only it corresponds sufficiently to our intuitive notion of a mathematical construction." By 'a constructive theory', on the other hand, Heyting means "a theory in which an object is only considered as existing after it has been constructed. In other words, in a constructive theory there can be no mentioning of other than constructible objects ... In [a] ... constructive theory there can be no reference to a preceding mathematical system; it must, by its nature, be self-contained. The

[1]*Constructivity in Mathematics,* ed. A. Heyting (North-Holland Publishing Co., Amsterdam: 1959), pp. 69-71.

notion of a constructible object must be a primitive notion in this sense that it must be clear what it means that a given operation is the construction of a certain object ... Also there can be nothing arbitrary in the notion of a constructible object." Thus for a constructive theory, the requirements (i), (ii), and (iii) for a theory of the constructible are explicitly denied.

Heyting goes on to note (p. 70) that "though mathematical constructions are originally mental operations, symbolization is necessary to a certain extent, for practical reasons. However, in a constructive theory the symbolic language will be considered to express mathematical constructions, so that every formula will admit an immediate and unique interpretation. For instance [the crucial one], the interpretation of the existential quantifier will be determined by the exigency of constructivity. A formula of the form $(Ex)A(x)$ can have no other meaning than: A mathematical object $x$ satisfying the condition $A(x)$ has been constructed." Finally, Heyting comments that "it is sometimes clarifying to formalize a chapter of constructive mathematics, but it is never necessary. Formalization is not an essential feature of constructive mathematics . . ."

A few comments are in order. Strictly, as soon as we move beyond mathematics, there is a very considerable difference between constructing an object and the notion of its existence. Existence may be presumed to be accommodated by the existential quantifier quite irrespective of the results of human acts. That the sun exists is not the result of any construction. For a human being to construct an object is for him to perform a human act. To accommodate such acts variables over human beings must presumably be available. This at once leads into pragmatics. Existence is a logico-semantical notion, whereas construction is a pragmatical one. A "constructive theory" for Heyting is then one in which every object covered by the existential quantifier is a constructed one.

Let '$p$ Constr $x$' express that person $p$ constructs object $x$ in some suitable way. Then

'Constr $x$'   may abbreviate   '$(Ep)p$ Constr $x$',

and may read '$x$ is a constructed object'. Heyting's requirement for the existential quantifier may be expressed by requiring that it be interpreted as 'there exists a constructed object such that'. More particularly, where '$(Ex)$' is the usual quantifier,

'$(Ex)$ $_cGx$' may for the moment abbreviate '$(Ex)(\text{Constr } x$ $\cdot$ $Gx)$',

where the subscript 'c' in the definiendum reminds us that the quantifier there is for constructed entities only.

The formula '$p \text{ Constr } x$' here may be construed howsoever one wishes, in many alternative ways. If we remain within a mathematical context, the requirement is only (recall (iii)) that it expresses "sufficiently . . . our intuitive notion of a mathematical construction." Of course there are many intuitive notions of a mathematical construction, and every one is free to choose his favorite, provided only that he makes sufficiently clear what it is. No matter whether 'Constr' is taken as a primitive or defined, the form '$p \text{ Constr } x$' is embedded within a "mathematical theory" in which the constructible objects may be discussed.

In view of these considerations it would seem that Heyting's requirement concerning the existential quantifier — that '$(Ex)A(x)$' "can have no other meaning than: A mathematical object $x$ satisfying the condition $A(x)$ has been constructed" — can be stated *only within a pragmatical metalanguage incorporating a theory of the constructible.* The very phrases 'has been constructed', 'satisfying', and 'condition' are metalinguistic phrases. A theory of the constructible is thus needed metalinguistically in order to formalize a constructive theory. In the language there may be some (non-linguistic) objects admitted other than the constructed ones, but not necessarily. It might obtain there that

$$(x)\text{Constr } x$$

and

$$(Ex)Gx \supset (Ex)_c\, Gx,$$

in which case the constructive theory becomes merely a part of a theory of the constructible. In any case, it seems that a theory of the constructible is the more fundamental, being incorporated within the pragmatical metalanguage within which the constructive theory is formulated or "interpreted."

Heyting thinks it is 'something clarifying to formalize a chapter of constructive mathematics (p. 70), but it is never necessary." Strictly of course it is never necessary to formalize any portion of mathematics at all, constructive or otherwise, nor indeed any branch of science, nor any theory at all. To do so, however, is to help make our ideas clear, to help make them consistent, to show explicitly how they are interrelated, to enunciate what is assumed, and so on. Particularly where our ideas are somewhat obscure, formalization of them is often helpful. Our notions of the mathematically constructible are notoriously sticky and a considerable formalization of them is no doubt needed for even a minimal clarity.

In getting at mathematical constructions, we must of course start out with some primitives and with some values for variables. These latter may be taken *ad hoc* as the very constructed objects we wish, as already noted, or they may be taken in a wider sense as comprising entities in some sense already available. Here mathematicians and philosophers will divide, the former taking only mathematical objects *sensu stricto,* the latter something else in addition or perhaps something altogether different. One good candidate here would be linguistic expressions (sign designs or sign events), which provide a useful way of getting at arithmetical objects within a general theory of counting.[2] As to the primitives, there is of course always enormous choice. One usually has a pretty clear set of logical primitives if in general one sticks to the standard truth-functional connectives and quantifiers, with the addition cf such non-logical primitive predicates as are needed for the desired domain of theory.

Arithmetic as based on the pragmatics of counting is a

[2] As evidenced in IV above.

nominalistically oriented theory, with sign events and other "concrete" objects as the only values for its variables, and formalized upon the basis of a first-order logic only. The *tertium non datur* therefore holds, as well as both principles of double negation. Likewise the quantification theory is of the classical kind, with none of the restrictions upon its laws of the kinds that occur in intuitionistic logics. The resulting system is thus perhaps not an intuitionist system in any strict sense, although a kind of "theory of the constructible" can be formulated within it.

In his "On Various Degrees of Constructivism"[3], Mostowski explicitly identifies nominalist with constructivist systems. "The constructivist trends in the foundations of mathematics are nearer to the nominalistic philosophy [than to the "idealistic (in the platonic sense of the word)"]," he writes (p. 178); "I would even venture to say that they represent the nominalistic trend in the foundations of mathematics." Systems built in accord with nominalism, however, need not be intuitionistic in the sense of presupposing an intuitionistic logic. Rather they may, and perhaps in some sense *should,* be formulated wholly on the basis of a first-order logic. Perhaps intuitionist systems should also be so formulated — a point to be urged in a moment.

Mostowski makes several further comments relevant to these considerations. "One should not think that the constructivistic [or nominalistic] arithmetic of integers allows us to get rid altogether of the abstract notions of sets and functions," he writes (p. 179) "We are forced to reintroduce them as soon as we come to a description of the process of counting. Indeed, counting consists in establishing a one-one relation between the counted objects and numbers. If the counted objects are symbols themselves, we can express the relation between them and the numbers again by means of certain symbols without departing from the nominalistic attitude; this is the approach described by Lorenzen.[4] No such device is possible if we want to count non-linguistic objects. For this reason it seems to me that even the constructivists must admit the existence of some

---

[3] In *Constructivity in Mathematics,* pp. 178-194
[4] In his *Einführung in die Operative Logik und Mathematik* (1955).

abstract entities if not in pure mathematics, then necessarily in the description of procedures of applied mathematics. I shall not dwell upon this subject as it does not seem a very important one and lies outside the topics [degrees of constructivism in mathematics] we are concerned with."

The subject may not be important for mathematics, but it is of course crucial for the philosophy of mathematics. And unfortunately, most of the statements in the paragraph cited are erroneous. We are by no means "forced" to reintroduce abstract notions of sets and functions when we return to a description of the process of counting. The use of the primitive form '$p$ Crrlt $a,x,F$' of IV above, with suitable axioms upon it and employing some notions from the calculus of individuals, enables us to do this without sets and functions as values for variables. Mostowski thinks that "counting consists in establishing a one-one-relation between the counted objects and numbers." According to the theory here, one does not *establish* a one-one relation, one rather *exemplifies* the relation Crrlt, and the counters are not numbers but arbitrary marks of some kind, which can be concatenated with each other. Numbers emerge only in contexts in which it is said that such correlation takes place. Nor is Crrlt in any even remote sense one-one, as noted. Moreover, Lorenzen does not confine himself merely to counting as between numbers as symbols and other linguistic objects, nor is there any such confinement in the treatment of the paper above. All manner of non-linguistic objects may be counted as well. Thus Mostowski is by no means justified (p. 179) in thinking that "even the constructivists must admit the existence of some abstract entities" either in pure mathematics or in "the description of procedures of applied mathematics."

Constructivism and intuitionism, howsoever formulated, look to epistemology for suitable foundations. Almost all writers on the subject are more or less in agreement on this. One will look far and wide, however, for a sophisticated discussion of the epistemological issues involved or for a clear delineation of the kind of epistemology needed. In fact, none seems ever to have been given. The following comments are aimed to provide some first steps in this direction.

212

# LANGUAGE OF MATHEMATICAL INTUITIONISM

The most suitable approach to epistemology no doubt is via pragmatics, as seems now almost universally agreed upon. If one sticks to a first-order basic logic without increasing the values for variables, a good way of proceeding is to introduce as needed suitable predicates for relations between human users and the objects of their knowledge and activity. 'Crrlt' is such a predicate.

It is interesting that certain pragmatical predicates have in recent years crept into the formal literature on intuitionism almost unawares. In his "Informal Rigour and Completeness Proofs",[5] for example, Kreisel explicitly introduces the form

$$\text{(K)} \qquad\qquad `\Sigma \vdash_m A\text{'}$$

to express that the "creative subject" $\Sigma$ has evidence at stage $m$ of his procedure to assert $A$. The form (K) is taken as primitive and certain axioms concerning it are given. Other writers have used similar forms. At best, however, these forms seem rather *ad hoc* and not very clear. The "creative subject" is the human user of language — all well and good. But what is a stage of his research? How is one demarcated from another? Can two "stages" be combined to form a complex stage? In any case, stages are taken as values for the variable '$m$' and the ontology of the language of intuitionism is accordingly increased with the admission of a rather obscure kind of object.

Perhaps, however, stages can be regarded as certain events in the life histories of the creative subjects. If so, event logic may be used and a constructed object becomes one for which there is an event or act of someone's constructing it. Thus

'Constr $x$' would now abbreviate '(E$e$) (E$p$) $\langle p,\text{Constr},x \rangle e$',

where '$\langle p,\text{Constr},x \rangle$' is a predicate form of event logic. The succession of stages may then he handled in terms of the temporal order of events.

[5] In *Problems in the Philosophy of Mathematics,* ed. by I. Lakatos (North-Holland Publishing Co., Amsterdam: 1967), pp. 138-186. See also relevant papers by B. van Rootselaar, A.S. Troelstra, D. van Dalen and J. Myhill.

# EVENTS, REFERENCE, AND LOGICAL FORM

Now what about the evidence? Only *good* or *adequate* evidence is relevant. A natural variant of (K) would thus be one in which an evidential variable is admitted also. Thus

(K′)                           '$\Sigma \vdash^e_m A$'

is perhaps a more explicit form, expressing that the creative subject $\Sigma$ has at stage $m$ good or adequate evidence $e$ for asserting $A$. Once (K′) is admitted, the problem as to just what good evidence is arises as a matter of course. How good must it be? And do we mean here *inductive* evidence of the kind studied in the theory of confirmation? If so, intuitionism becomes complicated with inductive logic at its very roots, a complication presumably not to be wished.

If forms such as (K) or (K′) seem too complicated, what is to take their place? The problem becomes especially acute if one wishes the intuitionistic logical connective '$\multimap$' itself to be definable rather than primitive. In fact an ideal language for intuitionism would be such as to have all its intuitionist *content,* so to speak, packed into the special predicates such as 'Constr', and so on. There should then be no need of any special connectives or quantifiers other than the usual ones. Once the special predicates are suitably axiomatized, whatever one wishes to assert intuitionistically should then be forthcoming upon the basis of first-order logic. Whether such an ideal can be achieved or not, whether such a language can be adequately formulated or not, remains yet to be determined. In any case, it seems, only such formulations of either intuitionist or constructivist mathematical theories could be regarded as acceptable nominalistically.

Let '$p$ Prv $a$' express that person $p$ constructs an intuitionatistically acceptable *proof* of formula $a$. Some such form should presumably be definable within syntax. If it is not, let it be taken as a primitive and axiomatized. Perhaps '$p$ Prv $a$' could then be made to do the work of (K) or (K′). 'Crrlt and 'Prv' seem reasonable notions, of a nominalistically acceptable kind, in terms of which a good deal anyhow of intuitionism should be expressible. Stages of procedure are then events of proof, correlations, and the like.

214

'$\langle p, \mathrm{Prv}, a \rangle e$' expresses that $e$ is an event or act of $p$'s proving $a$.

The language of intuitionism is a language, and its symbols (sign events) must obey the usual laws of inscriptional syntax. There seems to be no way to avoid this situation at all, even if one should wish to. Thus an operation of concatenation is needed as well as structural-descriptive predicates for the basic symbols of the language. Further, the language of intuitionism is a part of the wider language of science. Intuitionist mathematics is not a subject apart, but must base itself upon a well-grounded epistemology, which in turn will be but a fragment of a wider philosophical system. Perhaps some form of intuitionism provides *the* one acceptable way of doing mathematics, as many are convinced. To substantiate such a claim we must become much clearer about its language, and as to how this language is grounded in systematic pragmatics, than we have been heretofore.

# XIII

# SOME STRICTURES OF
# THREE SELLARSIAN THEMES

*"Sine pennis volare haud facile est."*

"The most difficult portion of any inquiry is its initiation," Northrop noted at the beginning of his *The Logic of the Sciences and the Humanities.*[1] "One may have the most rigorous of methods during the latter stages of investigation, but if a false or superficial beginning has been made, rigor later on will never retrieve the situation. It is like a ship leaving port for a distant destination. A very slight erroneous deviation in taking one's bearings at the beginning may result in entirely missing one's mark at the end regardless of the sturdiness of one's craft or the excellence of one's seamanship." It is for this reason that a secure logic, not only in the sense of a theory of valid inference but in the sense of a sound set of unit or root ideas or notions given coherent form with their interrelations explicitly characterized, is indispensable in discussing general methodological and philosophical problems, and nowaday in particular, those in the theory of reference (semantics) and metaphysics as well.

Modern logic and the new metaphysics in fact have become integrally interrelated in this age of sophisticated methodologies and of concern with the deep structure of natural language. Current

---

[1] (The Macmillan Co., New York: 1947), p. 1.

formulations of metaphysical views may be based on propositions (Fitch), on states of affairs (Chisholm), on physical objects (Quine), on qualia (Goodman), or on events, and so on. To be "based on" one particular kind of object is not necessarily to exclude other kinds, nor is it to exclude abstract objects such as classes and relations. In any case, all of these views presuppose, or contain in some fashion, a more or less explicit logic as an integral part. Gone are the days, it would seem, when a metaphysical view can be formulated in disregard of the niceties of modern logical theory including syntax and semantics.

Sellars' work raises interesting problems concerning metaphysics and its logical underpinning, a few of which will be examined in this paper.

The phrase 'values for variables' has been bandied about a good deal in the recent literature, but usually it seems for the wrong reasons. The values for the variables of a theory, of whatever kind, are precisely the objects or entities taken as fundamental or basic in that theory. Other kinds of entities may then be introduced as constructs in terms of the basic ones. Here is the whole point of having variables at all. The values for them are the fundamental individuals "about" which the theory deals. If we have no values for variables, we simply have no theory all.[2] We are thus legitimized in asking Sellars at every stage what the values for his variables are, what predicates are applicable to them, and finally, what precisely is assumed by way of characterizing those predicates. Sellars is much too acute a thinker not to wish these questions asked, and not to be willing in principle to try to provide adequate answers to them.

Sellars by-passes "technical semantics of the Tarski-Carnap variety, because of its original orientation towards the foundations of mathematics . . ." and its concentration on "extensions rather than intensions, on classes rather than properties, on truth values rather than propositions, and on truth-functional connectives rather than

---

[2] Cf. the discussion in *Belief, Existence, and Meaning.* See also Quine's "Variables Explained Away," in his *Selected Logic Papers* (Random House, New York : 1966), for an alternative.

218

modal predicates."[3] Instead of pressing extensional semantics for its fruits, however, Sellars contends that "extensions are limiting cases of intensions and cannot be understood apart from them. Thus, classes in the logistic sense cannot be understood apart from properties, nor truth apart from propositions." Whatever play is allowed here upon 'understood', however, one can surely understand "apart from" intensions the Zermelo set theory, say, or a class theory based on the simple theory of types, neither of which contains intensions. Likewise one can "understand" some well-formed axiom system for arithmetic quite apart from any talk concerning propositions. Surely mathematicians "understand" mathematics, and physicists physics, quite apart from all talk of intensions.

Even so, one may agree with Sellars that intensions are surely needed. He thinks these cannot be provided by the "Tarski-Carnap variety" of semantics. There are other closely related varieties, however — the garden of semantics has become a lush one — that do the trick, even in the kind of way that Sellars condones, as we shall see in a moment.

Part of Sellars' argument on this point seems to be the contention that the Tarski-Carnap semantics cannot handle sentences such as

(1)                    ' 'Not' stands for negation.'

" 'Not' has a sense in a sense of 'sense' to which intensions belong," Sellars claims (p. 95), and "if we can get clear about 'not' and negation we will have the key to the status of senses generally . . ." Let us examine Sellars' way of introducing intensions, and then try to be as clear as we possibly can about 'negation' and 'not'.

The first item to note is Sellars' use of dot quotes. "To be a 'not' in our language," he says (p. 96), "an item need not have the visual shape illustrated between the quotes. It can have an auditory shape, or, even, a different visual shape. This permissiveness, however, is

---

[3] See Wilfrid Sellars, *Science and Metaphysics,* the John Locke Lectures for 1965-6, Nos. 3 and 4 (MSS., p. 93).

compensated for by the requirement that to be a 'not' in this permissive sense, a linguistic design must function with other designs in a way which parallels the functioning of 'not's in our language. Let us use dot quotes to embody quotation thus construed." The difficulty with dot quotes, however, seems to be that they are too permissive and that clearcut rules governing them have never been given. Just what is involved when we say that a word in a language "parallels the functioning of" a word in a language (perhaps the same or a different one)? The notion of being a translation of, or perhaps of being a paraphrase of, seems needed to make Sellars' explanation clear, but these in turn are very difficult notions indeed, posing all kinds of problems of their own. Before we can accept Sellars' use of dots, a good deal of spade work must be done. If one spares the spade work with permissiveness, the child is spoiled and no helpfully explanatory doctrine emerges.

Sellars does not tell us precisely how 'stands for' is to be construed in (1) other than that it is not a surrogate for 'designates' or 'denotes' or whatever. This is like saying that however 'cardinal number' is construed, it is not to be as 'set of sets in one-to-one correspondence with a given set' but rather as something else *on ne sait quoi.* Perhaps 'stands for' is to be construed merely as ordinary English, in which case Sellars might well appeal to a characterization of the deep structures of sentences containing this phrase. It seems very unlikely, however, that by such appeal he would ever arrive at a Fregean intension. There is not a shred of evidence, at the present stage of research anyhow, that such an entity would ever be found.

Intensionality for Sellars is accommodated by means of dot quotation and in the use of 'stands for' or 'means' or the like. The latter are not to be taken as phrases for undefined semantical relations, however. In effect Sellars proposes a *definition* of these phrases in terms of dot quotation. Thus, he contends that

(2)  "·Himmel· (in German) means sky

has the sense of

(3)  ·Himmel·s (in German) are ·sky·s

or, in PMese

(4)  ·Himmel·s (in German) ⊂ ·sky·."[4]

This one quotation is picked out more or less at random and articulates a point made several times; it may be taken as as good a statement of the doctrine as any. Let us attempt a kind of "rational reconstruction" of it as follows.

We must carry out this reconstruction in a metalanguage of great breadth, perhaps even in terms of a universal metalanguage containing variables over the object language. The formulation of such a metalanguage would raise considerable difficulties of its own. Instead let us restrict attention, as Sellars does in effect, to just a handful of languages, including German and English. Within the comparative metalanguage of this handful of languages, we could presumably define the dot quotes by enumeration. Thus perhaps

(5)  '·sky·' may be regarded as short for '$\hat{a}(a$ = 'sky' v $a$ = 'der Himmel' v ····)'.

Here single quotes are used in the customary sense of forming sign designs rather than sign events. This definition is given within the comparative metalanguage, and hence the outer single quotes are quotes within the metametalanguage. The inner single quotes occurring in the definiens are special signs of the metalanguage itself and take the place of introducing structural descriptive names.

This definition is significant only on the assumption that *classes* of expressions are available in the metalanguage as values for its variables. It is not clear that Sellars wishes to make use of such real classes, however, and no doubt the use of virtual classes of expressions here would enable us to achieve pretty much the same end. Thus we could perhaps define

---

[4] See his *Philosophical Perspectives* (Charles C. Thomas, Publisher, Springfield, Illinois: 1967), p. 311.

(6)   '·sky·'   as   '$\{$ $a \ni (a$ = 'sky' v $a$ = 'der Himmel' v $\cdots)\}$ '

equally well.

How now is '·der Himmel·' defined? Presumably with the same definiens? If so then of course it follows trivially that, where '$\epsilon$' is the sign for membership,

$a \epsilon$ ·sky· if and only if $a \epsilon$ ·der Himmel·, for all $a$,

from which both (3) and (4) follows.

A doctrine of "meaning" emerges then by taking (2) itself as a definiendum with (3) as its corresponding definiens. And similarly for other cases.

It might be objected that too much has been packed into the definientia here that needs unpacking. What needs unpacking is of course Sellars' key phrase 'plays the same role in $L_1$ as is played in $L_2$ by' or 'parallels in $L_1$ the functioning in $L_2$ of'. No analyses of these phrases are given, without which the doctrine of dot quotes with its attendant account of meaning seems a mere "promissory note." And even if a doctrine concerning 'plays the same role in $L_1$ as is played in $L_2$ by' were worked out, it is by no means clear that any such thing as a Fregean intension would emerge anywhere along the line.

Let us try now to be as clear as we possibly can about (1), that is, about 'negation' and 'not'. In order to avoid the complexities of examining the deep grammar of these as words of English or the elaborate definitions of them in the *Oxford English Dictionary*, let us take as paradigmatic or authoritative Church's account of them in Runes' *Dictionary of Philosophy*.

First under 'negation' we read:

The negation of a proposition $p$ is the proposition $\sim$ p. The negation of a monadic propositional function $F$ is the monadic propositional function $\lambda x [\sim F(x)]$ ; similarly for dyadic propositional functions, etc.

Or the word *negation* may be used in a syntactic sense, so that the negation of a sentence (formula) A is the sentence $\sim$ A.

Here we are being very clear, surely, concerning 'negation'. The word 'not' is more difficult. Church tells us that "the propositional calculus formalizes the use of the sentential connectives *and, or, not, if . . . then* . . . ." and that in particular the sign '$\sim$' is used "to denote negation ('$\sim p$' to mean 'not $p$'), . . ." Of course these statements are concerned with 'not' only as a sentential connective, and not with other of its many uses in English. Sellars' formula (1) is presumably restricted in the same way. These statements surely provide a reasonable account of them in terms of which to understand (1).

Even so, Church's account can be sharpened if the semantical predicate for truth is explicitly brought in. Let 'Tr $a$' express that the sentence $a$ is true. Let 'tilde' be the structural-descriptive name of '$\sim$' and let 'Sent $a$' express that $a$ is a sentence of some one of the languages under consideration. Then the principle

$$\text{`}(a)\ (\text{Sent } a \supset (\text{Tr } a \equiv \sim (tilde\ a)))\text{'}$$

enunciates as clearly as we can ever hope to do the desired property of *tilde*. Surely this principle is much clearer than Sellars' (1) and says explicitly and fully whatever it is that (1) is supposed to say. Similarly

$$\text{`}(a)\ (b)\ (\ (\text{Sent } a \cdot \text{Sent } b) \supset (\text{Tr } (a\ vee\ b) \equiv (\text{Tr } a \text{ v } \text{Tr } b)\ )\ )\ \text{'},$$

where '*vee*' is the structural-descriptive name of 'v', enunciates fully the desired properties of *vee*.

Sellars makes much of the contention that his account of meaning is *non-relational*, 'meaning' being defined away in terms of the dot quotes and notions of logic. Perhaps also he intends 'plays in $L_1$ the same role as is played in $L_2$ by' to be defined in the same way. To define this by enumeration in the manner of (5) or (6) would not be satisfactory in a metalanguage involving more than a handful of object languages and in which languages themselves figure as values for variables. If the enumeration cannot be carried out, some relational notion would seem to be needed fundamentally either as defined or primitive. A non-relational semantics of some kind is essential for Sellars substance-property metaphysics, yet no such semantics seems yet to have been developed.[5]

Let us turn now to Sellars' views concerning abstract entities. The view is in essentials (*Philosophical Perspectives*, p. 229) that "qualities, relations, classes, propositions and the like ... are linguistic entities. They are linguistic expressions. They are *expressions,* however, in a rarified sense, for they are distinguishable from the linguistic materials (sign designs) which embody them in historically given languages." More specifically, abstract entities are to be handled by the dot quotes. And in order to avoid using an abstract entity in the definiens or definientia of the definitions (5) of the dot quotes, the definition (6) above is no doubt to be preferred to (5). (6) utilizes only a virtual class, it will be recalled, whereas (5) makes reference to a real one as a real abstract entity.

In 'The lion is tawny' the phrase 'the lion' refers to a universal, and this entire sentence is construed by Sellars as meaning that necessarily all lions are tawny. If necessity is construed in terms of logical or analytic truth (as seems natural), then 'The lion is tawny' becomes

'The sentence 'All lions are tawny' is analytic',

and this latter is a statement in the semantical metalanguage concerning the linguistic expressions 'lion' and 'tawny'. Sellars does not word his thesis in just this way, but this seems essentially what it amounts to. His schema

(S)          'The $K$ is $f$ ≡ All $K$'s are $f$†',

he says, "represents an identity of sense," the dagger indicating that

---

[5] Non-translational semantics perhaps provides an exception to this remark, with 'Tr' for truth as a primitive.

224

'All $K$'s are $f$' is itself analytic. "Notice particularly," we are warned (pp. 233-234), "that although the commentary represented by the dagger is in the metalanguage, the two sides of the equivalence and, specifically, the expressions 'the $K$' and '$K$'s' are at the same level of discourse—discourse about the lion being at the same level as discourse about lions." This last phrase is perhaps not literally the case but embodies rather the intended proposal, which is to make 'The lion is tawny' at the same level of discourse as 'The sentence 'All lions are tawny' is analytic'.

This proposal is interesting and bears some similarity with the author's treatment of *nominal virtual entities* in the theory of intensions. This may be seen by construing the sentence 'The lion is tawny' in terms of *L-designation* as follows. Let '$(x) (Lx \supset Tx)$' express 'All lions are tawny', using the customary symbolization. Then we may let

(S')    'T($\imath$L)'    abbreviate    '(E$a$) (E$b$) ($a$ LDes L $\cdot$ $b$ LDes T $\cdot$ $a$ AnlytcInc $b$)',

using 'LDes' for L-Designation and 'AnlyticInc' for analytic inclusion (of one-place predicates) as in *Belief, Existence, and Meaning.* The definiendum here reads 'The lion is tawny' and '$\imath$' plays the role here of the so-called "institutional" 'the' of English.[6]

The question arises, however, as to whether Sellars' kind of proposal can be made to work at large, so to speak, or whether it is capable of providing only a rather limited theory. The use of nominal virtual entities was restricted only to the theory of intensions, of connotation, and the like, it will be recalled, and was not intended as a general doctrine of universals. Sellars, however, it would seem, proposes to handle *all* universals as "rarified" linguistic entities. It would thus be consonant with his theory to regard all universals in this way, including universals of higher logical types.

Sellars restricts his examples for the most part to *named* or *designated* universals, universals for which a specific name or

---

[6] See *Belief, Existence, and Meaning,* Chapter VII and C. H. Langford, "The Institutional Use of 'The'," *Philosophy and Phenomenological Research* 10 (1949): 115-120.

linguistic description of some kind is available. The question arises now as to how *variables* and quantifiers over universals are to be introduced. Without variables and quantifiers over them, one cannot go very far in developing a doctrine of universals of sufficient power to be useful in the philosophy of science and mathematics. Without them one must restrict oneself to the virtual theory of classes and relations, which may be interesting enough on its own account and for various purposes. It is not clear, however, that the virtual theory can be made to suffice for a full theory of universals of the kind Sellars apparently wishes. If one holds to the virtual theory, one's doctrine is presumably some variant or other of nominalism. It is not clear that Sellars' view is intended to be such, however, being more oriented, it would seem, to some form of realism.

Sellars discusses in some detail the connection between his doctrine of universals and the Russell paradox.[7] Again, however, this seems to be wholly in terms of designated universals rather than in terms of universals as values for variables.

Without variables over universals there would be no means of introducing the quantifiers upon them. In accord with Sellars' proposal, one might attempt to try to make quantifiers over linguistic expressions somehow provide for quantifiers over them. It is by no means clear whether this could be done, however, especially in the absence of any concrete suggestions. And of course, one could not use in the metalanguage variables over classes of linguistic expressions (as is customary) to help out here, for this would involve one in a theory of universals of a non-linguistic kind in the metalanguage. Thus, for Sellars' proposal to work, a way must be found to express the various principles of, say, the simplified *Principia Mathematica*, without using variables over classes or relations, but only over individuals and linguistic expressions. It is clear that the syntax and semantics of the metalanguage could not be of the classic Tarski-Carnap kind, but would presumably have to be of the more nominalistic kind studied in *Truth and Denotation* or in II and III above. The situation would be similar also if one were to

---

[7] *Philosophical Perspectives,* Chapter X.

handle mathematics set-theoretically rather than on the basis of type theory. It is far from clear, to cite just one example, how Sellars would propose to accommodate the Zermelo-Skolem *Axiom of Sums,* to the effect that

$$(x) \, (Ey) \, (z) \, (z \; \epsilon \; y \; \equiv \; (Ew) \, (z \; \epsilon \; w \; \cdot \; w \; \epsilon \; x)),$$

where '$\epsilon$' is the symbol for class membership.

Note that these comments concerning the need for variables and quantifiers in no way depend upon Quine's criterion for ontic commitment, that we are ontically committed to regard the entities over which our variables range as real entities. The play here is upon the phrase 'ontic commitment'. According to Quine it is commitment to "what there is." The view here, however, as mentioned earlier, is merely that variables are needed to range over whatever our theory is supposed to be about. The use of variables and quantifiers is needed, indeed in practice indispensable, in helping us to articulate our theories. Whether what our variables are taken to range over are "real" or not, or really "exist" or "subsist" or not, is quite another matter. Unfortunately these two quite separate points are usually confused with one another.

Let us turn now to a third Sellarsian theme, concerning substance-oriented as over and against process-oriented metaphysics. The issues are vast and complex and cannot all be discussed here. Instead, let us consider only a few salient points.

Sellars starts with the suggestion that "although it is correct to say that episode-expressions . . . [refer] . . . to *episodes,* . . . episodes are *derivative* entities and rest on the referring expressions which occur in tensed statements about things (or 'substances')."[8] Again, where the 'is' of

$$\text{'}E_1 \;\; \text{is earlier than} \;\; E_2 \text{'}$$

"is in the 'tenseless present', [it] is a mistake *if it is supposed that*

[8] "Time and the World Order," in *Minnesota Studies in the Philosophy of Science,* Vol. II (University of Minnesota Press, Minneapolis: 1957) pp. 527-616, p. 543.

## EVENTS, REFERENCE, AND LOGICAL FORM

*this 'tenseless present' is logically independent of the use of tensed verbs.*" Also (p.550) "statements about events are, in principle, translatable into statements about changeable things." In short, Sellars argues for a metaphysics in which "substances" are the fundamental entities as opposed to one in which events are.

"The more (p. 594) one appreciates the systematic character of the difference between the framework of things and the framework of 'events,' " he writes, "the more one comes to realize that the latter is *in the first instance* simply a reaxiomatization of the former, and differs from it only as a Euclidean geometry axiomatized with one set of primitives differs from one which has been axiomatized with another set of primitives." The difference seems, however, ontically rather more fundamental. No matter what set of primitives is used in the two axiomatizations of Euclidean geometry, the ontology, the values for variables of the two theories is essentially the same. Not so for thing metaphysics as over and against event metaphysics. Here the ontologies are very different—otherwise Sellars would have no argument—and the primitive predicates of one differ *in kind* from the primitive predicates of the other, being applicable to different sorts of entities as arguments. "Which is the correct axiomatization?" Sellars asks (p. 594). "If this is interpreted as a question concerning the structure of 'ordinary' temporal discourse, it seems to me perfectly clear that the basic individuals of this universe of discourse are things and persons—in short the 'substances' of classical philosophy." In accord with this, Sellars apparently wishes the *justification* for his view to rest upon its mirroring "the structure of 'ordinary' temporal discourse" better somehow than the alternative. Does it really do so?

Let us examine a little Sellars' handling of tenses in order (a) to determine if possible its logical character and (b) to ascertain if we can the extent to which it accords somehow with ordinary discourse. Neither (a) nor (b) is easy to achieve, and Sellars has not helped us too much with regard to either. He has given us merely a few sign-posts along the way, but has left most of the trudging up to us. Let us follow his sign-posts to try to characterize his theory a little more precisely *logistice*, as he puts it. Logistic is of course our great

228

tool in helping to make our theories clear, and we ought therefore as philosophers to use it as much as we can.

In addition to variables over things Sellars admits variables over *propositions.* (Occasionally he uses a property variable, but these need not concern us here.) Some propositions express (or are (?)) *facts,* and those that do should be tensed. The three tenses, past, present, and future, are presumably to be handled in terms of predicates or operators applicable to atomic propositions. In accord with this, we might let 'P$p$', 'N$p$', and 'F$p$' express respectively that it *was* a fact that $p$, it *is* (now) a fact that $p$, and it *will be* a fact that $p$. Sellars does not explicitly introduce predicates such as 'P', 'N', and 'F', but it is helpful to do so. No further tenses are introduced. Perhaps it is intended that all others should be definable in terms of these. There are a good many other kinds of tenses, some of which are introduced in Reichenbach's rather sophisticated theory, referred to above.[9] Sellars sticks to just these three, apparently regarding them as metaphysically or linguistically basic.

Numerous examples of tensed statements of various kinds are given, all of which, it would seem, can be construed in terms of 'P', 'N', and 'F'. For a *theory* of tenses, it would be reasonable to expect some axioms characterizing 'P', 'N', and 'F' and their interrelations. These we are not given, however. It is true of course that Reichenbach provides no axioms either, but his theory is embedded in a wider theory of events, so that the basic principles governing tenses are presumably provable. In the absence of an axiomatization, or a well-developed prior theory in which they are definable, it is really very difficult to determine just what the theory of tenses here is supposed to be.

Sellars frequently makes reference to metalanguages. The notion of a metalanguage is best viewed always relative to a well-developed language *system* as object language. Sellars is exclusively concerned with natural language, but it is by no means clear what a metalanguage of a natural language is. To be sure, there is increasing metalinguistic talk in the recent writings of linguists. Sellars seems to want the advantages of being able to use metalinguistic talk when he

[9] *Elements of Symbolic Logic,* Chapter VII.

229

needs it, but with almost no indication of its constraints, form, and structure.

Consider again (S) and (S') above. Recall that (S') was proposed as a kind of "rational reconstruction" of (S). (S') is clearer, it is thought, and the full character of the metalanguage in which it occurs may readily be determined. What is needed now for Sellars' handling of tenses is a kind of full rational reconstruction, similar to that which (S') gives of (S). Without this, the theory here also seems one more "promissory note." The "cash value," Sellars says (p. 593) "is to be provided not by metaphysics . . ., but by the advance of science (physical theory of time)." It would seem more reasonable for Sellars here to have referred to the advance of linguistics in its search for the deep structure of tensed sentences, the motive of his theory being to accord with ordinary tensed discourse.

That the advance of the science of linguistics in its search for deep structure supports Sellars thing metaphysics is very doubtful. It is perhaps premature to claim that it supports the event view. What can be claimed at the present time is that the deep structure of many types of sentences of ordinary language can easily be given in terms of events, and that the character of event logic can at the moment be made reasonably clear. This latter might therefore be regarded as providing a tentative system of deep structures of the kind linguists are seeking. Of course there will be alternative systems, just as there are in all areas of science.

Sellars is happily one of the few writers who recognizes the important role that logical syntax and semantics must play in metaphysics and the philosophy of language. Hence of course his interest in metalanguages. Metalanguages are of two kinds, as noted above, those in which the expressions of the object language are regarded as sign designs or shapes, and those in which they are regarded as sign events or inscriptions. Sign designs are presumably abstract objects, shapes, more specifically, classes of similar inscriptions. If, however, abstract entities are to be handled as linguistic entities, as Sellars wishes, the linguistic entities themselves must somehow be concrete—otherwise an infinite regress would ensue. *Ergo,* it would seem reasonable for Sellars to regard expressions as

230

inscriptions or sign events. In this way he seems driven back to an event ontology of inscriptions. Of course, he could perhaps regard inscriptions as things, but ink marks, utterances, and the like, surely are very different from the simple "substances" of classical philosophy. An utterance, what is uttered, is rather a momentary occurrence or happening in the world of events. The very terminology of 'sign events' helps to bring out their ontic status. A dilemma for Sellars is then that he must regard expressions either as sign designs or sign events; if sign designs, his syntax and semantics must be based on "abstract" entities reducible (for him) to other linguistic entities, in turn further reducible, and so on; if sign events, syntax and semantics must presumably be left out of his scheme altogether, being based on events not substances as values for variables.

Out of a plethora of technicalia that could be commented on, let us consider now only one item concerning 'existence'. "The crucial point," he writes (p. 563), "is that statements of the form

$$\text{`}(Ex)\cdots x\cdots\text{'}$$

are not as such in any ordinary sense existence statements. They correspond to existence statements, where they have the force of

(7)          '$(Ex)x$ is properly called (an) S'

where 'S' is a proper or common name," or equivalently,

(8)          '$(Ex)x$ satisfies the criteria for being called S'.

Strictly, in order not to confuse use and mention, quotes are needed here around 'S'. Sellars thinks that 'S exists' is then to be construed as (7) or (8) (with quotes around 'S') rather than as

(9)          '$(Ex)x = S$',

as is more customary. The difficulty is not that this latter is usually construed as analytic, but that the existential quantifier and '=' are not tensed. He wishes to provide for 'S existed' and 'S will exist' as well as for 'S exists'. To do this, he construes (9) as the metalinguistic statement (7) or (8) (with quotes around 'S'), gaining the effect of tense by allowing 'satisfied' to be tensed. Thus 'S existed' becomes (Ex)x satisfied the criteria for 'S' ', and 'S will exist' becomes '(Ex)x will satisfy the criteria for 'S' '. Satisfaction is a very exact relation of semantics, however, studied especially by Tarski, and thus presumably has the same tenseless status as any notion of logic. Satisfaction should be no more tensed than quantifiers or identity. In fact, an expression for satisfaction is defined by Tarski in terms wholly of the untensed notions of higher logic, together with structural-descriptive names and concatenation. To tense the notion of satisfaction is to alter rather fundamentally the structure of semantics. This is precisely what Sellars in effect must do, if the proposal concerning (7), (8), and (9) is to be made workable. Unfortunately we are told nothing as to what this alternation would consist of. Presumably it would involve introducing the predicates 'P', 'N', and 'F' in the metalanguage. Let '$x$ Sat $a$' be defined to express that $x$ satisfies $a$, where $a$ is a sentential function containing one and only free variable. Then 'P($x$ Sat $a$)' 'N($x$ Sat $a$)' and 'F($x$ Sat $a$)' would presumably provide forms for tensing the satisfaction relation.

Note that for Sellars 'P', 'N', and 'F' presumably take only *atomic* factual propositions (or propositional functions as here (?)) as arguments. Are forms such as 'P($p$ v $q$)', 'P($p \supset q$)', and so on, needed? Apparently not. But if not, Sellars would seem committed to a doctrine of atomic propositions with all the difficulties thereunto appertaining. Also the question arises as to whether the predicates 'P', 'N', and 'F' would themselves be *tenseless* predicates, or whether they too should be tensed, that is, whether forms such as 'PP$p$', 'PN$p$', 'PF$p$', 'NP$p$', and so on, should be admitted.

Sellars claims, it will be recalled, that "all statements about events are, in principle, translatable into statements about changeable things." To substantiate this claim would be a formidable task indeed. Nothing less than explicit rules of translation would have to be given showing in detail how it could be carried out. Sellars claims

(p. 572) that ". . . events have a derivative status in the sense that singular terms referring to events are contextually introduced in terms of sentences involving singular terms referring to things." In these translations, however, presumably some temporal dating is needed. Many of Sellars' examples make reference to a time $t$. If we are allowed in the translation to make reference to times, where these are values for variables, then Sellars' claim is in no way remarkable. If times constitute a species of substance, there is no problem. Expressions for events may be built up as ordered triples or whatever, with one factor a time. Such a theory has been developed by the author elsewhere, and has some kinship with the Kim-Brandt theory.[10] However, times are surely not substances, and Sellars does not claim that they are.

If times are available as values for variables, a theory of events may be built up. And if events are available as values for variables, with a suitable topology upon them, a theory of time may be built up. Times would be constructs in terms of events, perhaps handled as classes or virtual classes of simultaneous events. In any case, it behooves Sellars to renounce both times and events as values for variables, retaining only the substances of classical philosophy, if his method is to be made workable.

(There seem to be three metaphysical views with regard to events. Either substances alone are values for the thing variables with time handled somehow by means of suitable predicates, or substances together with either times or events, or events only. Sellars' view seems to be the first. The second, with times, has been developed somewhat in *Belief, Existence, and Meaning*. In *Logic, Language, and Meaning*, the second method is also used, but with events rather than times. The third method, with events and events only, was developed in I and II above.)

Sellars' claim takes on metaphysical point only if all reference to times is avoided, all power of speaking of time then residing in the use of 'P', 'N', and 'F'. If this latter is Sellars' claim, there would

[10] See *Belief, Existence, and Meaning*, Chapter IX, J. Kim, "On the Psycho-Physical Identity Theory," *American Philosophical Quarterly* 3 (1966): 1-9, and R. Brandt and J. Kim, "The Logic of the Identity Theory," *The Journal of Philosophy* 64 (1967): 515-537. See also *Logic, Language, and Metaphysics*, Chapters VII and VIII.

seem to be many kinds of sentences not easy to translate in the desired fashion, for example,

'Lightning never strikes twice',
'The events of World War II changed the course of Western European history',
'Her second performance of the Sonata left much to be desired',
'The sonata is merely the set of all its performances',
'Brutus kissed Portia twice of the Ides of March, 44 BC',
'Annette danced beautifully then, but even more beautifully the time before',

and so on. It would be interesting to know precisely how sentences of these kinds could be translated into thing sentences, without the use of time references except whatever is involved in 'P', 'N', and 'F'. In terms of the event logic of I and II these forms may readily be handled along the lines of the material of V and VI.

Sellars purports to take the physics of the special theory of relativity seriously and to show how sentences in the framework of things can be harmonized with it. Does he succeed in this? To do so he would be obliged to show us, not only how purely mathematical statements but also the statements of contemporary physical theory, including particle theory — particles are *very* different surely from the "substances" of classical philosophy — cosmology, relativity, and so on, could be translated into the thing language.

It has already been remarked that Sellars wants the justification of thing metaphysics to rest in part upon its mirroring "the structure of 'ordinary' temporal discourse." Suppose now that we had gotten the temporal part of our ordinary discourse all straightened out satisfactorily. Let us reflect for a moment on metaphysics as mirroring the structure of the *whole* of our discourse, including of course its temporal part. Clearly it would not do to claim that the *primary* aim of metaphysics is to elucidate this whole structure. It is not clear that Sellars makes this claim, but he does seem to come dangerously close to it. The point here is merely to note our natural language is merely one phenomenon among many that we should try to understand philosophically, but we should not give it our exclusive attention as metaphysicians. There is after all the non-verbal world, which is rather fascinating in its variety and multifariousness.

Sellars' thought is often complex and involved, and it may be that some of the foregoing remarks do not do it full justice. The remedy, if there is one, is of course, to formulate our philosophical statements *logistice*, for then at least we have something very explicit upon which we can agree or not. Many of Sellar's valuable remarks should perhaps best be viewed as prologemena to and commentary upon such formulations, as he himself often comes close to suggesting.

# XIV

## ON LORENZEN'S
## *NORMATIVE LOGIC*
## *AND ETHICS*

'*Si Pergama dextri defendi possent.*''

"Dialogic" logic and the provocative philosophy of logic encompassing it were discussed by Paul Lorenzen in his John Locke lectures at Oxford in 1967-68 under the title *Normative Logic and Ethics.*[1] It will not be amiss to examine some of the points raised in these lectures not only as regards general matters but points of detail as well.[2]

Lorenzen first discusses "elementary sentences" of the form '$S_1, \cdots, S_n \ \epsilon \ p$' or '$S_1, \cdots, S_n \ \epsilon' \ p$', where '$S_1$', $\cdots$,'$S_n$' are proper names, '$p$' is a predicator, '$\epsilon$' is used as the English 'is', and '$\epsilon'$' as 'is not'. An instance is 'Socrates is a philosopher'. Lorenzen writes (p. 15) that "we use proper names for naming objects and we use predicators to assert or deny properties of the named objects." Clearly Lorenzen intends to include *relational* predicators also, and it is a curious and unhappy use of terms to regard relational predicators

---

[1] (Bibliographisches Institut, Mannheim/Zürich: 1969).
[2] Cf. also "Truth and Its Illicit Surrogates," for further discussion of some of Lorenzen's views.

237

as standing for properties. They stand rather for relations, each of specified degree.

Why do we use elementary sentences? Lorenzen asks. "Because there are objects and because there are properties which the objects have or do not have." How is this known? "Well," we are told (pp. 15-16), "it is easy to *prove* [italics added] such existential sentences, beginning with 'there are objects', 'there are properties' by giving examples. 'Socrates is a philosopher' proves that there are objects: namely, Socrates, and that there are properties: namely, to be a philosopher." Merely to give examples, as is done here, is surely not an adequate means of "proof," however, in any proper logico-mathematical sense. From 'Socrates is a philosopher' the sentence 'there is an object' may well follow within a first-order logic. Just how the predicator 'is an object' is to be construed, however, is not clear from Lorenzen's account and he makes no reference to the voluminous literature on this subject. By 'follows logically' here one may mean in accord with the usual rules of quantification of first order. To contend that 'there are properties' follows logically from 'Socrates is a philosopher' is much more dubious and can be maintained only with 'logical consequence' construed on the basis of a second-order logic. The difference here is of course very significant, but no mention is made of it.

To the question 'Why do we use elementary sentences?' Lorenzen answers (p.15) that we "do not prescribe that there are objects—but we recommend to our children the use of proper names. We do not prescribe that there are properties—but we recommend to our children the use of predicators." This is surely an incomplete answer based on a faulty theory as to how language is learned. We do not — in the first instance anyhow — *recommend* to our children anything at all in any literal sense. We use language in their presence, they hear us, they mimic us, we help them to associate properly word with thing, complex phrase with complex circumstance, and so on. The full theory here is of course long and involved, and no one has pieced it together yet in a wholly satisfactory way. Even to spell out a comparatively simple theory of rote learning has turned out to be very difficult indeed, as the work of Hull, Fitch, *et al.*, has shown.[3]

Lorenzen confuses the use and mention of expressions throughout. This is particularly irksome in the discussion of truth. Instead of 'It is true that $S$ is $p$', it is said (p. 17) that "we may say '$p$ applies to $S$'—this is only a shift of emphasis to the predicator $p$." The correct use of quotation marks here would require that we say that the predicator '$p$' applies to $S$. It is not just a shift of emphasis, it is a shift from *using* an expression to *mentioning* it. The matter is of some import, because otherwise it is not clear whether Lorenzen is speaking about a semantical notion of truth or an absolute one.

The point of the shift of emphasis here is that Lorenzen wishes to introduce 'property' in effect by definition. "If [pp. 17-18] I am saying '$S$ has the property $p$', I am not only just asserting '$S$ is $p$' or 'It is true that $S$ is $p$', but I am in the same moment reflecting on my predicating, confirming that $p$ ['$p$'] applies to $S$, and, in addition, expressing that I am not interested in the particular predicator $p$ ['$p$'] of the English language but that I am interested in $p$ ['$p$'] only insofar as I may substitute for $p$ ['$p$'] any other sound with the same use . . . . . . In order to express this, I propose to say '$S$ has the property $p$' instead of speaking about the predicator $p$ ['$p$'] ."

To accomplish this, Lorenzen commits a multitude of technical sins. First, there is the confusion of use and mention, already referred to. Second, he uses an unanalyzed notion of *synonymity*. If '$p$' and '$q$' are synonymous predicators, he writes in effect, the sentence '$A$('$p$')' is said to be *invariant* with respect to synonymity if $A$('$p$') if and only if $A$('$q$'). It is then proposed (pp. 17-18) "to say '$A$(property $p$)' instead of '$A$(predicator $p$)'." The shift in level of language should be noted. The two formulae '$A$(property $p$). and '$A$(predicator $p$)' ['$A$('$p$')'] are, at first blush anyhow, formulae in quite different languages, the first in an object language, the second in its metalanguage. Sense can be made of Lorenzen's proposal only if '$A$(property $p$)' is regarded as a translation in the metalanguage of some formula of the object language. Lorenzen proposes to say that

---

[3]C. Hull, F. B. Fitch, *et alia, Mathematico-Deductive Theory of Rote Learning* (Yale University Press, New Haven: 1940).

the predicator '$p$' then *represents* the "abstract" object the property $p$. The suggestion that "properties" be "represented" in effect as abstractive classes of "synonymous" predicators is by no means novel, having been made on various occasions by Russell, Carnap, and others whose work Lorenzen summarily dismisses.

A host of problems arises as to how 'synonymous' is to be analyzed, none of which Lorenzen considers. First there are the purely structural matters concerning how the notion is either defined or characterized axiomatically. (Presumably there is no other way of introducing it.) There is also the question of how it is to be interpreted behaviorally if at all—the kind of question raised by Quine. There is, in addition, the question of how to construe synonymity as a relation between expressions of one language and those of another. From his examples it is clear that Lorenzen construes this notion interlinguistically — 'rot' and 'red' are for him synonyms. But it is by no mean clear that even an adequate *intra*linguistic account, for just one object language, of this notion has ever been given.

Thus far only synonymous predicators have been considered. Synonymity of proper names Lorenzen explicitly introduces by definition. "Different proper names are called synonyms," he writes, "if they are used to name the same object." This is of course an unsuitable definition. Proper names that name the same object are *coextensive* or *codesignative,* but not necessarily synonymous. Lorenzen here seems to have forgotten Frege's celebrated distinction between 'the morning star' and 'the evening star', and makes no effort to accommodate the important difference between coextensive and cointensive (in some sense) names.[4]

By a similar abstractive procedure, it is proposed to handle *propositions* as being "represented" by sentences. Again, this proposal is by no means novel. Lorenzen's way is inadequate, given his way of construing 'synonymous' as between proper names. Even if this were emended, difficulties would remain. To *accept* a proposition is by no means to accept every member of a class of

---

[4] Recall especially *Belief, Existence, and Meaning,* Chapter VII.

synonymous sentences, nor even to accept any one member as "representative." To *assert* a proposition is by no means to assert every member of a class of synonymous sentences — and so on.

A key point Lorenzen makes (p. 20) is that "either we accept the use of proper names and predicators or we do not speak at all." Clearly, this is not the case, however. We can "speak" in languages containing only variables but no proper names. Many of the well articulated logistic systems are languages of this kind. To be sure, some proper names might be introduced within them as abbreviations for descriptive phrases, although strictly it is not necessary that this be done. We can speak quite well without proper names and say what we wish within such systems.

Lorenzen draws a distinction (p. 20) between "proper descriptions" and what he calls 'indicator-descriptions'. "We use indicators such as 'this', 'you', and so on, and we use indicator-descriptions such as 'my dog'. Also the simple sentence 'the dog is barking' in its ordinary usage does not presuppose that there exists exactly one dog, only that there exists exactly one dog here and now in the situation in which the sentence is used. The definite article 'the' in 'the dog is barking' is not the logical operator ɿ. It is rather an abbreviated indicator 'this'." We are told nothing more concerning indicators, however, so that the whole subject is left somewhat up in the air. No sound reasons are given for not handling the 'the' in 'the dog is barking' by means of 'ɿ', as an incomplete or abbreviated description, the full description of the particular dog referred to being available if required.

Throughout Lorenzen really seems to think he is talking about "elementary sentences" in a natural language, rather than about those of an artificially constructed language system. It has been urged earlier, however, that the two kinds of language should be sharply contrasted with each other and that little advance in clarification is to be gained by confuting the two.

In the discussion of the logical "particles" 'or', 'and', and so on, Lorenzen proposes (p. 23) to start "in the tradition of Cartesian doubt. If namely I begin . . . to doubt whether I understand 'or', then it is of no help to teach me the use of 'or' with the help of

EVENTS, REFERENCE, AND LOGICAL FORM

meta-talk which contains 'or'. Thus . . . it is reasonable to insist on a method of introducing 'or' into that part of language which we are going to use — without already using logical particles on a meta-level." Two difficulties are involved in this passage. One is the confusion between a "teach-learn" situation concerning a given word and a "logical construction" or "reconstruction" of the proper syntactical and semantical behavior of that word. The other is that the contention concerning teaching seems inadequate. It is indeed often of great help to teach the use of a word with the help of talk already containing the word. If a child does not know how to use 'or', the best possible method to teach him is repeatedly to use it correctly in his presence.

In the discussion of truth and falsity (pp. 23-24), 'T' and 'F' are explicitly introduced *but not as predicators.* "The symbol T ['T'] is not a predicator. It only looks like one." By way of explanation we are told that "we do not understand an elementary sentence $S \epsilon p$ ['$S \epsilon p$'] unless we understand $S \epsilon' p$ ['$S \epsilon' p$'] also. Predication is the decision between affirming or denying the predicator $p$ of the object $S$." These three sentences do not seem to have much to do with one another. Perhaps 'T' here is intended to stand for the *absolute* notion of truth mentioned above. If so, of course, nothing is stated by using 'T' that cannot be stated without it. And similarly for 'F'. If a semantical account of truth were being used here, 'T' and 'F' would of course be predicators in a proper sense. Lorenzen's discussion of truth and falsity is at best obscure. This is regrettable because it is in terms of them that certain key statements concerning dialogues are made, as we shall see.

Predication, decision, and affirming and denying would seem to be quite separate matters. But surely predication is *not,* in any proper sense of 'is', "the decision between affirming or denying" anything at all. Predication is a purely linguistic matter, decisions are mental acts of a certain highly complex kind. A decision to affirm or deny a sentence, even an elementary one, may be expressed, or conveyed to an interlocutor, by means of the sentence. Here Lorenzen is committing one of Ryle's category mistakes.

The point of introducing 'T' and 'F' seems to be in connection

242

with understanding the existential quantifier. "To assert a some-sentence," Lorenzen goes on (p. 24), "is something different [from predication], because we have to defend such an assertion according to the given rule: we have to name an object $S$. Therefore the sequence of symbols $V_x A(x) \ \epsilon' \ T$ (or $V_x A(x) \ \epsilon \ F$) has no meaning up to now; it has no use that has been explicitly agreed upon." These contentions seems arbitrary. In the first place, we do not "have" to "defend" an existentially quantified statement '$V_x A(x)$' by naming an object $S$ such that $A(S)$. Who "has" to do this and why? Many statements we make we do not "have" to defend at all. And if requested to so do, we need not name a specific object. If one were asked to defend 'There is at least one grain of sand in the depths of the Pacific' one would not proceed to name one. To "defend" 'There is something I want to tell you but I cannot remember what it is' by naming it is to void the very sentence itself. And so on.

Lorenzen's contention that '$V_x A(x) \ \epsilon \ T$' has no meaning or use that has been agreed upon holds of course only if no meaning or use has been agreed upon. A meaning or use is not, however, given merely by the rule:

$$A(S) \ \epsilon \ T \Rightarrow V_x A(x) \ \epsilon \ T,$$

as Lorenzen contends. Quantifiers are incorporated in logical systems by means of suitable semantical rules governing them. Without such rules they remain merely mute sequences of symbols waiting to be interpreted. Such an account of the behavior of the quantifiers is spelled out in semantics, and no satisfactory alternative kind of an account seems ever to have been given.

Lorenzen goes on to state the rules of dialogic assertion, attack, and defense. It has been suggested that these rules are *ad hoc* devices of a highly artificial kind, much oversimplified if regarded as determinative of "dialogues" in practice. Only two players are involved, and only one sentence. The play is all simultaneous, so to speak, with no time differences brought in. There is no concern with probability considerations, with bringing in fresh evidence, with the modification of what is regarded as defensible in the course of the dialogue, with the discovery of new truth, and so on. Instead, rules are laid down to the effect that "the proponent may either attack a sentence asserted by the opponent or he may defend himself against the last attack of the opponent," and so on. Of course, as already suggested, such rules can be given to make the "dialogues" behave in a certain way. One is free surely to formulate such rules *ad libitum.* The point at issue is that they do not in any significant way characterize praxis in the way in which dialogists contend.

A theory of dialogues useful in praxis would surely allow for any number of players and any (finite or infinite) number of sentences. Sentences, even long conjunctions, are not asserted, attacked, and defended *solo* in praxis, but only as members of elaborate conceptual systems with all manner of criss-crossings, interconnections, and so on, among them. Further, they are not all asserted with equal strength. Some we are surer of than others. Some we are willing to "give up" readily, others we wish to hold on to at all costs. We should be ready to revise them at any point should compelling evidence to do so be brought in. And so on. Only by means of much more elaborate "rules" could Lorenzen's dialogues be made to be of interest in characterizing scientific praxis — for he claims that they are. To formulate such rules adequately would of course require going much more deeply into the theory of scientific method than the dialogists seem to care to do. Yet without doing so, they cannot readily protect themselves from the charge of extreme artificiality and oversimplification.

Just as there are difficulties with Lorenzen's account of the existential quantifier, so are there difficulties with his account of negation (pp. 24-25). "Let us introduce the assertion of $\rightarrow V_x A(x)$ [quotes needed throughout] by the following proposal: If I assert this, you may assert the affirmative part . . . . and then I shall ask you to defend it. If you succeed, I will have lost my assertion; otherwise I shall have won. In case you do not know how to defend $V_x A(x)$, it is advisable for you not to challenge the original thesis $\rightarrow V_x A(x)$ . . . . I do not propose to call $\rightarrow V_x A(x)$ true if *you* cannot refute the assertion of it: I would call it "true" [double quotes here mysteriously added] only if *no one* could refute it. This shows that in dealing with quantified sentences the classical disjunction "either true or false" no longer applies." On the contrary, it seems, this shows only that a sentence of the form '$\rightarrow V_x A(x)$' is *dialogically irrefutable* in a very special sense. But dialogic irrefutably is conceptually quite different from truth.

A proper account of negation, it would seem, cannot be given in terms just of *assertion* or *refutation* or the like. We might well use the negation sign in some of our assertions and it might well appear in some of the sentences we care to refute. But this is of course quite another matter. Further one might well in praxis not know how to defend an existentially quantified sentence and yet it would be inadvisable not to challenge its negation. For example, I might not know how to defend the sentence 'There exists an unconditioned conceptual valuation of the entire multiplicity of eternal objects' within the confines of the Whiteheadian cosmology, yet it would be inadvisable of me indeed not to challenge its negation. Another example. Out of sheer ignorance of the theory of real variables, I might not know how to defend the statement 'The bounded set $\Gamma$ of real numbers has a least upper bound', yet it would be inadvisable for me not to challenge the statement 'The bounded set $\Gamma$ has no least upper bound'. I might well "know" the principle of the least upper bound in some theoretical way but not be able in praxis to defend it. Examples of this kind can of course be multiplied *ad nauseam.*

Occasional historical remarks are made here or there, the point of which seems to be that Aristotle and the philosophers of the Platonic academy had something like dialogic logic in mind all along in their work in formal logic. "We need not assume that Aristotle had in mind exactly our dialogical game," Lorenzen tells us, "but in any case something rather like it." Of course we should not *assume* anything whatsoever about Aristotle's logic. Instead, by painstaking historical research, we should try to interpret the text *au pied de la lettre* as best we can in the light of what we now know.

Let us turn now to Lorenzen's account of arithmetic as a dialogic game. "In order to introduce arithmetic, I begin," he says (p. 41) "—— as mankind did at least 10,000 years ago with counting. To count means to invent a sequence of symbols called numerals and to use them in the well-known way . . . . The simplest sequence of numerals is made up with one symbol only, say

$$I, II, III, \bullet\bullet\bullet\bullet\bullet. "$$

"The sequence of stroke numerals," he goes on, "is constructed by the following rules:

(L1) $\Rightarrow I$
(L2) $n' \Rightarrow n\,I,$

with $n$ [quotes needed] as an "eigenvariable"; that is, as a variable for strings of symbols constructed by means of these rules themselves."

Although Lorenzen wants to begin with counting, somehow he immediately loses track of it. In fact, nothing he says beyond these introductory remarks in any way helps to illumine the intricate human procedure of counting. No matter—we can return to this in a moment. Instead he immediately proposes the following rules:

(<1) $\Rightarrow I, nI$
(<2) $m,n \Rightarrow mI, nI.$

In effect these are supposed to accommodate the notion of being *less than* so that '⊢$m,n$,' is supposed to mean that $m<n$. The use of '⊢' here is not clearly explained, nor is that of '$\Rightarrow$', but no matter. Lorenzen seems to think he has opened up "a new field of symbolic activity which is sometimes useful in dealing with groups of objects. Only practice can teach the value of such a technique. Terminologically, I would like to say that the <-*rules* have a *pragmatic* justification."

In the first place, nothing very new is said here. Stuart Mill attempted something rather similar, and Frege was not only brilliant,

246

but delightful as well, in this *Grundlagen*, in demolishing it and the attempt of others to formulate *ex nibilo* a "Pfefferkuchen and Kieselstein Arithmetik." Moreover, again, the rules (L1), (L2), ($<$1), and ($<$2) are formulated without regard to the distinction between use and mention. Actually they are concerned only with a single sign, the stroke, and an operation of *concatenation*. The sign 'I I', for example, consists of 'I' concatenated with itself. These last two statements are not quite correct, however, for they are stated in terms of sign designs rather than sign events. It is not clear precisely which Lorenzen intends, and in fact he fails to distinguish the two. This is unfortunate, for the distinction is an important one for his purposes. It is more in the spirit of his quasi-pragmatic view, however, to think it is the latter. If so, we should say here that a sign event of the shape 'I I' is the concatenate of a sign event of the shape 'I' with another similar sign event, where concatenation is now construed in terms of sign events.

Lorenzen starts out by talking about the signs or "numerals," as he calls them, but immediately goes on to identify these numerals with the numbers themselves. This is surely an illicit identification. But, for the moment, no matter. Somehow Lorenzen thinks that his rules have a "pragmatic justification" but that arithmetical rules in "the axiomatic approach" do not. Instead of the $<$-rules, one would have, in the axiomatic approach, the following:

(T1) $$\wedge n \cdot I < n \, I,$$
(T2) $$\wedge n \wedge m \cdot n < m \rightarrow nI < mI \, .$$

"The question: How do we know the truth of . . . [these] axioms?" he writes (pp. 42-43), "is not permissible; one refers vaguely to empirical verification or confirmations. Starting with the pragmatically justified $<$-rules, on the other hand, we see that the $<$-axioms are indeed true, in the sense that they can be defended as theses in a dialogical game."

Something here is very much amiss. In the first place, the "pragmatic justification" of the $<$-rules is never given nor is it ever made clear what a pragmatic justification of them would amount to.

247

Secondly, it is not clear why an answer to the question, 'How do we know the truth, in the axiomatic approach, of the T-rules?' is "inadmissible"? Who says? And why? Of course the question *is* admissible and one could attempt to give various answers to it. And one could do this hopefully without "referring vaguely to empirical verifications or confirmations." A *tu quoque a fortiori* is in order. Let Lorenzen (1) state his rules with the necessary clarity distinguishing between use and mention, (2) tell us precisely and clearly what a "pragmatic justification" of them would consist of and assure us that this is a sound requirement, and then (3) show that his rules may be justified in this sense. Perhaps he thinks he has done all three, but clearly not in accord with modern standards of logico-philosophic rigor.

Another point. The '*n*' and '*m*' Lorenzen calls 'Eigenvariablen', that is, variables "for strings of symbols constructed by means of the rules themselves." This is an inadequate explanation. We cannot understand the rules unless we understand what the variables in them range over. The only explanation is that they range over the very entities "constructed by means of the rules themselves." (This is like teaching a child 'or' by using it in meta-talk, which Lorenzen earlier berated.) The use of 'constructed' here is vague. What does it mean to say that a rule "constructs" an entity? Human beings may be said to "construct" cathedrals, ships, artifacts, and so on, but in no sense do "rules" do so. Human beings may write or utter strings of symbols, but rules do not do so. Rules have no power to make entities exist if they do not do so already. Lorenzen's explanation of how he wishes his variables to behave seems to rest upon a confused "philosophic grammar" concerning 'construction', 'rule', and 'exists'.

Lorenzen claims that his <-axioms are "true". Note, however, that the <-axioms are stated with *free* variables. Are we thus allowed to regard formulae containing free variables as significantly true or false? Ordinarily, and on the basis of either the semantical or absolute theories of truth, only *sentences* are significantly allowed to be true or false. Again, something is amiss in Lorenzen's account. To get around this, he might say that '*n*' and '*m*' are not to be "variables" at

248

all in the usual sense, but only *abbreviations* for strings of strings of strokes. An abbreviation is of course technically something very different from a variable.

In the development of this Pfefferkuchen and Kieselstein arithmetic, one must be careful that no quantifiers are introduced inadvertently. The theory would have to be an arithmetic *without* variables either bound or free. The '*m*' and '*n*' in (L1), (L2), (<1), and (<2) might then be regarded merely as abbreviations for sequences of strokes, and (L1), (L2), (<1), and (<2) themselves as chemata. Whence then come the quantifiers in (T1) and (T2)? — for quantifiers can be written only with genuine variables. One cannot here both have one's cake and eat it too.

Lorenzen's key point about arithmetic might then be para-phrased as follows. The principles of an arithmetic without variables (as based on (L1), (L2), (<1), and (<2)) can be used to "justify" the principles of an arithmetic with free variables (as based on (T1) and (T2) *inter alia*) in the sense that these latter can be "defended as theses in a dialogic game." The difficulty with this contention, how-ever, is that the theses and their defenses would no longer be for-mulae within the same language! The theses are stated in the arith-metic with free variables and quantifiers upon them. The defenses are formulae in the arithmetic without free variables, but only with abbreviations for strings of strokes.

If, on the other hand, genuine variables over numbers are admitted in the usual way, then of course '*n*l' *for variable* '*n*' is never defined. (L1) and (L2) would not suffice for this. They "construct" only 'l', 'l', and so on. And in this list we never find '*n*l' where '*n*' is a variable. All we ever find is 'lll ··· ll' where '*n*' is an *abbreviation* for 'lll ··· l'.

Similarly '(*m* + *n*)' for *variable* '*m*' and *variable* '*n*' seems never to be defined. '(α + β)' where 'α' and 'β are abbreviations for strings of strokes of course is defined. In the list of all expressions of the form '(α + β)', however, one will never find '(*m* + *n*)' for variable '*m*' and variable '*n*'.

These points are of course concerned with very fundamental

matters concerning notation, which Lorenzen neglects to consider. Many of these difficulties hark back to the failure to distinguish use and mention.

Another difficulty is that it is by no means clear how '⇒' in (L1), (L2), (<1), and (<2) are to be construed. In the first place, '⇒' as occurring in (L1) and (<1) must mean something quite different from what it means in (L2) and (<2). In (L1), for example, it seems to stand for creation *ex nihilo*. Behold, *ex nihilo*, there is a 'I'. But (L2) presumably is intended to state that *given* any sequence of strokes ' III ⋯ I ' there is another sequence ' III ⋯ II ' containing one more. Now just how are we to construe 'there is' in these informal statements? And what is it that is said to be? Sign designs or sign events? And in either case, are they to be regarded as human artifacts in some wise, explicitly made by a human user of signs, or are they mere physical or Platonic items in the whole cosmos quite independent of the human user? Merely to say, as Lorenzen does, that these are "constructive" rules carrying their own "justification" on their sleeve as it were, says very little, it would seem, without satisfactory answers to the foregoing questions.

Lorenzen proposes (p. 45) "to call arithmetical truths *synthetical* truths. They are non-empirical truths," he writes. "If we follow the Kantian usage and call all non-empirical truths 'a priori', we have with Kant the arithmetic truths as synthetic *a priori* truths." What does Lorenzen mean here by 'synthetic'? "In order to come closer to the traditional Kantian terms, I shall use 'synthetical' instead of 'constructive'," he notes by way of answer to this question. ". . . .To defend an arithmetical truth, we need not use the "empirical" truth of elementary sentences; we need only "synthesis" according to pragmatically justified rules."

There is of course an enormous literature concerning just what synthetic truths are, and Lorenzen's comments throw no new light on the matter. He merely proposes to use 'synthetic' where he might as well use 'constructive'. As already noted, Lorenzen gives no clear account as to just what "constructive truths" are nor as to what 'pragmatically justifiable' means.

In most discussions concerning analytic and synthetic truths the words 'empirical', 'a priori', 'non-empirical', and 'a posteriori' creep in almost unawares and usually without much indication as to how they are used. These hoary traditional notions, however, are not above suspicion and cry for analysis. So in Lorenzen's account also. These words creep in with no indication whatsoever as to how they are to be used or as to what they mean. Presumably we are supposed already to know—the kind of knowledge we all have unless asked to give an exact account of it.

It is thus very doubtful that Lorenzen has said anything new or interesting concerning synthetic a priori truths. Nor has he in any serious way challenged the traditional Frege-Carnap distinction between analytic and factual truth.

Limitations of space do not permit discussing Lorenzen's further classification of sentences ("formally analytic," "formally synthetic," "materially analytic," "materially synthetic," and so on) nor his remarks on set theory, protophysics (including geometry and chronometry), and modal logic. All of this he regards (p. 73) as "plain sailing." "No one has any serious difficulties with elementary sentences, with descriptions or abstractors, with the logical particles or modal rules, with rules for predicators or constructive rules for arithmetical symbols, or even with ideal norms in protophysics. Of course," he goes on, "most people still insist on doubting every step, but this is only a kind of philosophic amusement and the practice of the scientist is not disturbed by such verbal games." Now surely if "no one has any serious difficulties" with these matters, it cannot be true that "most people still insist on doubting every step." And who is the "scientist" whose practice is not disturbed by "such verbal games"? Perhaps the dialogist himself? Or is the view rather that *his* account of these matters accords with what the scientist does in practice and that alternative accounts do not? In any case, it is not shown that his account does accord in this way, and to do so adequately would be a long, arduous business. Nor is it beyond dispute that it is the function of logical analysis merely to explicate the practice of the scientist, although this may well be part of its function. Also, just as a matter of fact, some scientists *are* disturbed by logical analysis, for example at the moment some psychologists, social scientists, linguists, and others, and often feel they have much to learn from it.

Enough has been said surely to indicate that one cannot recognize in Lorenzen's work the use of a sound logical technique for the handling of the various mathematical and philosophical problems he considers. The technique is unreliable and itself unexamined, and the problems are oversimplified.

In spite of this critique of Lorenzen's views, however, we are all much indebted to him for calling attention again to constructive accounts of arithmetic, for emphasizing as few philosophers have its pragmatic aspect, for appraising freshly the role of numbers in science, and so on. By overcoming what appear to be the inadequacies of his account as quickly as possible, we hopefully can make progress on some of the topics he considers.

# XV

# IN DEFENSE OF
# NOMINALISM

*"Quod defertur non aufertur."*

Event logic is, as conceived throughout, a nominalistic theory in the strong sense of being of first order and of not admitting sets, classes, relations, numerical functions, and the like, as values for variables. Such abstract entities have simply not been needed, and it is perhaps a little surprising that so much can be achieved without them. Nonetheless, nominalism has its critics, and the most sustained recent attack upon it is that contained in Hilary Putnam's challenging *Philosophy of Logic.*[1] It will perhaps not be without interest to discuss this attack in the light of some of the foregoing material. The result will be not so much a defense of nominalism as an attempt to show that Putnam's attack rests upon pseudo-arguments that fail to make their point in view of the relevant literature.

Putnam urges (pp. 9f.) that "a nominalist is not likely to say:

(A)     "For all *classes S, M, P:* if all $S$ are $M$ and all $M$ are $P$, then all $S$ are $P$".

He is more likely to write:

[1] (Harper and Row, New York: 1971).

EVENTS, REFERENCE, AND LOGICAL FORM

(B)   "The following turns into a true *sentence* no matter what *words* or *phrases* of the appropriate *kind* one may substitute for the latters S, M, P: if all S are M and all M are P, then all S are P'." "

"The reason is clear if not cogent," Putnam continues: "the nominalist does not really believe that classes exists; so he avoids formulation (A). In contrast to classes, "sentences" and "words" seem relatively "concrete," so he employs formulation (B)." Putnam thinks, however, "that formulation (B) [and its ilk] cannot really be preferable to (A)." His reasons are roughly four-fold. (1) By 'words or phrases of the appropriate kind' in (B) must be meant "all *possible* words and phrases of some kind or other, and . . . *possible words and phrases* are no more "concrete" [and hence nominalistically acceptable] than classes are." (2) There is the problem of defining 'logically valid' in wholly nominalistic terms. (3) There is also the problem of defining 'truth' in wholly nominalistic terms. (4) And finally, there is the problem of accommodating mathematics in wholly nominalistic terms. Let us consider these items one by one and then return to the differences between (A) and (B).

Putnam worries that for the nominalist (p. 13) there "is not *one* notion of validity but an infinite series of such notions: validity in $L_1$, validity in $L_2$," and so on. A similar situation of course holds for the notion of truth. Even the realist, as Putnam himself observes later on (p.22), is in the same boat of being unable to explicate an intuitive notion of truth applicable to all languages, but must be content "to provide a battery of alternative notions ['true in $L_1$', 'true in $L_2$', and so on] that he can use in all scientific contexts. . . . . . But − today, at least − the nominalist cannot even do this much." This last statement is clearly false. Nominalistically acceptable definitions of 'true in $L_1$', 'true in $L_2$', and so on, may readily be given, so that realists and nominalists are in this regard also in the same boat.[2] They are, moreover, in the same boat also with regard to 'valid in $L_1$', 'valid in $L_2$', and so on. Nominalistically acceptable definitions of these notions are available, as Putnam himself in effect

[2] Cf. *Truth and Denotation* and III above.

254

argues (pp. 16-17). He fails to note, however, that even the realist can do no better. The latter too must be content with a battery of notions here just as for truth. Of course there are readily discernible family resemblances in both cases. The points (2) and (3) are thus inconclusive and no more favor nominalism than realism.

Not as to (1). Of course by 'words or phrases of the appropriate kind' in (B) the nominalist means such and such kinds of sign events or inscriptions. He does not require. however, that these be just those that "happen to be written down." Nominalists to a man have been careful to avoid so stringent a requirement.[3] In effect then all inscriptions whatsoever, here, there, everywhere, past, present, and future, whether explicitly exhibited or not, are admitted as values for the nominalists' syntactical variables. The point (1) thus rests merely upon a misunderstanding of what nominalistic syntax takes as values for its variables.

Now as to (4). There have been successful nominalistic renditions of portions of mathematics, including a standard constructivistic theory of real numbers,[4] to which Putnam makes no reference. There are also other types of constructivistic systems more or less nominalistically acceptable[5] to which no reference is made. The point (4) thus seems to rest merely upon neglecting the relevant literature. The material of "The Pragmatics of Counting" above helps to strengthen the nominalists' claims. The nominalist is here in essentially the same boat with the mathematical constructivists, sharing alike the distrust of set theory and interest in purely constructivitic procedures. Curiously Putnam does not argue against constructivism. The point (4) thus seems wholly gratuitous.

The points (1)-(4) are directed primarily against Goodman. Putnam notes rightly (p. 15) that "Goodman has never tackled the problem of defining logical validity at all." Nor has Goodman ever tackled the problem of defining 'true in $L$', either nominalistically or

---

[3] Cf. the Goodman-Quine "Steps toward a Constructive Nominalism," *Truth and Denotation,* and more recently, V. F. Rickey, "Axiomatic Inscriptional Syntax," *Notre Dame Journal of Formal Logic* 13 (1972): 1-33.

[4] See the author's "On Virtual Classes and Real Numbers," *The Journal of Symbolic Logic* 15 (1950): 131-134.

[5] See, for example, the work of Lorenzen referred to above.

otherwise. Nor has Goodman anywhere presented suitable nominalistic foundations for arithmetic or geometry. Thus points (2), (3), and (4) may cogently be urged against Goodman, but not against more catholic kinds of nominalism in which truth, logical truth, and mathematics are explicitly provided for.

As a kind of corollary of (4) Putnam claims (p. 38) that "no nominalist has ever proposed a device whereby one might translate arbitrary statements of the form "the distance $d$ is $r_1 + r_2$' into a nominalistic lanuage." In fact "a nominalistic lanugage is *in principle* inadequate for physics." This claim rings hollow in view of the gratuitousness of (4) and the material of IV above and of "Towards a Pragmatic Protogeometry."

To see this more clearly, let us attempt to provide a nominalistically acceptable rendition of 'the distance $d$ between points $a$ and $b$ is $r_1 + r_2$ units'. Let us follow here Putnam's lead (p. 41) and carry the discussion no deeper than he does. He lays down five requirements for distance, in terms of suitable geometric primitives. Let

$$\text{'}e \ \text{Dist} \ e', e_1, e_2\text{'}$$

express that physicist $e$ assigns the real-number expression (inscription) $e'$ to the two "points" $e_1$ and $e_2$. By use of such a sentential function, the measurement of distance is handled as a certain kind of human activity. Physicists assign numerical expressions to certain phenomena or entities or processes or whatever in certain ways. The notion of distance is not something heaven-made but is a human artifact or construct needed for the purposes of science. For 'Dist' to accomplish what is required of it, axioms may be laid down providing for Putnam's five conditions. Let 'NR $e'$' express that $e'$ is a real-number expression. (This notion is readily definable in terms of "The Pragmatics of Counting.") Then the following are postulated:

(1)  $(e_1) (e_2) ((\text{Pt}_e \ e_1 \cdot \text{Pt}_e \ e_2) \supset (Ee)(Ee')(\text{NR} \ e' \cdot e \ \text{Dist} \ e', e_1, e_2))$.

256

'$Pt_e \ e_1$' here expresses that entity $e_1$ is taken by person $e$ to be a point.

(2)    $(e) \ (e') \ (e_1) \ (e_2) \ (e \ \text{Dist} \ e',e_1,e_2 \ \supset \ (e' \approx \text{'O'} \equiv e_1 =_e e_2))$.[6]

Let '$e \ \text{Cngr} \ e_1,e_2,e_3,e_4$' express that physicist or geometer $e$ takes the distance between points $e_1$ and $e_2$ to be *congruent* to that between $e_3$ and $e_4$, Then

(3)    $(e) \ (e') \ (e'') \ (e_1) \ (e_2) \ (e_3) \ (e_4) \ ((e \ \text{Dist} \ e',e_1,e_2. \ \cdot \ e \ \text{Dist} \ e'',e_3,e_4) \ \supset \ (e \ \text{Cngr} \ e_1,e_2,e_3,e_4 \equiv e' \approx e''))$.

Let '$e \ \text{Colnr} \ e_1,e_2,e_3$' express that $e$ takes the points $e_1,e_2,e_3$ to be *colinear*, and '$e \ \text{Bet} \ e_1,e_2,e_3$' to express that $e$ takes the point $e_2$ to be *between* points $e_1$ and $e_3$'. Then

(4)    $(e) \ (e') \ (e'') \ (e_1) \ (e_2) \ (e_3) \ ( \ (e \ \text{Dist} \ e',e_1,e_2 \ \cdot \ e \ \text{Dist} \ e'',e_1,e_3 \ \cdot \ e \ \text{Dist} \ e''' \ e_2,e_3 \ \cdot \ e \ \text{Colnr} \ e_1,e_2,e_3 \ \cdot \ e \ \text{Bet} \ e_1,e_2,e_3) \ \supset e' \approx (e'' + e'''))$.[7]

Finally let $a_1$ and $a_2$ be particular points (for example, the end points of the standard meter stick in Paris), such that

(5)    $(e) \ (e') \ (e \ \text{Dist} \ e',a_1,a_2 \ \supset e' \approx \text{'1'})$.

These rules are somewhat oversimplified, but they suffice to sustain the point that theories of measurement may be nominalistically accommodated in event logic in terms of protogeometry. The measurement of other physical magnitudes may be introduced similarly. Putnam's challenge here is thus without further interest.

At the very beginning and throughout Putnam fails to distinguish

---

[6] '$e' \approx e'''$ here expresses that $e'$ and $e''$ are expressions that stand for the same real number, and '$e_1 =_e e_2$' expresses that person $e$ takes the entities $e_1$ and $e_2$ to be the same.

[7] $(e'' + e''')$ here is the numerical expression standing for the result of adding the number for which $e''$ stands to the number for what $e'''$ stands.

clearly the use and mention of expressions. Sometimes he uses quotes correctly, sometimes he does not. This is harmless enough. The danger is, as Frege well pointed out in the Preface to the *Grundgesetze*, in immortal words that bear continual repeating, that "it is remarkable how an inexact mode of speaking or writing, which perhaps was originally employed only for greater convenience or brevity and with full consciousness of its inaccuracy, may end in a confusion of thought, when once that consciousness has disappeared. People have managed to mistake numerals for numbers, names for the things named, the mere devices of arithmetic for its proper subject-matter. Such experiences teach us how necessary it is to demand the highest exact in manner of speech and writing." If use and mention are not clearly distinguished at the outset, it is astonishing with what regularity confusion between object and metalanguage, and hence of course between object-linguistic statements and metalinguistic ones, sets in.

Consider a schema

$$(5') \quad '((x) -\!\!- (Sx \supset Mx) \cdot (x)(Mx \supset Px)) \supset (x)(Sx \supset Px)'.$$

Putnam contends (pp. 31-32) that if a logician "is making assertions at all in writing down such schemata as (5'), the logician is making assertions of validity, and that means he is implicity making second-order assertions: for to assert the validity of the first-order schema (5') is just to assert $(S)(M)(P)$ (Schema (5')) — and this is a second-order assertion." Leaving aside any quibble about the proper analysis of 'assertion', note that Putnam is using the word here in three senses: asserting (5'), asserting that (5') is valid, and asserting $(S)(M)(P)$ (schema (5')). In the first usage, 'is asserted' is a metalinguistic predicate. It is the expression (5') that might be asserted by a logician. According to this usage $(S)(M)(P)$ (schema (5')), whatever object this is, cannot be the object of an assertion, but only the formula '$(S)(M)(P)(-\!\!-\!\!-\!\!-\!\!-)$' with the blank appropriately filled in. A statement asserting that (5') is valid is itself clearly a metametalinguistic statement of the form '(5') is valid'. Asserting $(S)(M)(P)$ (schema (5')) is something quite different —

presumably asserting a *proposition.* Putnam regards this latter as "a second-order assertion." Therewith he confuses propositional assertion with a metalinguistic statement. The two can no more be the same, even "implicitly," than 'toad' can be a toad. What starts out as a harmless convenience in not putting in quotes correctly ends up in a very considerable confusion in doctrine. If a logician intends to assert (5′) we might prefix to it the Frege assertion sign '⊢', or something of the sort. The result is then most certainly a metalinguistic statement, but this is a very different statement from '(S) (M) (P) (————)' and in a very different language. If 'S, 'M', and 'P' are taken as schematic letters, as with Quine, then of course they cannot be quantified at all. The moment one quantifies them, one has surreptitiously stepped into a language system with an altogether different logical structure.

Putnam wishes to call statements such as (A) above statements of *logic,* even though classes are covered by the quantifiers. A way to allow this, not mentioned by Putnam, would be to bring in virtual classes. If S, M, and P are taken as virtual classes, (A) could be construed rather as

(A′)   '( (x) (Sx ⊃ Mx) · (x) (Mx ⊃ Px)) ⊃ (x) (Sx ⊃ Px)'.

where in place of 'S', 'M', and 'P' any virtual-class expressions are inserted. (A′) belongs clearly to logic and has essentially the same content as (A) itself.

Putnam contends (p. 18) "that 'true' makes no sense when applied to a physical object, even if that physical object be an inscription of a sentence; it is not the physical sentence that is true or false, but *what the sentence says.* And the *things* sentences say, unlike the sentences (inscriptions) themselves, are not physical objects." Of course one can make such a contention, but one then needs a theory of *just what it is that sentences say.* Such a theory Putnam nowhere supplies nor does he even so much as give us a hint of what it would be like. In fact he seems no happier with presupposing "the existence of nonphysical entities such as propositions, meanings, or what have you " than the nominalist is. His view is thus at best not clearly articulated. On the one hand 'true' is not adjectival of sentences or statements but, on the other, it is not clear what else there is (for him) for it to be adjectival of. Not of sets or classes, certainly, yet the main thrust of his argument is to the effect that "at present references to "classes," or at least something equally "nonphysical," is indispensable to the science of logic." Perhaps Putnam would be content so long as we squeeze in something "nonphysical," no matter what.

Curiously Putnam's actual usage of 'true' does not accord with his contention. Throughout he speaks of "true sentences" or "true statements" without qualms. The phrases are after all grammatically well formed, and deep-grammatical accounts of 'true' would surely have to account for such usage *inter alia.*

Logico-metaphysical views die hard, and improved renditions render them increasingly invulnerable to attack. If nominalism is to be shown unacceptable, it must be on the basis of much deeper arguments than Putnam presents.

In one important respect the nominalist is the most fortunate of men. The notions and principles, either logical or non-logical, that he regards as acceptable are also acceptable to the realist. It is the realist who is on the defensive here. He has the difficult task of justifying *on philosophical grounds* the additional notions and principles. Goodman's injunction here is to the point: *Don't do anything that I wouldn't do.*[8] It is difficult enough, as we all know, to do just this much. The nominalist has no enemies, only detractors. The only criticisms launched against him are of the form 'You can't do this or that'. But these, as we have seen, are ill founded and are quickly becoming out of date.

A basic methodological *minimax* principle should obtain: *with a minimum of means a maximum of results.*, with mini-means to maxi-ends. This is in fact may be regarded as *the* basic methodological maxim, the real point of the Ockamite principle that *frustra fit per plura quod potest fieri per pauciora.* Maximax (Putnam) is *frustra*; minimin (Goodman) is too narrow; Maximin (Eberle[9]) is

[8] In "The World of Individuals," in *Problems and Projects,* p. 171.
[9] R. Eberle, *Nominalistic Systems* (Reidel, Dordrecht: 1970).

metalinguistic extravagance. Event nominalism proceeds in accord with the minimax principle and thus, it would seem, within the confines of a proper methodology.